Contents

International Capital Markets

Developments, Prospects, and Policy Issues

By a Staff Team from the
International Monetary Fund

led by
Morris Goldstein and
David Folkerts-Landau

INTERNATIONAL MONETARY FUND
Washington, DC
September 1994

ISBN 1-55775-426-8
ISSN 0258-7440

Price: US$20.00
(US$12.00 to full-time faculty members and
students at universities and colleges)

Please send orders to:
International Monetary Fund, Publication Services
700 19th Street, N.W., Washington, D.C. 20431, U.S.A.
Tel.: (202) 623-7430   Telefax: (202) 623-7201

recycled paper

			Page

The following symbols have been used throughout this paper:

...   to indicate that data not available;

—   to indicate that the figure is zero or less than half the final digit shown; of that the item does not exist;

-   between years or months (e.g., 1991–92 or January–June) to indicate the years or months covered, including the beginning and ending years or months;

/   between years (e.g., 1991/92 to indicate a crop or fiscal (financial) year.

"Billion" means a thousand million.

Minor discrepancies between constituent figures and totals are due to rounding.

The term "country," as used in this paper, does not in all cases refer to a territorial entity that is a state as understood by international law and practice; the term also covers some territorial entities that are not states, but for which statistical data are maintained and provided internationally on a separate and independent basis.

Preface

This report was prepared under the direction of Morris Goldstein, Deputy Director of the Research Department of the International Monetary Fund, together with David Folkerts-Landau, Chief of the Capital Markets and Financial Studies Division of the Research Department. The co-authors of the report are Liliana Rojas-Suárez, John Montgomery, Victor Ng, and Michael Spencer of the Research Department, and Robert Rennhack and Paul Mylonas of the Policy Development and Review Department.

This report was prepared in connection with the annual surveillance of international capital markets conducted by the International Monetary Fund. It draws, in part, on a series of informal discussions with commercial and investment banks, securities houses, stock and futures exchanges, regulatory and monetary authorities, and the staffs of the Bank for International Settlements, the Commission of the European Communities, the European Bank for Reconstruction and Development, the International Swaps and Derivatives Association, the Japan Center for International Finance, and the Organization for Economic Cooperation and Development. These discussions took place in Belgium, Canada, the People's Republic of China, France, Germany, Hong Kong, Ireland, Italy, Japan, New Zealand, Sweden, the United Kingdom, and the United States, between October 1993 and March 1994.

Subramanian S. Sriram provided extensive research and editorial support and, together with Kellett W. Hannah, prepared the data presented in the report. Norma Alvarado and Janet Shelley provided expert word processing assistance. Esha Ray of the External Relations Department edited the manuscript and coordinated the production of the publication.

The study has benefited from comments by staff in other departments of the Fund and by members of the Executive Board. Opinions expressed, however, are those of the authors and do not necessarily represent the views of the Fund or of the Executive Directors.

List of Abbreviations

ADRs	American Depository Receipts
AIL	Approved Issuer Levy
BIS	Bank for International Settlements
BOC	Bank of China
BSA	Bank Support Authority (Sweden)
BTANs	Bons du Trésor à taux annuel (France)
BTFs	Bons du Trésor à taux fixe (France)
CAD	Capital Adequacy Directive
CBOE	Chicago Board Options Exchange
CBOT	Chicago Board of Trade
CCPC	Cooperative Credit Purchasing Company (Japan)
CFTC	Commodity Futures Trading Commission (United States)
CHAPS	Clearing House Association Payments System (United Kingdom)
CHIPS	Clearing House Interbank Payments System (United States)
CITIC	China International Trust and Investment Corporation
CME	Chicago Mercantile Exchange
CSRC	China Securities Regulatory Commission (China)
DCH	derivatives clearing house
DITIC	Dalien International Trust and Investment Corporation
DMO	Debt Management Office (New Zealand)
DTB	Deutsche Terminbörse (Germany)
EC	European Community (former name of European Union)
ECP	Euro-commercial paper
ECU	European currency unit
EMTN	European medium-term note
ERM	(European) exchange rate mechanism
EU	European Union
FAS	Financial Accounting Standard
FASB	Financial Accounting Standards Board (United States)
FDIC	Federal Deposit Insurance Corporation (United States)
FRN	floating rate note
GDP	gross domestic product
GDRs	Global Depository Receipts
GEMMs	gilt-edged market makers (United Kingdom)
GGF	Government Guarantee Fund (Finland)
GITIC	Guangdong International Trust and Investment Corporation
GNP	gross national product
GSCC	Government Securities Clearing Corporation (United States)
ICBC	Industrial and Commercial Bank of China (China)
IFC	International Finance Corporation
ISDA	International Swaps and Derivatives Association
ITIC	International Trust and Investment Corporation (China)
JGB	Japanese Government bond (Japan)
KOP	Kansallis-Osake-Pankki (Finland)

LIBOR	London interbank offered rate
LIFFE	London International Financial Futures Exchange
MATIF	Marché à Terme International de France
MMI	Major Market Index
MTS	Mercato Telematico Secondario (Italy)
NAFTA	North American Free Trade Agreement
NASDAQ	National Association of Securities Dealers' Automated Quotations (United States)
NETS	National Electronic Trading System (China)
NTMA	National Treasury Management Agency (Ireland)
Nymex	New York Mercantile Exchange
NYSE	New York Stock Exchange
OATs	Obligations Assimilables du Trésor (France)
OCC	Office of the Comptroller of the Currency (United States)
OECD	Organization for Economic Cooperation and Development
OFD	Own Funds Directive
OTC	over the counter
OTS	Office of Thrift Supervision (United States)
PBOC	People's Bank of China
PCBC	People's Construction Bank of China
QIBs	qualified institutional buyers
RTGS	real time gross settlement
S&P	Standard and Poor's
SAEC	State Administration of Exchange Control (China)
SCRES	State Council for the Reform of the Economic System (China)
SCSPC	State Council Securities Policy Committee (China)
SDB	Shenzhen Development Bank (China)
SEB	Skandinaviska Enskilda Banken (Sweden)
SEC	Securities and Exchange Commission (United States)
SEHK	Stock Exchange of Hong Kong
SFA	Securities and Futures Authority (United Kingdom)
SIB	Securities and Investment Board (United Kingdom)
SITCO	Shanghai Investment and Trust Corporation (former name of SITICO)
SITIC	Shangdong International Trust and Investment Corporation
SITICO	Shanghai International Trust and Investment Corporation
SRD	Solvency Ratio Directive
SSE	Shanghai Stock Exchange (formerly Shanghai Securities Exchange)
STAQS	Securities Trading Automated Quotation System (China)
SURFs	step-up recovery floaters
SVTs	Spécialistes en Valeurs du Trésor (France)
TITIC	Tianjian International Trust and Investment Corporation

I

Introduction

The period running from the beginning of 1993 through the first quarter of 1994 was an eventful one for global capital markets. In the industrial world, the long rally in bond markets since 1990 suffered a particularly sharp reversal in the first quarter of 1994;[1] indeed, the surge in government bond yields among the Group of Ten countries from the beginning of February through the end of March 1994 was one of the largest two-month increases recorded during the postwar period. Meanwhile, 1993 turned out to be a boom year for private financing to developing countries, marked by a sharp increase in the volume of flows, an improvement in the terms of borrowing, strong increases in equity prices in many local stock markets, and a significant broadening of the investor base. That market too, however, suffered a sharp dip—some would say, correction—during the first quarter of 1994. Last but not least, the past twelve months has witnessed heavy involvement by policymakers in regulatory and supervisory issues. The spate of large losses suffered by some hedge funds (e.g., Granite Partners, Steinhardt Partners, and Quantum Fund), by some large banks (e.g., Banesto and Crédit Lyonnais), and by some end-users of derivatives (e.g., Metallgesellschaft, Codelco, and Procter and Gamble) has only served to underline the heterogeneous nature of risk in today's global financial markets.

This year's international capital markets report takes its cue in part from these recent developments, and in part from some structural changes in capital markets that will have an important influence on the financial landscape over the longer term. The rest of the report is organized into six sections. Section II analyzes the origins of the recent turbulence in government bond markets in the major industrial countries, and considers whether the role of hedge funds in that episode argues for altering present regulatory arrangements. Section III addresses recent initiatives to reduce systemic risk in the rapidly growing market for derivatives, as well as two ongoing debates about the most appropriate way to design and to implement supervision over banks and nonbanks. Section IV reviews recent trends in external financing for developing countries, with particular reference to the pricing of risk and to the volatility of financial flows. Sections V and VI turn to longer-term structural issues. Specifically, Section V takes stock of the evolution of government securities markets in the industrial countries over the past decade and identifies the main characteristics of recent reforms. Section VI moves the discussion from industrial countries to developing countries by highlighting as a case study China's emerging capital markets. Finally, Section VII presents the conclusions of the report.

Following the report, a series of annexes provides background information. One of these annexes discusses government securities markets and another the role of capital markets in financing Chinese enterprises. Other annexes report on recent developments in international financial markets, on the regulation of international banking, and on private market financing for developing countries.

---

[1]In the United States, long-term bond yields troughed earlier—in the fall of 1993. This bout of bond market turbulence was the second major shock to financial markets in industrial countries in the past twelve months. The first was the renewal of exchange market pressures within the European exchange rate mechanism (ERM) during the summer of 1993, which ultimately resulted in a considerable widening of the margins.

II

Bond Market Turbulence and the Role of Hedge Funds

Factors Underlying the Turbulence

As illustrated in Chart 1 and Table 1, yields on ten-year benchmark government bonds increased sharply in many industrial countries between the beginning of February 1994 and the end of March. In Japan, Germany, Switzerland, and Belgium, the increase was on the order of 50–70 basis points, while in the Netherlands, Italy, France, and the United States, increases were in the 70–100 basis point range. The United Kingdom, Canada, Sweden, and Australia recorded the largest run-up in yields (130–167 basis points). On the whole, movements in major currency exchange rates were much more modest during this period, although in mid-February and again in early March there were some exceptionally large movements in the yen/dollar exchange rate (with the rate on February 14, 1994 falling from 106.5 yen/dollar to an intraday low of 101, close to its historic low).[2]

If Sherlock Holmes were brought in to work on the case of the fickle bond markets, he would presumably have at least four questions:
• Why did long-term interest rates increase so much over such a short period?
• Why was the increase in long-term interest rates so widespread across industrial countries?
• What accounts for the nontrivial differences across countries in the magnitude of interest rate increases?
• If there were large spillover effects from one industrial country to another, why did those spillover effects occur primarily through bond markets and not through currency markets?

As with many episodes of turbulence in financial markets, it is not possible to provide unambiguous answers to all these riddles—even with the benefit of hindsight. Nevertheless, there is by now enough of a collection of clues and suspects to provide a credible overall story of what happened and why.[3]

Chart 1. Yields on *Financial Times* Benchmark Government Bonds, January 1993–March 1994

(In percent)

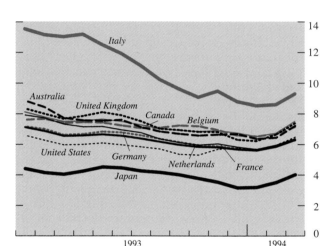

Source: The WEFA Group.

Probably the best place to begin is with the large, gradual buildup of interest rate—and to some extent, exchange rate—positions in the latter half of 1993 by hedge funds, proprietary traders (at banks and securities houses), institutional investors, and dealers. Just as "convergence plays" provided a key prologue to the ERM crisis, this latest round of large-scale position-taking set the stage for the bond market turnaround in the first quarter of 1994. Ever since the widening of margins in the ERM in the summer of 1993, a wide spectrum of investors had been expecting a fairly rapid and significant fall of interest rates in Europe. It has been estimated that U.S. investors alone may have put as much as $75 billion into Europe in 1993.[4] In the eyes of many international investors, the U.S. and U.K. experiences had demonstrated how helpful lower interest rates could be in spurring economic recovery. With consensus forecasts of weak economic activity and of high and growing unemployment in Europe, with inflationary pressures seemingly in

---

[2]Equity prices showed some marked declines in industrial countries (with the exception of Italy, where they actually increased) during this period; see Table 1.

[3]In addition to the factors discussed below, there is also the possibility that, at least to a certain extent, increases in long-term interest rates reflected some element of overreaction of the markets, in the sense that interest rates may have been pushed above what could be attributed to economic fundamentals; see International Monetary Fund (1994).

[4]It has not been possible to obtain quantitative estimates of the total cross-border interest rate positions built up in European bond markets during 1993.

Table 1. Developments in Financial Markets of Selected Industrial Countries

(Changes between February 3 and March 30, 1994)

	Long-Dated Bond Yields[1] *(Basis point change)*	Equities[2] *(Percent change)*	Exchange Rates *(Percent change local currency/ U.S. dollar)*
United States	96	−8.6	. . .
Japan	51	−3.0	−4.7
Germany	59	−0.2	−3.3
France	94	−10.3	−2.7
Italy	78	2.9	−3.4
United Kingdom	130	−11.4	1.3
Canada	144	−5.4	3.9
Netherlands	76	−7.5	−3.1
Australia	167	−10.6	−1.7
Switzerland	63	−8.1	−2.2
Belgium	69	−3.8	−3.8
Sweden	147	−11.3	−0.2

Sources: *Financial Times,* various issues; and Bloomberg Financial Markets.

[1]Ten-year Benchmark Government Bonds. (Bonds mature in 2004 except for German 6 percent bonds, which mature in 2003.)

[2]Share indices used are FT-SE 100 (United Kingdom), Dow Jones Industrials (United States), DAX (Germany), CAC 40 (France), Nikkei 225 (Japan), MIB General (Italy), Composite (Canada), AffarsvardnGen (Sweden), SBC General (Switzerland), BEL20 (Belgium), CBS TtlRtnGen (Netherlands), and ASX All Ordinaries (Australia).

check, with recovery in Germany still uncertain, with wider margins providing more room for maneuver for monetary policy in other ERM countries, and with elections not far down the road, they saw a long position in medium- and long-term European bonds—be it in the cash or derivative markets—as a winning hand.

Turning to the U.S. economy, the perception in the latter part of 1993 (at least to judge from interest rate projections in the forward market) seemed to be that the U.S. cyclical rebound was gaining strength and that it would bring with it (in 1994) a steady but gradual rise in interest rates; however, the containment of inflationary pressures and some progress on fiscal consolidation were regarded as factors that would keep the rise in rates from being too sharp. Confidence in interest rate forecasts had also been buoyed by the considerable profits made on long U.S. bond (and equity) positions in 1993. In Japan, continuing weakness in the banking system and falling share prices may have been regarded as setting the stage for further interest rate cuts. This projected international configuration of interest rates, in turn, led to a seemingly obvious currency play. Since interest rate differentials would increasingly favor dollar-denominated fixed income assets, go long on the U.S. dollar—particularly with respect to the Japanese yen, but also with respect to the

deutsche mark.[5] Some participants even combined these interest rate and currency plays by funding long European bond positions in the low-cost yen. On top of all this, long bond and equity positions in emerging markets (including Brady bonds) were on the rise, under the assumption that the increasing recognition of the yield and diversification attributes of emerging market investments, alongside significant policy reforms in some developing countries, would allow impressive returns to be earned in 1994, just as in 1993.

In the event, a set of unforeseen developments combined to derail the projections that had previously been so profitable. Five such developments deserve specific mention.

First, European interest rates did come down—but at a much slower pace than expected; from December 1993 on, the process of interest rate reduction seemed to have stalled. As this gulf between expectations and reality persisted, market participants came under increasing pressure to close out their long European bond positions, which of course pushed rates higher. Somewhat later, the decision by the Bundesbank not to lower official rates at the February 17, 1994 Council meeting, in concert with the announcement a few weeks later of a 20 percent increase in M3 for January, may well have increased pessimism about prospects for future German interest rate reductions.

Second, the small (25 basis points) upward adjustment of interest rates induced by the Federal Reserve on February 4, 1994—in tandem with the very strong fourth quarter U.S. GNP figure (announced as 7.5 percent on March 1) was apparently interpreted as a harbinger of future increases in U.S. interest rates and as an indicator of stronger than expected inflationary pressures.[6] Although futures data suggest that the market had been expecting interest rates to rise in the first quarter, the timing of the "turn" in monetary policy was uncertain and the Federal Reserve's action seems to have been widely interpreted as a message that "the

---

[5]Some market participants identified a second yen/dollar currency play. Here, the underlying assumption was that the yen/dollar rate would fluctuate over a relatively narrow range—bounded on the upside by the concern that too high a yen would hamper unduly Japan's recovery, and hemmed in on the low side by the concern that a very weak yen would frustrate a reduction in the United States/Japan bilateral trade imbalance. This second currency play called for "going short on volatility" by issuing dynamically hedged, customized, over-the-counter (OTC) derivatives, known in the trade as "strangles," that pay off if the yen/dollar rate stays within a certain range over the relevant time period.

[6]Some analysts also regard the coincident publication of inflation indicators by the National Association of Purchasing Managers and the Philadelphia Federal Reserve Bank, along with congressional testimony by Federal Reserve Chairman Alan Greenspan, as reinforcing the revised forecast of stronger inflationary pressures and of higher interest rates.

turn is now"—with an implication that a series of further increases was in the offing; perhaps the markets also took the increase as a wake-up call that long-term interest rates had been pushed down too low in 1993 by an excessively optimistic reading of inflationary and budgetary trends.[7] A further tightening of the federal funds rate (by 25 basis points) on March 22 was followed by a further increase in long-term bond yields.

Third, the intensification of the trade dispute between the United States and Japan—in mid-February and again in early March—was seemingly read by the market as a signal that the U.S. authorities would be more inclined to tolerate a higher yen as a mechanism for inducing Japan to either implement greater macroeconomic stimulus (than proposed hitherto) or grant greater market-access concessions. The dollar's depreciation against the yen was followed by some (more modest) depreciation against the deutsche mark and some other European currencies.

Fourth, prospects for further interest rate declines in Japan were dampened when Japanese equity prices proved to be more buoyant than expected and when reports surfaced that certain Japanese Government trust accounts would switch from being net purchasers to become net sellers of Japanese Government bonds (JGBs); yields on ten-year JGBs rose sharply in January.

And fifth, bond and equity prices in the emerging markets of the Far East and Latin America declined in February, providing yet another reason for some funds to pull in their horns. It is worth noting that these developments leading to a revision of expectations would have caused an increase in bond yields, even if there had not been a buildup of interest rate and exchange rate positions in 1993. Financial markets do not necessarily require that transactions take place before prices change; if the same revision of expectations is shared by almost all market participants, the price can move almost immediately to the new equilibrium.[8]

In any case, once investors had revised their outlook for interest rates and exchange rates, several

institutional practices operated to encourage a sell-off of previous positions. More and more, institutions that engage in aggressive position-taking use mark-to-market accounting methods and explicit loss limits (supplemented by programmed trading) as integral elements of their risk-management systems. When actual trading losses exceed loss limits, the positions are automatically liquidated in the cash market or in the futures market. In addition, the timing of losses was not conducive to sticking with a deteriorating position: many traders had reported their positions marked to market at the end of 1993 and began the year with a zero profit position; hence, there was no cushion of gains to offset losses in January, February, and March 1994. Such risk management guidelines are just what the doctor ordered to reduce the incidence of large losses and of outright failures of institutions, but those same guidelines—in a situation when the change in market sentiment is very one-sided—can contribute to large asset price swings.

Liquidity was another key factor. Although liquidity in practically all European government bond markets has been on the rise over the past decade in response to sets of reforms (see Section V), the fact remains that liquidity in the smaller ones is not yet sufficient to permit the turnaround of a very large, accumulated position in a short time, without a significant change in yields. Even in the largest European government bond markets (German Bunds, the French Obligations Assimilables du Trésor (OATs), U.K. gilts), liquidity is lower than in the market for U.S. Government securities. In a few cases, liquidity considerations may have prompted several European authorities to engage in some limited intervention.

Liquidity also speaks to why large positions in some European bonds were built up a piece at a time (to avoid driving up the price), and why, once the decision was made to exit, many participants rushed for the widest door available, namely, the larger futures exchanges (which frequently offer better liquidity on government bonds than is available on the local cash markets). Trading activity and open interest on European futures exchanges increased markedly during the first quarter of 1994; for example, the total volume of contracts grew by 115 percent on the London International Financial Futures Exchange (LIFFE) and by 83 percent on the Marché à Terme International de France (MATIF) (compared with growth in the fourth quarter of 1993). March was a particularly heavy month. MATIF actually had to briefly suspend trading on the ten-year government bond futures on March 3 (because the contract price dropped by more than the 250 basis points daily limit), and LIFFE, MATIF, and Deutsche Terminbörse (DTB) had to increase their margin requirements. The two largest

---

[7]If the Federal Reserve had not tightened monetary conditions in early February, it is likely that U.S. interest rates would still have increased significantly as evidence on the unexpected strength of the U.S. recovery accumulated; in fact, the Federal Reserve's action in early February probably advanced somewhat the timing of the interest rate increase but may well have reduced the size of the increase relative to what it would have been in the absence of any action.

[8]In some countries (the United States and Japan), this pure expectations effect may have had more to do with the increase in interest rates than the sell-off of previous interest rate positions, whereas in some others (European countries), the increased selling pressure associated with the liquidation of previous positions may have been the key.

U.S. futures exchanges—namely, the Chicago Board of Trade (CBOT) and the Chicago Mercantile Exchange (CME)—likewise experienced record trading volumes in March.

Leveraging was another element in the volatility picture. By taking full advantage of the high degree of leverage available in repurchase (repo) markets, in foreign exchange, and on futures exchanges, hedge funds, proprietary traders, securities houses, and other market participants were able to use their limited capital to build up very large positions in interest rate and exchange rate contracts, thereby contributing to the 1993 run-up in bond prices. But once bond prices began to decline, losses on investment positions relative to capital were multiplied by this same high leverage. This of course increased the pressure to liquidate losing positions.

But how does one explain the widespread nature of the increase in the long-term rates? Here, four factors are relevant. First, as detailed above, there was a coincident revision of expectations about future interest rates in each of three industrial country regions (Europe, North America, and Japan), driven initially by forces that were largely specific to that region. Second, market participants are not unaware of the increasing correlation of long-term interest rates across the major industrial countries, as shown in Table 2. Capital market integration has been on an increasing secular trend for some time,[9] and a co-movement of long-term interest rates among the industrial countries has long since ceased to be a unique event. Thus, when U.S. long-term rates increased sharply in early February, market participants may well have reasoned that rates would soon be driven up elsewhere in the industrial world. From the timing of interest rate movements, it does indeed look like there was significant positive transmission of the U.S. interest rate increase in early February to other major industrial countries (with the exception of Japan). Third, many of the larger players in today's capital markets operate in many markets simultaneously. Given their risk management systems, losses sustained in one market may call for liquidations in other markets to keep total losses from hitting prespecified limits. In this connection, the large losses suffered on wrong yen/dollar currency plays may have spurred further retrenchment in European bond markets or in emerging market securities. Fourth, in countries where the cash market was not liquid enough to cope comfortably with large selling pressure and where a liquid futures market was also not available, investors resorted to cross-hedging; that is, they built proxy hedges by exploiting the relatively high covariance among certain subsets of country bond yields (particularly within the ERM). Again,

[9]See Mussa and Goldstein (1993).

Table 2. Government Bond Yield Correlations[1]

	1970–79	1980–89	1990–94
Canada	0.930	0.947	0.962
France	0.409	0.907	0.928
Germany	0.191	0.908	0.934
Italy	0.660	0.851	0.593
Japan	0.182	0.826	0.965
Netherlands	0.405	0.866	0.913
United Kingdom	0.590	0.793	0.949

Source: Bank of England.
[1]Correlation coefficient for ten-year bond yields (monthly levels) with U.S. ten-year bond yield.

this proxy hedging increased the correlation of interest rate movements across markets.

As regards the quiescence in foreign exchange markets relative to bond markets, several developments appear to have contributed to that outcome. For one thing, some market participants who wanted to take long European bond positions in countries with relatively high nominal bond yields apparently hedged their currency exposure from the outset; that is, they separated the interest rate play from the currency play. As such, when news induced them to revise their expectations about interest rates, there was no need to take parallel action on the currency front since they were already hedged there. The exceptionally high liquidity of foreign exchange markets (where average daily turnover is now in the neighborhood of $900 billion), relative to that in government bond markets, would also suggest that shifts in asset preferences could be accommodated in the former with less price change than in the latter. It is likewise well to note that the revision of expectations about the future path of interest rates in the United States was in the same direction to the revision in Europe (i.e., the news was that interest rates in the United States would increase faster than previously assumed, while those in Europe would decline slower than previously assumed), thereby leaving the interest differential—presumably the key variable for exchange rate caculations—little changed. In the U.S./Japan case, the revisions to the interest rate forecasts also went in the same direction, but there the breakdown of the trade framework talks may have altered the market's forecast of the current account and hence of the future exchange rate as well. Finally, it may be that the significant exchange market intervention undertaken in a few cases dampened exchange rate movements relative to what they would have been in its absence. In any case, one can observe from implied volatilities in option and futures markets that uncertainties in exchange markets in February and March 1994 did not show the same upward jump as uncertainties in bond markets.

Probably the toughest of Mr. Holmes's four questions is what explains the cross-country variation in the size of the interest rate increase. The difficulties here are that the list of suspects is reasonably long (including, intercountry variations in the scale of earlier capital inflows, in risk premiums associated with fiscal or political developments, in changes in real rates associated with revisions of growth forecasts, in changes in inflationary expectations associated with revisions of central bank behavior or revisions of output gaps, and in revisions of real exchange rate forecasts) and that several factors relevant for bond yields can be changing at the same time. For this reason, one can only advance some tentative observations.

In the Swedish case, the inflow of nonresident investors engaging in interest rate plays was large relative to the size of the market. The trigger was probably interest rate increases abroad, but the backdrop of a still extremely high fiscal deficit and a relatively high variance in inflation performance over the past decade may well have prompted these nonresident investors to reverse their position in Swedish bonds more readily than if these latter risk-premium factors had been absent. In Canada, the high degree of integration with the U.S. capital market makes it particularly sensitive to U.S. interest rate developments. But here too a negative turn in investor sentiment in the first quarter may have had something to do with adverse fiscal and political news—after a period in 1993 when the fundamentals looked increasingly positive.

In the United Kingdom, aside from external influences, a comparison of the behavior of indexed and nonindexed bond yields seems to suggest that a rise in both inflationary expectations and in real rates occurred in February and March 1994.[10] In view of the accumulating strength of the recovery and the small reduction of official short-term interest rates in February, markets apparently became more uncertain as to whether the stance of monetary policy was consistent with the maintenance of low inflation over the medium term. In the United States, the main factor would seem to have been the relatively large size of the revision of expectations about the growth of the economy—perhaps supplemented by a relatively large correction of earlier long-term yield developments in the first three quarters of 1993.

In most of the continental European countries, there did not seem to be any evidence of increased inflationary expectations. Political uncertainties in Italy, uncertainties surrounding the release of large M3 figures for January 1994 in Germany, and some deterioration of the fiscal position in France—in concert with the spillover effects from the U.S. rate increase—may have been at work. In Japan, a more positive reassessment of prospects for the economy—with its implications for future interest rate cuts—was probably the dominant factor in pushing bond yields higher.

Some might be tempted to look for a more economical way of explaining the country pattern of increases in long-term rates. More specifically, it might be argued, for example, that the size of interest rate increases was systematically greater for those countries with the lowest degree of anti-inflationary credibility, or with the largest (positive) revisions to growth forecasts, or with adverse news about budget deficits, or with the highest levels of budget deficits or of debt stocks, or with the lowest degree of liquidity in the bond market. Based on some simple bivariate analysis, it seems clear that while each of these variables captures part of cross-country pattern, none of them provides a convincing explanation. For each of them, there are at least two or three dogs—and often more—that did not bark. In the end, there is no alternative but to embrace a more eclectic explanation of the cross-country pattern of rate increases.

Turning to the performance of markets, while some of the more aggressive position-takers suffered considerable losses in February and March 1994, there were no systemic consequences of difficulties at individual institutions. Payments and settlement systems coped well with the increased volume of activity. To be sure, there were unusually large price swings, but that was in part a reflection of an unusually large and sudden revision of expectations. What is more, in contrast to the two big bouts of turbulence in ERM foreign exchange markets, this time the authorities did not act forcefully to supply liquidity to the markets. As such, more of the adjustment to a new equilibrium was taken up by price changes.

Role of Hedge Funds

Because hedge funds have been active participants in the ERM crises of 1992–93, as well as in the recent bout of turbulence in bond markets, and because their potential market influence has been growing over the past decade, it is not altogether

---

[10]In countries which either do not offer indexed bonds or have offered them only for a short time, recourse has to be made to other methods for separating the inflationary expectations component from the real component in observed nominal interest rates. One such method is to look at the contemporaneous behavior of nominal interest rates and nominal exchange rates. The idea is that if a rise in the nominal interest rate mainly reflects an increase in inflationary expectations relative to other countries, then the nominal exchange rate should depreciate; alternatively, if it is primarily due to a rise in the real interest rate, then the exchange rate should appreciate.

surprising that their activities have come under increased scrutiny.[11]

Defining what is and what is not a "hedge fund" is problematic. The term hedge fund carries no formal definition in securities law, and the private investment vehicles that make up this industry are extremely diverse. While there is no comprehensive data base yet available on hedge funds, it has been estimated that there are 800–900 such firms, with aggregate capital somewhere on the order of $75–100 billion; by way of comparison, there is approximately $27 billion of equity capital in large U.S. securities firms and $90 billion of capital in U.S. money-center banks. A large hedge fund might have as much as $10 billion under management, whereas a small fund might manage only $75–100 million. The fund's investment portfolio could span government securities, foreign exchange, financial futures and options, commodities, real estate, mergers and acquisitions arbitrage, mortgage-backed securities, or even other hedge funds. Alternatively, it could specialize in only one or a few of these markets. More than half of the total capital in the industry is thought to lie in "macro" hedge funds, whose managers seek to profit by betting on changes in interest rates, exchange rates, and equity prices in global markets.

A key question is what is special about hedge funds? After all, the proprietary trading desks of large banks and of large securities houses, as well as some mutual funds, also engage in aggressive position-taking. Several factors warrant explicit mention.

First, hedge funds are less regulated than other large players in financial markets. Because they are private companies with less than 100 partners and are frequently chartered offshore, they escape from many of the registration and reporting requirements and investment guidelines that apply to broker-dealers, mutual funds, and other investment advisers in the United States.[12] For example, hedge funds are not required to and generally do not, report their positions and trading activity to shareholders. Hedge funds are subject in full to antifraud and market manipulation statutes. They are also covered in some major industrial countries by recent "large trader" reporting and information legislation (see below).

The relatively light regulatory burden of hedge funds permits them to have greater flexibility in their investment strategies than do other financial market participants. This operating flexibility of hedge funds is also enhanced by their own limits on redemption and transferability of shares. The most important constraint on their operating flexibility is their own risk-management practices.

Second, hedge fund investors are wealthier and presumably have a higher tolerance for risky investments than the public at large. Hedge funds generally require that 65 percent of their shareholders be accredited, that is, they must have a net worth of at least $1 million or an income in the previous year of at least $250,000. In addition, most hedge funds require a minimum investment, ranging from $250,000 to $10 million. Most investors are simply not willing to allow someone else to take large risks with their money. They would prefer to accept a lower rate of return in exchange for a reduction in volatility.

Third, hedge funds are generally regarded as the most leveraged players in major financial markets. Indeed, it is largely this use of leverage that gives hedge funds their market clout (though the propensity of others to regard them as market leaders also contributes to this clout). Hedge funds are said to leverage their capital by anywhere between 5 and 20 times, with the average for macro funds being closer to the lower end of the range. While a certain degree of leverage is available to any investor who wants to purchase financial assets on margin, hedge funds routinely use collateralized borrowing in the repo markets for government securities to generate very high leverage ratios. The lender is typically a large bank or large securities house. For example, a hedge fund could borrow $1 billion from a bank and purchase a like nominal amount of government securities. The bank would take possession of the securities as collateral, and in addition the fund would be asked to deposit anywhere from $20 million to $40 million (2–4 percent of principal) as interest-bearing margin money—the only actual capital investment of the fund—usually in the form of treasury bills. The size of the margin will depend on the bank's forecast of interest rate volatility and on its assessment of the creditworthiness of the fund. The lending bank may call in further margin or reduce the margin over the life of the contract. Although the maturity of the bonds purchased by the funds will depend on their view of the future shape of the yield curve, the maturity of the repo contract tends to be only a few days.[13]

---

[11]To say that hedge funds have participated in the recent bout of bond market turbulence should not be taken to imply that their participation was approximately uniform across countries; for example, it has been reported that hedge funds were much less active in Japanese bond markets than in, say, European ones.

[12]By limiting the number of investors, hedge funds avoid registration under the Securities Act of 1933 and the Investment Company Act of 1940. By limiting the frequency with which they trade, they avoid having to register as dealers under the Securities Exchange Act of 1934.

---

[13]Smaller or less creditworthy hedge funds may not have bank lending available to them. They often use the futures markets to set up risk positions. Margins in the OTC market for foreign exchange positions tend to be higher than on interest rate positions, reflecting the greater volatility of the former.

Yet a fourth distinguishing characteristic of hedge funds—and the one that has most accounted for the industry's explosive growth over the past seven years or so—is their superior performance. Despite their much-publicized recent losses, hedge funds have been extremely successful in their investment activities, and they have handily outperformed the major market indexes and publicly offered mutual funds (see Table 3). For 1993 as a whole, the return to hedge capital was 23 percent, compared with 14 percent for mutual funds and 10 percent for the Standard and Poor's 500. Market developments in the first quarter of 1994 apparently inflicted a 13 percent loss on macro hedge funds, with most of the loss occurring in February and March, after returning 53 percent in 1993. The entire hedge fund industry reportedly lost only about 2 percent of its capital during the turbulent first quarter of 1994. Money flows to performance. That is how funds are marketed, and that is how investors decide where to put their money.

There are at least three areas in which authorities might harbor concerns about the activities of hedge funds.

The first concern lies in the area of credit risk. Since the larger hedge funds receive loans from banks and securities houses to help fund their position-taking, there is the concern that large losses in hedge funds could generate significant loan losses for their creditors. The bulk of lending to hedge funds is thought to be fully collateralized, with the lender holding the financial instrument.[14] From the point of view of the supervisory authorities, they need to be assured that margin requirements on loans to hedge funds are set at the appropriate level, that margins are increased when the market price of the collateral falls, and that there is adequate information on the current, consolidated exposure of hedge funds to their lenders. As indicated above, the historical record on performance of hedge funds suggests that they should be a good credit risk. To this point, we are not aware of banks or securities houses taking large losses on loans to hedge funds. Systemic risk could arise if the price of the collateral took a very large fall (relative to historical experience), or if some lenders in the system had not properly collateralized their exposure. Otherwise, a failure of a number of hedge funds would simply represent a loss to their wealthy shareholders.

Table 3. **Comparative Returns: Hedge Funds Versus Other Investments**

(*Annual percentage return*)

	Hedge Funds	S&P 500	Mutual Funds
1993	23.2	10.1	14.3
1992	15.8	7.7	6.8
1991	25.4	30.4	36.1
1990	10.9	−3.1	−3.8
1989	24.9	31.6	28.5
1988	22.9	16.5	15.8
1987	14.5	5.2	1.0

Source: Republic New York Securities (1994).

Two questions arise with respect to credit risk. One is whether lenders have been (and will be) sufficiently strict in setting and enforcing margins on hedge funds when the latter are under pressure—now that hedge funds have become such important customers of some banks and securities houses. Not only do hedge funds generate substantial commission and interest income for lenders, but the order flow may also provide lenders with useful information for their own proprietary trading activities. Recall that on futures exchanges, initial and maintenance margins are set by predetermined formulas and failure to maintain margin results in an automatic closing out of positions by the clearinghouse. This is not necessarily so in the OTC market, where there is more room for discretion and negotiation. If lenders were too lax in calling for increased margins when the price of collateral deteriorated for fear of losing the business to a competitor, one of the protective mechanisms against systemic risk would be weakened. A second question is whether lenders—or for that matter, the central bank—know the consolidated exposure of individual hedge funds. If consolidated exposure is greater than each lender realizes, then again, risk is increased because aggregate calls on capital for increased margins could (at times of historically large asset price movements) exceed the ability of the hedge fund to meet its obligations. Bank supervisors are increasing their efforts to get a better picture of the exposure of their banks to hedge funds, but this is not likely to cover positions of the funds vis-à-vis securities houses and foreign lenders. How large the gaps are for estimating consolidated exposure remains to be seen.

A second potential concern is that hedge funds—because of their market clout and reported high turnover of positions—could generate excessive volatility in government bond markets. This is an issue on which the jury is still out. Presumably, the presence of hedge funds adds to the liquidity of these markets. Discussions with country authorities also confirm that there have been cases when hedge funds' presence on the buy side of the market (dur-

---

[14]U.S. Comptroller of the Currency Ludwig reported (statement to Congress, April 13, 1994) that for the eight banks supervised by the Office of the Comptroller with exposure to hedge funds, most exposure is collateralized by cash and government securities. According to Federal Reserve Governor LaWare (statement to Congress, April 13, 1994), uncollateralized exposures to hedge funds are "considerably" less than 2 percent of the equity capital at each of three major banks supervised by the Federal Reserve.

ing times of declining conditions) has worked to stabilize yields, just as their presence on the sell side has sometimes acted to increase volatility. When there is a major price break in the market, hedge funds may be more inclined to go against the market than other institutional investors that are subject to stricter regulatory restrictions and/or to closer oversight by shareholders. In the view of one supervisory authority, "hedge funds have become the 'buyer of last resort' in some of these markets." In the most deep and liquid markets—U.S. Government securities, the foreign exchange markets for the major currencies, and the larger futures exchanges—the influence of any single set of players is apt to be limited. In less liquid markets, however, it could not be ruled out that hedge funds might exacerbate volatility. In any case, there is little indication from looking at the short-term behavior of government bond yields over the past decade or so that volatility has increased systematically across the Group of Ten countries. Nor is there a firm link in the empirical literature between turnover and price volatility. There is, however, a question of whether margin requirements and leverage in the financial system are currently at appropriate levels.

Potential concern number three is that hedge funds could engage in market manipulation and thereby compromise the integrity of markets. As mentioned earlier, hedge funds are subject to standard antifraud and market manipulation regulations. In addition, there are already some limits in effect on the size of positions or share of the issue that any firm can take in futures markets or in gov-

ernment bond auctions. While hedge funds often seem to react similarly to a given set of market opportunities, we are not aware of any evidence that they have colluded to manipulate prices. Moreover, some authorities have stepped up their surveillance of government securities markets over the past few years, and many have in place issuance techniques (e.g., taps or reopenings of issues) that make it difficult to engineer market squeezes. All that being said, the absence of regular information on large trades and positions makes it problematic to ascertain the market impact of hedge funds, or to detect instances of market manipulation. It could be argued that such information would be particularly useful in the smaller government securities markets where the actions of a set of players is likely to have a larger potential impact on prices. In the United States, enabling legislation has been in place since 1990 that permits activity-based large trader reporting in publicly traded equity securities and options;[15] that legislation includes hedge funds as "large traders." More recently, a similar large position reporting requirement covering U.S. Government securities was included in the reauthorization of the Government Securities Act.[16]

---

[15]U.S. Securities and Exchange Commission, June 12, 1992.

[16]The reauthorization passed in December 1993. The regulation for government securities reporting will be written and administered by the U.S. Treasury Department. The law permits the Treasury to request reports of all large positions in a recently issued security when a pricing anomaly exists in that security; large positions are defined as those above $1 billion.

III

Derivatives and Supervisory Issues

Last year's *International Capital Markets* report examined the growth of derivative markets, the role of wholesale banks in these markets, and the benefits and potential systemic risks associated with their continuing development.[17] The losses incurred recently by several commercial firms undertaking derivative transactions (see Box 1) reinforces oft-repeated concerns that when a financial activity is growing very rapidly and attracting many new entrants, the probability of less experienced players getting into difficulty rises, with potentially adverse spillover effects for their lenders and counterparties. The first part of this section reviews the response of regulators to these challenges. The second part looks at two other timely issues in supervision, namely, the role of the central bank in banking supervision, and the adequacy of the existing approach to the supervision of nonbanks.[18]

Derivatives: Recent Supervisory and Regulatory Initiatives

Over the past year, the total notional value of OTC and exchange-traded derivative products has grown by 47 percent to exceed $12 trillion (about twice U.S. nominal GDP). It is well recognized both by the industry itself and by central banks and other supervisory agencies that the continued stability of the derivative markets can only be sustained if the implementation of "best practices" in risk management is accelerated and if continued progress is made toward reducing the sources of systemic risk.[19] An important initiative has been the extension of the Basle Capital Accord to include, inter alia, a more comprehensive treatment of the market risk of derivative positions. This parallels the adoption by the European Community (EC) of a new Capital Adequacy Directive (CAD) in March 1993 to modify and extend the 1989 Solvency Ratio and

Own Funds Directives, which are similar to the 1988 Basle accord.[20] In addition, efforts have been made to improve disclosure and accounting standards, as well as to strengthen the settlement and payments infrastructure in money markets.

Although the 1988 Basle accord covered credit risk for both on- and off-balance sheet positions, its focus on credit risk was increasingly viewed by supervisors as too narrow.[21] Market risk—especially, interest and exchange rate risk—has tended to become more important as the trading books of banks have increased in size relative to loan books.[22] In addition, some derivative positions, such as currency forward contracts or interest rate swaps, initially do not have a credit exposure; instead, potential credit exposure evolves as exchange rates and interest rates change over the duration of the contract.[23] In an effort to deal with these limitations of the 1988 accord, the Basle Committee on Banking Supervision proposed, in April 1993, a new set of capital requirements for banks, which are largely similar to the capital standards under the European Union's (EU's) CAD.[24] The proposals—featuring capital requirements for market risk, measurement of interest rate risk, and a recognition of netting—are now being considered by national supervisors and by the banking industry.

The main innovations in the 1993 proposals are the separation of banks' loan and trading books, the isolation of market risk from specific risk, the adoption of a portfolio perspective, and the conversion of fixed-income derivative positions into combinations of simple debt securities for purposes of computing capital requirements.

---

[17]See Goldstein, Folkerts-Landau, and others (1993b).

[18]A number of other issues—including the resolution of banking problems in some industrial countries—are considered in Annexes II and III.

[19]A compendium of best practices in risk management for derivatives is contained in the report by the Global Derivatives Study Group (1993). Central banks and other supervisory agencies in some of the major industrial countries have recently issued extensive reports on developments in derivatives markets, with particular emphasis on sources of systemic risk.

[20]For a more detailed discussion of the EC directives, see Goldstein, Folkerts-Landau, and others (1993b), Section V.

[21]Credit risk is the risk of counterparty default.

[22]Market risk is the possibility of losses stemming from asset price changes that are unrelated to changes in the credit standing of any particular counterparty.

[23]Banks are not exposed to credit risk for the full face value of these contracts, but only to the cost of replacing the cash flow if a counterparty defaults.

[24]The 1993 Basle proposal and the CAD follow the same approach in the measurement of interest rate risk and the same building block approach in aggregating market and specific risk. But the Basle proposal is more stringent than the CAD in the treatment of foreign exchange risk and equity risk.

Box 1. Futures Shocks

One of the central recommendations of the Group of Thirty report on derivatives was that senior management must be kept fully informed of a firm's operations in derivatives markets.[1] Two announcements in December 1993 and January 1994 demonstrated the importance of this principle. In late January, the Chilean copper mining company Codelco—which accounted for 6 percent of Chilean GDP in 1993—announced that it had suffered losses of $206.8 million on copper futures trading in 1993. These losses apparently originated in a clerical error by the head futures trader who entered some of his transactions in his computer incorrectly. Despite a requirement to inform his superiors and to close positions when losses reached $1 million, he apparently kept this knowledge to himself and attempted to regain the original $30–40 million in losses by speculating in the futures markets. At one point in this operation, which proved disastrously unprofitable, he had taken positions that represented requirements to deliver twice Codelco's annual production.

Six weeks earlier, similar problems at German metals and mining conglomerate Metallgesellschaft AG had come to light. MG Corp, a U.S. subsidiary, had sold five- and ten-year contracts to its customers to provide petroleum products at fixed prices. These contracts gave the customers the option to terminate the contract, at a cost equal to half the resulting profit, at any time—that is, if the spot price rose above the forward price. To hedge the exposure from these long-term options, MG Corp took a long position in the near-month futures contract, which is generally the most liquid contract, and rolled this position over each time the futures contract expired. Such a hedging strategy is profitable as long as the market is in "backwardation"—that is, the spot price exceeds the futures or forward price. However, by the end of November, the market had moved into "contango"—that is, the futures price exceeded the spot price—and MG Corp incurred losses when it rolled over its futures position. The fall in futures prices was reportedly due in part to MG Corp's own transactions, which were swamping the market. By that time, MG Corp had an estimated 55,000 outstanding contracts in the New York Mercantile Exchange (Nymex)—almost twice the usual limit—and even more OTC positions (where the latter represented commitments to deliver 160 million barrels of oil—80 times the daily output of Kuwait).

At the end of November, MG Corp faced a margin call from the Nymex. It met the call only with the help of a DM 1.5 billion loan from Deutsche Bank and Dresdner Bank. Reportedly, it was only at this point that Metallgesellschaft's supervisory board was made aware of both the hedging strategy and the resulting losses. By that time, these losses had reached DM 800 million and further losses of at least DM 1.5 billion were expected. Metallgesellschaft's 1993 pretax loss, estimated at DM 347 million at the end of November 1993, was revised upward to a loss of DM 1.9 billion in January 1994, when a DM 3.4 billion rescue package of equity injections and debt/equity swaps was agreed with its creditor banks.

---

[1]Global Derivatives Study Group (1993).

The loan book continues to be treated as specified in the 1988 accord, while risk in the trading book (including derivative trading) is separated into specific and general market risk. The specific risk of a position includes credit risk, settlement risk, liquidity risk, and the risk of adverse movements in specific securities that are unrelated to market-wide factors (such as the general price level, the exchange rate, or the whole term structure of interest rates). The portfolio approach was adopted because the market risks of different securities are related; this approach permits offsets for positions that are negatively correlated. The so-called building block approach embodied in the new proposals computes total capital requirements as the sum of a specific risk charge and a general market risk charge.

The general market risk applicable to all debt securities (including the decomposed derivative positions) is the risk of unexpected interest rate changes. The Basle Committee has proposed a simplified "ladder approach" to measuring such risk. Fixed income instruments are divided into 13 maturity bands, and instruments within the same maturity band are treated alike. Net unhedged positions are computed for each maturity band, and then capital charges are applied. The Committee also adopted a shorthand method for computing foreign exchange risk. A net overall position is computed for each currency, and all net long currency positions are then added together; the same procedure is applied to all net short positions. The overall foreign exchange position is defined as the greater of the total long position and the total short position. A capital charge of 8 percent is then applied to the overall forex position.[25] The Basle Committee is

---

[25]A simple numerical example may be helpful in understanding how capital charges for market risk are computed. Suppose a bank has a long position in deutsche mark of $50 million and a long position in sterling of $30 million. The total long position in foreign exchange is then $80 million. Likewise, assume that the bank has a short position in yen equal to $40 million; the total short position in foreign exchange is then the same $40 million. The overall foreign exchange position—the greater of the long and short positions—would be $80 million, and the capital charge would be 8 percent of this overall position, or $6.4 million. Capital charges for equity and traded debt portfolios are arrived at in a similar manner. In the case of equity, positions in individual stocks replace positions in currency, whereas for traded debt, aggregated positions in each maturity class replace positions in currency. The 8 percent capital charge for foreign exchange positions is to be added to the capital required to cover the credit risk on the same items, whereas the capital charge for debt securities and equities is substituted for the capital charge required by the 1988 accord to cover credit risk.

also proposing to allow banks to reduce credit exposures through bilateral netting, as long as such netting meets existing laws and complies with the minimum standards set out in the 1990 Lamfalussy report.[26]

The industry's response to the capital proposals has been mixed. Banks in the United States, Canada, France, and United Kingdom—increasingly joined by their supervisors—have argued that the new proposals fail to recognize banks' effort in exploiting more complicated risk-reducing correlations among their on- and off-balance sheet positions. Indeed, they maintain by making the "least common denominator" the industry standard, the new Basle proposals reduce incentives for banks to adopt more advanced risk management systems. They certainly do not want to maintain two risk-reporting systems. Further, as more and more of the assets of banks become tradable, the distinction between a loan book and a trading book could become increasingly artificial. Major money center banks in the United States have therefore proposed that they be allowed to use their own proprietary risk-management models to come up with prudential capital charges for derivative positions. This would require bank supervisors to evaluate the key assumptions contained in these proprietary risk-management models (particularly those related to the choice of pricing models, the length of estimation periods for obtaining volatility parameters, and the estimated holding periods). Banks in other industrial countries seem somewhat more favorably inclined to the Basle proposals. They do not want the best to become the enemy of the good. They regard the Basle proposals as practical, and as providing a decent approximation to true portfolio risk; in some cases, the Basle proposals are close to the kind of risk management systems they employ on their own behalf. While it is too early to tell, perhaps a compromise on market risk will emerge under which banks would be able to choose between the off-the-rack Basle method and their own custom-tailored models. It is not yet clear which of the two approaches would yield higher capital requirements on average.

The new Basle proposals apply to banks only, and not to securities houses. This is not a problem in EU countries where most securities house functions are performed by banks. However, in the United States and Japan, the lack of harmonization of capital requirements may lead to discrepancies between capital standards for banks and securities houses. Given that many of the distinctions between banks and securities houses are quickly disappearing, more uniform standards are called for. To unify

standards, the International Organization of Securities Commissions has devoted substantial efforts to setting up global capital standards, but serious disagreements between securities supervisors remain, primarily over the appropriate capital charges for equity trading books. However, most market participants did not expect a failure to reach agreement on uniform capital standards to result in large changes in market shares between banks and securities houses, or between countries.

In addition to extending capital requirements, efforts are under way to improve disclosure and accounting standards and to strengthen market infrastructure. Supervisors have encouraged banks to provide more detailed accounts of their derivative operations. Banks appear to see greater disclosure as largely in their own long-term interest, and in any case, as probably inevitable—but worry that (unless implemented on a universal basis) it could aggravate differences in national accounting procedures and further disadvantage them relative to some nonbanks. U.S. bank regulators have proposed that banks disclose their income from derivative operations, as well as the level of their counterparty risk. One strong motivation for greater disclosure is that the present lack of transparency of consolidated positions in the derivative markets increases the likelihood of precautionary runs based on faulty information; that is, market participants may test the solvency of a bank when they suspect that it is having problems in its trading book. The better the information available to market participants, the better the chances of pricing risk appropriately and of avoiding instabilities induced by rumors. The issue of disclosure and the marking-to-market of off-balance sheet positions is currently under study at the Bank for International Settlements, and it has found support within the Financial Accounting Standards Board and the Group of Thirty.

As desirable as stricter disclosure standards for derivatives are, it needs to be acknowledged that thorny questions remain about what to disclose, how often to disclose, and to whom to disclose. Should, for example, disclosure cover only notional or marked-to-market exposure, income from derivative operations, and the level of counterparty risk—or should the institution go further and provide information on the maximum loss that it would be prepared to sustain in its trading activities under adverse market conditions, and on what measures have been put in place to ensure that this loss limit is respected? Is it adequate to describe the institution's risk management strategy for derivatives in broad qualitative terms or does this strategy need to include specific quantitative information (e.g., capital at risk)? Since derivative positions can change rapidly during a short time period—unlike a

---

[26]See Bank for International Settlements and Group of Ten (1990).

bank's loan book—the frequency of disclosure is likewise a very relevant issue. A marked-to-market statement that is three months old may not provide an accurate guide to what the institution's exposure is today. Should this timing problem be handled by more frequent disclosure or instead by providing the maximum and minimum exposure during a given period? How much information should be made available to the public, and how much should only go to the regulators? If the concern is about runs based on misinformation, then priority ought to be given to public disclosure. Alternatively, if the emphasis is on detecting problems at an early stage—while safeguarding proprietary material, the tilt might be toward timely disclosure to supervisory authorities. On the whole, it seems that the authorities are concentrating much of their effort—and appropriately—on evaluating the quality of risk management in banking institutions, rather than on trying to track and to assess exposure on a day-to-day basis.

The growth of derivative markets has also added significantly to the strains on the infrastructure of financial markets, particularly wholesale payments systems.[27] The rising volume of intraday credit exposures generated in end-of-day net-settlement payments systems and the moral hazard such systems create have been important considerations for moving to real time gross settlement (RTGS) systems. RTGS provides immediate finality of payments and thereby reduces settlement risk. Moreover RTGS provides a basis for achieving delivery versus payment in securities settlement. By 1996 all but two EU members will have RTGS for domestic payments. In particular, Belgium, France, Ireland, and Italy will replace their existing net payments systems, and, in the United Kingdom, the Clearing House Association Payments System (CHAPS) will be modified to provide RTGS in 1995.[28]

The U.S. Federal Reserve has also set up a fee structure for daylight overdrafts that is currently being implemented. It is expected that this measure will, inter alia, increase netting and thereby reduce systemic risk, as the volume of credit generated in the net payment system declines.

In order to reduce the systemic risk associated with the pyramiding of gross transaction volumes created by derivative and other money market transactions, some authorities are studying the feasibility of adopting a clearinghouse structure for netting and for settling some of the more standardized OTC derivatives. The model would be similar to mechanisms that already exist on futures exchanges. One such clearinghouse—the Delta Government Options Corporation—already clears OTC options written on U.S. Treasury securities. A derivative clearinghouse would become a counterparty itself between the two contracting parties; it would monitor the value of each side of the contract and see to it that margin accounts are maintained. Support for such a clearinghouse in the banking community may however still be some time in coming, given the large costs required to set up new institutions, the loss in market power of AAA-rated dealers, and the narrow range of contracts that could be covered.[29]

Role of the Central Bank in Banking Supervision

A few years ago, when the statutes for a future European central bank were being formulated, a contentious issue was the role, if any, that this new central bank should play in the supervision of banks.[30] This question could not be resolved by reference to the practices of national central banks within the (then) European Community since those practices differed; for example, the Bank of England and the Bank of France had substantial formal responsibilities in the banking supervision area, whereas the Bundesbank did not. During this past year, this same issue surfaced on the other side of the Atlantic. Specifically, the new U.S. administration proposed that the responsibility for supervision of banks and savings and loans (now shared among the Federal Deposit Insurance Corporation (FDIC), the Office of the Comptroller of the Currency (OCC), the Federal Reserve, and the Office of Thrift Supervision (OTS)) be streamlined by replacing the four supervisory authorities with a single federal banking supervisor. The Federal Reserve System opposed that proposal, arguing that it is important as a matter of public policy for the Federal Reserve to maintain a hands-on involve-

---

[27]This was also the subject of the International Symposium on Banking and Payment Services organized by the U.S. Federal Reserve Board in Washington on March 10–11, 1994.

[28]While there is a general consensus in favor of RTGS, there is no such consensus with respect to cross-border payments. Some argue that such risk could be eliminated by extending the hours of operation of domestic RTGS systems to provide RTGS and delivery versus payment for cross-border payments, and the recently announced decision to increase the hours of operation of Fedwire is designed to increase the overlap of the Japanese and United States settlement periods. Others favor the netting of cross-border multicurrency payments. Direct links between national RTGS payments systems could easily result in the transmission of liquidity disturbances across borders.

[29]A potentially more successful proposal is the introduction of a derivatives collateral manager who would be a neutral third party to a bilateral collateral agreement, but who would not assume responsibility for contract performance as the derivatives clearinghouse would.

[30]See Folkerts-Landau and Garber (1992).

ment in bank supervision.[31] Meanwhile, in the Pacific, the Reserve Bank of New Zealand has taken the position that supervision of banks should lean more heavily on market forces, with a reduced role for the central bank or any other authority.[32]

Those who favor making the central bank the lead supervisor of banks maintain that (i) the central bank's role in resolving financial crises makes it imperative for it to have a close and continuous knowledge of the position and workings of banks—knowledge that can only be gained by hands-on supervision; (ii) when the central bank has close proximity to markets and to banks, there are important synergies for the formulation of monetary policy because the central bank will be more sensitive to key financial sector developments (e.g., the Federal Reserve has argued that its supervisory role helped it to be more sensitive to the "credit crunch" in 1991/92); and (iii) the central bank's supervisory role makes it easier for the central bank to get information from banks.

Proponents of this view note that fundamental and ongoing changes in the financial system—the growth of short-term money markets (interbank repurchases, negotiable bank liabilities, commercial paper, treasury bills, derivatives, and money market mutual funds), the ascendancy of quote-driven, dealer-based securities markets, and the spread of arbitrage-driven portfolio management (including dynamic hedging)—require that the relevant markets remain liquid under adverse circumstances. In order to manage liquidity shocks—which will arise from time to time under even the best monetary management—the central bank needs hands-on, up-to-date knowledge of the working of the financial system, of the linkages among financial institutions, of the exposures of institutions and of the quality of their balance sheets, and of the right personnel to contact at times of emergency; it also is necessary to have close ties with other central banks to facilitate the flow of information. It is argued that without this knowledge and these contacts, the central bank will find it more difficult to distinguish illiquidity from insolvency, and to determine in real time the most appropriate form of intervention.

---

[31]The Federal Reserve has proposed that the four agencies be consolidated into two, through the merger of the OCC and OTS into the Federal Banking Commission. Moreover, the Federal Reserve suggests that the FDIC be removed from examining healthy institutions and that all independent state-chartered banks and all lead state-chartered banks in holding companies be put under the supervision of the Federal Reserve. The Federal Reserve would also retain supervisory jurisdiction over large holding companies. See Greenspan (1994).

[32]Some countries—for example, Argentina, Costa Rica, Finland, Lebanon, and Uruguay—have opted for yet another approach, in which banking supervision is elevated to semi-independent status within the central bank.

The opposition to placing banking supervision in the central bank emphasizes that (i) the central bank can get the information it needs about the health of both the banking industry and of individual banks from the banking supervisor (e.g., both the Bank of Canada and the Bundesbank—neither of which has responsibility for bank supervision—report that they receive adequate information for their needs); (ii) the central bank can get its views on bank regulation heard (e.g., in an interagency council) without being the formal supervisor of banks; (iii) a lead role in supervision might induce the central bank to pull its punches (for financial fragility reasons) in the implementation of monetary policy; (iv) the need to close banks often involves an element of expropriation of private property, which is best left to a democratically elected body; and (v) banking supervision inevitably takes too much time away from what should be the main task of the central bank, namely, the design and implementation of monetary policy.

Moving farther on the spectrum toward less involvement by the central bank in banking supervision, we have the market approach proposed by the Reserve Bank of New Zealand. Here, regulatory constraints on banks would be reduced—though not eliminated—in favor of public disclosure and market discipline. Prudential requirements (e.g., large exposure limits and limits on open currency positions) would be abolished, with the exception of capital standards. There would be increased emphasis on the role of bank directors in taking responsibility for the sound management of their banks. Each bank would be required to display prominently a credit rating on its premises if it has a rating; if not it must disclose this fact. Public disclosure requirements (relating to risk concentration and capital) would be increased, and the infrastructure of the financial system would be strengthened (by moving to a RTGS system for wholesale payments), so as to reduce the systemic consequences of a bank failure.

Supervision of Nonbanks

Who should supervise banks? Interesting as that question is, it can legitimately be seen as only one part of the broader and logically prior issue of how best to supervise and to regulate the entire financial services industry in the industrial countries. While a full treatment of that issue would go beyond the manageable scope of this study, there is one aspect of it that emerges as particularly relevant for this year's report, namely, whether the traditional separation in some major industrial countries between the supervisory approach to banks and that toward nonbanks remains appropriate.

Box 2. Developments in Mutual Fund Investments

Investment in mutual funds has grown rapidly in recent years, particularly in the United States. This growth in mutual funds has generally been at the expense of bank deposits, as households searched for yields higher than those offered by banks.

The term "mutual fund" refers in the United States to regulated funds that invest in a wide variety of financial instruments. Many of these funds are open-end, in that investors can withdraw their funds at any time directly from the fund.[1] Mutual funds differ widely according to their investment strategy, but they may be divided into two large groups. One group consists of funds that invest in longer-term assets, especially stocks and bonds. The other group consists of funds, known as money market funds, that invest in short-dated money market instruments, including certificates of deposit, commercial paper, and Treasury bills. Mutual funds are tightly regulated in the United States, under the authority of the Securities and Exchange Commission (SEC). The chief governing statute is the Investment Company Act of 1940. This act allows funds to avoid some forms of taxation and permits public marketing, but imposes restrictions on leverage.

In 1993—for the third consecutive year—there were massive net inflows into mutual funds in the United States. About $280 billion flowed into U.S. nonmoney market mutual funds in 1993, compared with inflows of $200 billion in 1992 and $121 billion in 1991; such inflows had averaged only $41 billion in each of the previous four years. From 1990 to 1993, the assets of these funds grew at an annual average rate of 38 percent (from $569 billion at the end of 1990 to $1.10 trillion at the end of 1992 and to $1.51 trillion at the end of 1993). Such growth is not unprecedented, however. Mutual fund assets expanded at an annual average rate of 50 percent between 1981 and 1986.[2]

With the market turbulence of February and March 1994, net inflows into nonmoney market mutual funds fell sharply. After a $37 billion inflow in January (and an average of $24 billion a month in 1993), inflows fell to $22 billion in February and $14 billion in March—the lowest monthly inflow in a year and a half.[3]

Over the last three years, mutual funds have expanded their share of U.S. financial assets. The ratio of fund assets (excluding money market funds) to savings and small time deposits in banks grew from 21 percent in 1986 to 65 percent at the end of 1993.[4] There has thus been a considerable shift from bank deposits into mutual funds as a component of personal savings. U.S. banks are becoming increasingly involved in the mutual fund business. There is a trend toward bank sales of mutual funds, and some banks have also taken steps to acquire mutual fund managers. Most notably, Mellon Bank has recently been given approval to purchase Dreyfus, which manages funds holding $80 billion in assets.

The growth of mutual fund assets in other major industrial countries appears less pronounced than in the United States. For these countries, data are available only through 1992.[5] They show that the growth of U.S. funds outpaced those of the other countries. Annual rates of growth during 1990–92 for open-end investment companies in the other five major industrial countries range from a high of 13 percent in Italy to a contraction of 5 percent in Japan.[6] Growth of funds' assets in the United States was 22 percent over the same period, and more if money market funds are excluded.[7]

[3]Board of Governors of the Federal Reserve System, *Federal Reserve Bulletin*, various issues, Table 1.47.
[4]Board of Governors of the Federal Reserve System (1994), Table 1.60.
[5]A consistent data series is not available for Canada.
[6]Funds in Luxembourg expanded at a 28 percent rate during this period.
[7]These data are from Investment Company Institute (1993). See Goldstein, Folkerts-Landau, and others (1992) for a discussion of longer-term trends and of regulations governing mutual funds in Europe and Japan.

[1]Closed-end funds differ in that shares cannot be redeemed, but investors instead can sell their shares on the secondary market.
[2]Investment Company Institute.

Those who wonder about the traditional approach make the following argument. The muscle in financial markets in many industrial countries is increasingly being provided by institutional investors (mutual funds, pension funds, insurance companies, and hedge funds) and by securities houses—not by banks (see Box 2 for a discussion of mutual funds). Merrill Lynch, the world's largest broker-dealer, now has approximately $500 billion in client assets, and Fidelity Investments, the largest mutual fund, has about $300 billion under management. In the United States, the share of credit assets intermediated by commercial banks has fallen from about 60 percent at the end of World War II to slightly over 20 percent today. Meanwhile, the lines of demarcation that once separated the activities of banks from those of nonbanks have become increasingly blurred.

More and more, these institutions are offering similar products to the same customers. In some cases, by looking at the balance sheets, list of activities, and funding sources of large wholesale institutions, one would be hard pressed to tell which ones were "banks" and which ones were "securities houses." Moreover, the activities of large financial institutions—be they banks or nonbanks—are progressively becoming more "international" in character.

Yet the regulatory structure in much of the industrial world is segmented in a way that does not recognize these growing similarities and trends. Not only are regulatory lines drawn according to the type of provider of a financial service—and not to the type of service provided—but the attention to macro-prudential considerations is very different. On the bank side, considerable resources are being devoted to the supervision of banks. Bank supervisors have the authority to obtain at short notice—if they do not already possess it—any information on banking activities that they deem necessary to fulfill their responsibilities. They can issue cease-and-desist orders, and they can use moral suasion to influence what banks do and how they do it. Important strides have also been made in achieving international coordination and harmonization of supervisory practices. The Basle accord on capital standards and the existing agreements on the sharing of information among home and host country supervisors are outstanding examples of this process. Banking supervisors of the Group of Ten meet monthly in Basle to discuss current developments of mutual interest, including the identification of any potential systemic threats. The emphasis is on the safety and soundness of individual institutions, and on limiting systemic risk. In contrast, the supervisory framework for nonbanks is oriented toward investor protection and market integrity. Disclosure of financial positions and exposures tend to be more limited than in the case of banks. There is some degree of international sharing of information through memoranda of understanding, and some efforts at international harmonization of capital standards and the like under the auspices of the International Organization of Securities Commissions—but less so than for banks. There is no international group of nonbank supervisors that meets frequently to review developments in markets and to identify at an early stage potential sources of systemic risk.

Concerns about the adequacy of the existing approach to supervision of nonbanks fall into three categories. First, there is a worry that failure of some kinds of nonbanks, say, a large securities house, would have adverse spillover effects on other financial institutions and players that would not be much less serious than those associated with failure of a large bank. Underlining this concern is the thought that banks are less "unique" relative to nonbanks than they used to be.[33] Second, even if it were still true that it would be considerably easier to wind down a group of large, troubled nonbanks (say, mutual funds) because of the higher marketability of their assets, there is the concern that large-scale redemptions could initiate large, abrupt asset price swings that would in turn cause difficulties for risk-management at other institutions (where the assumption for dynamic hedging and other risk management practices is that asset prices will not be subject to large gaps or jumps). The difficulties experienced by equity brokers at the time of the 1987 stock market crash is a dramatic case in point. Third, the seg-

mented structure of regulation may well impede the efficient delivery of financial services and retard the competitiveness of those providers that face a relatively high burden of regulation.

Suggestions for altering the current supervisory framework for nonbanks fall into two camps. One would be to extend some of the safety and soundness and macro-prudential considerations that now apply to banks to particular classes of nonbanks. The other, much more ambitious way to go is to redraw the regulatory map by moving toward functional regulation.[34] Under this approach, banks and nonbanks alike would be free to provide either a wide range or narrow subset of financial services, depending on their comparative advantage. For each type of functional activity (e.g., derivatives trading, banking, insurance) market participants would develop codes of conduct and other elements of self-regulation; these codes of conduct would be different for retail business (small investors) than for wholesale business (large, professional firms). Supervisory authorities would conduct market surveillance in an effort to uncover wrongdoing. Firms with higher capital and better risk management systems would be subject to less oversight than those with weaker internal lines of defense—but there would not be regulatory distinctions by legal classes of financial institutions.[35]

Enough to say that there are many who doubt the need for such a different approach to the supervision of nonbanks. They emphasize that (i) thus far, there is precious little evidence that winding down troubled nonbanks has created adverse systemic effects—suggesting that differences between banks and nonbanks are still important; (ii) where liquidity problems at certain kinds of nonbanks (large securities houses) threaten to induce systemic concerns, these institutions can be given access to the central bank's discount window (as already implemented in the United States); (iii) these potential problems with nonbanks are much less serious in countries where universal banks carry out banking, securities, and insurance activities under one roof; (iv) information sharing and international coordination among nonbank supervisors has recently expanded substantially; (v) adding new prudential requirements for nonbanks will only shift risky activities to other, less-regulated institutions and locations—leaving systemic risk unaffected and reducing the international competitiveness of regulated nonbanks in the process; and (vi) functional regulation will create its own inefficient patchwork of regulatory burdens, particularly for financial firms that engage in many functions.

---

[33]The uniqueness of banks is usually attributed to their joint provision of liquid liabilities and of nonmarketable, illiquid business loans.

[34]See McDonough (1994) and Miller (1993).

[35]The U.K. authorities have probably gone farthest in implementing a functional approach to regulation.

IV

Developing Country Finance Issues

Broad Trends

The year 1993 was a boom year for private financing to developing countries, with a sharp increase in the volume of flows, a further improvement in the terms of borrowing, and strong increases in equity prices in many local stock markets. Most of this financing took the form of securitized flows. Bonds continued to be the financing instrument of choice, with almost $60 billion issued. For the third year in a row, bond placements in 1993 doubled relative to the preceding year. International equity placements rose only moderately (to $12 billion, up from $9 billion in 1992), although direct purchases of equity in local stock markets are thought to have displayed stronger growth. Most of the bond and equity flows went to Latin America, Asia, and Europe. Other regions received significantly less financing from international capital markets, although the range of countries accessing the market continued to expand in 1993. Banks continued to participate in this market primarily through short-term trade credits, although their medium- and long-term lending to most developing countries also picked up in 1993. The market ran into turbulence in the first four months of 1994, as the increase in U.S. interest rates, as well as the political uncertainty in Mexico, helped bring bond and equity flows down sharply from their peaks of the last quarter in 1993.[36]

The strong expansion of this market in 1993 reflected a significant broadening of the investor base to include more active participation by mainstream institutional investors in providing financing to a wider range of developing countries. In particular, assets from a number of Latin American countries, which had previously appealed mainly to flight capital investors and wealthy individuals, began to make the transition to an investment acceptable to even the more conservative of the institutional investors. In this sense, they joined a group of Asian countries that have maintained access to international capital markets and that have been able to attract pension funds, insurance companies, and the like from a relatively broad spectrum of investor countries.

Hedge funds and other highly leveraged speculators have generally remained on the sidelines of this market, but have entered for short periods when they have perceived a good profit opportunity. Starting in late 1992, some U.S. pension funds, and to a lesser extent insurance companies, reportedly began to purchase investments in Latin America, including Brady bonds. In mid-1993, U.S. mutual funds, even those with no specific mandate to invest in emerging markets, reportedly made sizable increases in their investments in many emerging markets. Pension funds and insurance companies increased their participation further. European institutional investors also invested more in this market, although more moderately, perhaps taking a cue from the heightened interest of the U.S. institutions.

These investors were attracted by the high yields on these assets compared to returns in most industrial countries, particularly after the decline in U.S. long-term interest rates early in 1993. U.S. mutual funds experienced a net inflow of about $250 billion in 1993—the largest annual increase ever—as households and other investors shifted savings out of bank deposits. The returns available in emerging markets were so high and so well publicized that many institutional investors simply could not afford to ignore these assets. Some private pension funds were reported to be motivated also by the prospect of unfunded liabilities, which created the need to target a higher total return on the funds' portfolio. The strong policy track record of many developing countries and the availability of several developing countries with investment grade ratings gave investors some confidence that the risks in this market were manageable. Also, there was a growing perception that developing country assets offered good possibilities for risk diversification, because returns in these countries have been relatively uncorrelated with industrial country returns. Institutional investors in source countries are often subject to limitations—ranging from government regulations to self-imposed prudential restrictions—on their holdings of paper from developing country issuers, but in most cases their investments in developing countries were still meager enough to render these restrictions not binding.

This further expansion of the investor base could help many countries consolidate the gains they have

---

[36]The decline in bond and equity flows was particularly marked in April 1994.

made in regaining and improving their access to private international capital markets. The entrance of major institutional investors greatly enlarges the potential pool of resources developing countries can tap to finance productive investment, particularly if many of these countries sustain sound policies and gain investment grade ratings. U.S. mutual funds currently manage about $2 trillion of assets, while the combined portfolios of U.S. pension funds and insurance companies stand at almost $6 trillion.[37] Institutional investors in other countries likewise manage large portfolios; the combined assets of pension funds and insurance companies in France, Germany, Japan, and the United Kingdom are in the vicinity of $5.7 trillion (as of the end of 1991).[38] Moreover, many large U.S. investors—such as pension funds and insurance companies—still invest probably less than 1 or 2 percent of their portfolios in emerging markets; a modest increase in that share would be a significant boost in the financing available to developing countries. Investors in Japan, Canada, Europe, and many developing countries have a large scope for increasing their participation. After all, over the long term, the potential returns to capital should be higher in developing countries than in industrial ones, and industrial country investors are becoming increasingly familiar with the nature of the risks associated with investing in these markets. Also, to the extent that major institutional investors do increase their participation in developing country financial markets, this could serve as an impetus for improvements in disclosure, as well as in the regulatory and legal environment.

By now, there is sufficient diversification of the creditor base that supervisory authorities in the industrial countries no longer regard financial flows to developing countries as presenting a serious potential source of systemic risk; that is, any losses arising on financial holdings in developing countries would likely be spread widely enough throughout their financial systems to keep the impact of any disruption fairly modest.[39] These authorities noted that the banking systems in their countries have substantially cut their exposure to developing countries since the early 1980s, more reflecting banks' own preference to avoid risky claims than the need to maintain provisions on loans to certain countries.

While an expanded investor base holds out the promise of large benefits to the developing country

recipients of such financial flows, this market is also likely to remain vulnerable to significant risks—risks that would be reflected not only in the risk premiums that these countries pay in the market but also in the volatility of financial flows. The market correction observed in the fourth quarter of 1992, as well as the volatility in emerging-market bonds and equities in early 1994, are illustrative of the reactive nature of this market. The sources of this volatility are numerous and well known; they include fluctuations in the pace and scope of policy reform in the host countries themselves, terms-of-trade shocks, and variations in industrial country growth, imports, interest rates, exchange rates, and trade policies.

With a combined portfolio probably amounting to $10–15 trillion or more, the pool of funds managed by the major financial institutions in the major industrial countries easily dwarfs the market capitalization of all emerging markets countries, which is approximately $1 trillion. As such, changes in investor preferences, particularly when these preference changes are one-sided, can have a significant impact on the financial markets of the issuing countries. Also, major institutional investors are not necessarily long-term "buy and hold" investors. U.S. mutual funds need to meet performance standards over a very short time horizon, and open-ended funds face the risk of sizable net redemptions if their quarterly performance lags behind their competition. As a result, these funds actively trade their holdings in order to meet their performance standards; there is little reason to suggest that they would hesitate to sharply cut their holdings of emerging markets assets if they considered that a deterioration in the risk/return outlook was in the offing. In fact, a number of mutual funds were reported to have reduced substantially their holdings of emerging markets assets in the recent market downturn. The investment performance of pension funds is often measured in terms of annual return or the average return over several years; they thus tend to hold assets for somewhat longer than mutual funds—a practice that is also encouraged by their desire to hold longer maturity assets so as to match the maturity structure of their liabilities. Insurance companies too tend to have a somewhat longer-term perspective, but take very seriously the need to preserve their reputation as safe investments—to say nothing of constraints imposed on their holding of risky assets by their charters. This more conservative branch of the institutional investor community has little incentive to repeatedly trade in and out on their emerging market holdings, but again, if a perceived deterioration in the underlying quality of those assets were in store, they would move quickly to reduce their holding of emerging market bonds and equities.

---

[37]Board of Governors of the Federal Reserve System (1993). The information on mutual funds includes open-end and closed-end funds and money market mutual funds.

[38]Chuhan (1994).

[39]The impact of any disruption of financial flows to developing countries would of course not be modest for the host countries themselves.

Pricing and Assessment of Risk

It needs to be kept in mind that the recent growth of emerging market securities notwithstanding, this market as a whole is still in its formative years and remains less familiar to industrial country investors than their own capital markets. Although many of the large banks and securities houses in industrial countries have recently expanded substantially their market research on emerging markets, foreign investors report that they find it a challenge to assess risk/return prospects when large-scale structural changes like privatization reduce the inferences that can be drawn from historical data, when standards of disclosure—though improving steadily—are lower than in some other markets, and when the number of bond issues is expanding so rapidly.

Because of the complexities of processing information, the market appears to look for certain benchmarks to help decide on an appropriate price for a particular bond. During discussions, market participants noted that Mexico, as the first debt-restructuring country to regain access to voluntary financing in recent years, came to serve as a benchmark for measuring the risk of new sovereign debt issues in Latin America and in other regions, particularly for those with subinvestment grade ratings. The sovereign bond issues in each country then serve as a benchmark for the bonds issued by other borrowers in that country, which trade at some margin above the sovereign. The spread paid on Mexican sovereign bonds has come down from about 800 basis points over the comparable U.S. Treasury interest rate in 1989 to roughly 200 basis points in late 1993. Many market participants saw no particular logic to a spread of 200 basis points for Mexico. Others disagreed and noted that this spread was similar to the spread paid by a U.S. corporate issuer of roughly the same credit quality.

Examination of spreads on developing country bonds—in both the primary and secondary markets—suggests that the market displays a broad rationality—albeit one characterized by frequent trial-and-error adjustments. Countries that are generally regarded as weaker economic performers tend to pay higher spreads and the spreads themselves appear to react over time to new information about the borrower's prospects. Of the major Latin American borrowers, Mexico has consistently paid the lowest spread, while Brazilian bonds have consistently paid the highest ones. Bonds from countries that avoided debt reschedulings tend to carry a lower spread than bonds from restructuring countries, and spreads are usually higher on private sector issues than on sovereign issues. Many market participants felt that spreads—both between sovereign borrowers and between sovereigns and corporates—should be much wider than they have been to capture accurately the differences in risk; by the same token, many participants felt that the levels of the spreads sometimes got out of line with risk considerations, especially during periods of euphoria or extreme pessimism about emerging markets more generally.

V

Government Securities Markets in Industrial Countries

Internationalization and Institutionalization

Large and recurring government fiscal deficits in the industrial countries have pushed up ratios of government debt to GDP. For the major industrial countries as the group, the ratio of general government debt to GDP was about 43 percent in 1980; the corresponding figure for 1994 is projected to be on the order of 68 percent. Moreover, the presence of large, unfunded public pension liabilities in many of these countries will complicate the already difficult task of reducing those debt ratios over the next decade.[40]

All of this has forced authorities to think hard about how they could minimize the cost of placing and servicing government debt. And the more they thought about that problem, the more convinced they seemingly became about three conclusions.

First, one could no longer rely almost exclusively on domestic investors. Given the size of the debt, crowding-out factors would push up domestic interest rates too high, and relaxation of capital controls cum the increasingly global competition for saving had rendered domestic investors less captive than before. No, if the debt was to be sold at low cost, governments would have to tap the international market. Moreover, in that international market, it would be the institutional investor that would be prime customer for these bonds. The share of public debt of the seven major industrial countries held by nonresidents now exceeds 20 percent, and this share is on the increase. For example, during 1993, on the order of one half of all domestic and foreign deutsche mark bonds were purchased by nonresidents, and they now hold over 30 percent of all deutsche mark bonds outstanding. Similarly, non-residents now account for approximately 30 percent of the French Government's negotiable debt and for roughly 50 percent of bond positions taken on MATIF. So too with the trend of institutional holdings, which have generally risen at the expense of the share held by households. Here, the U.K. figures are instructive. In 1980, households held 16 percent of gilts; by 1992, the household share had fallen to 9 percent.[41]

Second, if government debt was to be attractive to the international institutional investor, it would be necessary to institute a series of reforms in government bond markets. Those reforms, in turn, would be patterned on the standards of liquidity, transparency, issuing and trading efficiency, and tax treatment established in the world's premier government securities market, namely, the market for U.S. Government securities.[42]

Third, if government debt management was to be more clearly formulated in terms of cost minimization and if these reforms in government securities markets were to be implemented effectively, government debt management would need to gain greater independence from the rest of government, and particularly from monetary and exchange rate policies. While much has been made in recent years of the trend toward increasing independence of central banks, this trend toward increasing independence of debt management has been just, if not more, in evidence. Where this has been done, the underlying assumption is that there are sufficient monetary policy instruments available to sterilize the impact of debt management operations on the monetary base. Under this approach, management of the maturity and currency composition of debt also cease to send signals about future monetary and exchange rate policy.

Probably the best examples of efforts to grant debt management formal autonomy from the rest of government and to orient it around explicit performance criteria are found in some of the smaller industrial countries. Since 1988, debt management in New Zealand has been placed in a Debt Manage-

---

[41]In sharp contrast to many other countries, households reportedly hold the dominant share—about two thirds—of government debt in Italy. Only about 3 percent of Italian debt is issued on international markets, although more may be held by foreigners. Portugal is another country with little foreign-held debt.

Discussions with market participants and authorities revealed that institutional holders turn over their security holdings more frequently than retail holders, but that turnover does not depend particularly on the holder's country of residence. The impact of turnover on market volatility is also unclear.

[42]The market for U.K. Government securities—for gilts—has also served as a model for some of the reforms.

---

[40]See International Monetary Fund (1993), Table 10, p. 60.

ment Office (DMO) that, although formally part of the Treasury, has a distinct mandate regarding debt management. It has been charged with maximizing the Crown's net worth subject to some constraint on the risk it can assume. Ireland created the National Treasury Management Agency (NTMA) in 1990. Its debt management objective is to fund the Government's debt at a lower cost than that of a benchmark portfolio. Sweden has been one of the most innovative sovereign issuers for some years now; the Swedish Debt Office has had responsibility for all key aspects of debt management since the late 1980s.

Reform of Government Securities Markets

While the sequencing and precise nature of reform in government securities markets inevitably differ across the industrial countries, there is enough of a consistent pattern of these reforms to talk about a consensus. Obviously, the features of the market are not all that counts. If a country has poor macroeconomic fundamentals, the debt management office is going to have more difficulty selling the bonds at a high price—no matter how they improve the market—than if the fundamentals are sound. That being said, the following practices and trends are widespread. The watchwords are liquidity and transparency. Liquidity in the secondary market is especially valued because nothing seems to frighten professional investors more than the prospect of "not being able to get out" when they want to without changing the price significantly. Professionals also do not like surprises. The more they can know in advance what the government intends to do in the bond market, the more comfortable they are about participating in that market.

Primary dealer systems. Authorities in many countries have designated a group of securities houses (or banks) as principal participants—primary dealers—in the government securities market. These firms obtain privileges in exchange for accepting certain obligations. The privileges variously include the right to submit noncompetitive bids at auctions, access to inter-dealer broker screens, designation as counterparties for the central banks' open market operations, access to repo financing, and bond borrowing/lending facilities with the central bank. In addition, a certain cachet attaches to being a primary dealer. The obligations almost always involve requirements to place "reasonable bids" in auctions, to make a continuous secondary market in a range of issues, and to provide the central bank's trading desk with market information. Although primary dealer systems restrict entry into the market, the beneficial effect on liquidity—particularly in bear markets and in

countries with thin markets—appears to outweigh the drawbacks in most cases.

Issuance techniques. The methods of issuing government securities have undergone significant changes in recent years. The main change is the move away from issuing at fixed prices through syndicates, in favor of auctions. Auctions are now used to issue the bulk of domestic government debt; in contrast, when governments issue in the Euromarket or issue global bonds, underwriting by syndicates is the preferred option. Germany and Japan still rely on a syndicate to market a portion of their domestically sold debt.[43] Of the seven major industrial countries, only Italy—a regular issuer on the Euromarkets—uses underwriting syndicates as a regular issuance technique. The gathering consensus seems to be that auctions, by opening up the bidding to a wider base of investors, produce a better price for the government—at least once the market gains a certain maturity; syndicate shares tend to remain fixed for too long, and often unduly favor domestic firms—both of which reduce competitive forces. Once the decision is made to opt for auctions, a choice has to be made between uniform-price and discriminatory methods. Under the former, the issue is sold to all participants at the same price as that of the lowest successful bidder, while in a discriminatory system, each bidder pays the price individually bid. Canada, France, and Germany use discriminatory auctions exclusively, while other countries use a mix of methods, generally with discriminatory auctions used for most of the issue volume. The United States has recently adopted on an experimental basis uniform-price auctions for sales of some Treasury notes (the lessons from that experiment are not yet in). There is no clear presumption—be it based on theory or practice—that one auction-pricing method is superior to the other. Although discriminatory auctions might be thought to increase revenue for traditional price discrimination reasons, critics have argued that this is offset by the tendency of this method to exacerbate the "winners' curse" phenomenon (whereby successful bidders overestimate the value of the securities).[44]

Issue calendar. In response to calls from market participants, many countries have adopted a firm, preannounced issue calendar. Increased certainty about issue dates and about amounts of government securities to be issued is said to help market participants to place the issue. It allows institutional investors to structure the maturity of their investment portfolios in line with the issuing calendar. It

---

[43]Syndicated bonds in Japan are issued at the weighted-average price from auctions for the other tranche of the issue.

[44]For a review of different auction formats, see Feldman and Mehra (1993).

Box 3. Withholding Taxes and Government Borrowing

Some countries levy a withholding tax on government securities. The revenue yielded by these taxes is often substantially offset by an increase in the interest rate paid by governments, while the taxes often create administrative burdens for foreign investors in government securities (including the rebating of such taxes). These burdens reduce the willingness of these investors to hold a country's securities and can therefore increase the cost of debt service by more than the revenues raised by such a tax.[1]

Usually, such a tax is part of a tax on all interest income in the economy and is imposed on government securities partly as a way to treat government and private borrowing equitably. Both foreigners and residents are likely to be subject to the tax, although sometimes at different rates. Foreigners can get the tax rebated or reduced if their countries have tax treaties with the withholding country.

Among the seven major industrial countries, only Italy and Japan impose interest withholding taxes on nonresident holders of government securities. In Italy, the tax rate is 12.5 percent for foreigners, and in Japan the rate is 15 percent.[2] The rate can be reduced for

residents of some countries; German residents, for example, pay no tax in Italy, and German and U.S. residents pay a 10 percent rate in Japan. The United Kingdom and Germany impose withholding taxes on domestic residents, but exempt all foreign residents. A key issue with all such full and partial exemptions is the ease with which nonresidents can obtain a refund; market participants report that this process has in the past been cumbersome in Italy, although authorities have recently made efforts to improve the efficiency of the rebate process. Other industrial countries that impose withholding taxes include Australia and Switzerland.

The United States eliminated a 30 percent withholding tax in 1984; by then, it had come to be regarded as an ineffective means of taxing private capital flows. Loopholes and tax treaties meant that the effective U.S. tax rate on interest paid abroad was only 2 percent in 1983. One commonly used loophole permitted U.S. corporations to borrow on the Euromarket through subsidiaries in the Netherlands Antilles, which was tax exempt because of a tax treaty.[3]

Germany imposed a 10 percent withholding tax briefly in 1989. Borrowing by foreign residents in deutsche mark was exempt from the tax, and investors in deutsche mark shifted their assets toward these loans and away from debt issued by German residents. The result was an increase in the interest rates paid by domestic residents.[4] The tax was undermined by large-scale evasion and was abolished after only six months. In 1993, Germany reimposed a 30 percent withholding tax on interest income; interest on gov-

---

[1]Similar effects can occur with taxes on transactions of securities. Such taxes often lead investors to modify their behavior to avoid the tax, either by trading related but untaxed instruments, or by trading offshore; in other cases, investors simply reduce their trading volume, directly shrinking the tax base. The experience of Sweden and the United Kingdom with such taxes is described by Campbell and Froot (1993). In Sweden, a tax on domestic equity transactions led to increased offshore trading, while the tax on fixed income transactions, including government bonds, led to domestic trading in related—but untaxed—instruments. Total turnover of Swedish fixed-income instruments also fell by two thirds with the imposition of the tax. Although the effects of the British stamp tax on transactions in U.K. equities are less clear, it appears to reduce the number of transactions and to cause a switching into untaxed derivatives and American Depository Receipts (ADRs).

[2]See Huizinga (1994).

[3]See Goulder (1990).

[4]See Goulder (1990).

---

is often maintained that greater predictability lowers the cost of issues. Some countries, such as France, have become strong believers in such a firm issue calendar and have shown great determination to stick to it, even during periods of extreme turbulence (e.g., during the ERM crisis). Some others (the United Kingdom, for one) are more skeptical; they emphasize the wisdom of having enough leeway in timing to take advantage of opportunities for obtaining the best price, as well as the need to prevent the market from changing the environment in their favor just before an auction.

Position financing. The key consideration here is the ease with which market participants can finance their securities positions. The most common financing vehicle is the repurchase agreement (repo); in a repo, an investor sells a security to another party, while at the same time agreeing to repurchase the security at a future date and at a prespecified price. Repos are in essence collateralized borrowing (which obviates the need for credit risk assess-

ment): the trader that held the original security and executed the repo remains exposed to price movements on the securities used in the repo. The ability to execute repos is particularly important to foreign firms who do not have access to a domestic deposit base. The standardized, short-dated repo is becoming the main instrument for position funding in the major markets. It facilitates the taking of leveraged, long positions in securities. Where there are no repo markets, funding has to be in the form of uncollateralized lines of credit from the banking system.

The largest repo market is, not surprisingly, located in the United States. In October 1993, primary dealers alone had open repo contracts in government securities of $852 billion, equivalent to 30 percent of U.S. marketable debt outstanding. Most repos tend to have a short maturity of a few days. The repo market in Japan (Gensaki) accounts for about 30 percent of transactions volume in government securities. Repo markets elsewhere tend to be substantially smaller. In the United Kingdom, only ernment securities paid to residents is to be withheld by the bank transmitting the payments. Nonresident depositors and bond holders are exempt from this tax, but the new tax does not exempt borrowing by foreign residents. There have been ongoing efforts among countries in the European Union to harmonize withholding taxes across countries. Such a harmonization would, for example, significantly reduce the incentive for German capital markets business to flow through neighboring countries to avoid withholding tax.

A withholding tax has different effects on private and government borrowing. For a private borrower, the tax raises the interest the borrower must pay to give lenders the same net return. On the other hand, a withholding tax does not necessarily raise the cost of the government borrowing, since the government also collects the tax revenues. If lenders continued to demand the same net return, the government would have the same debt costs as before, once its new tax revenue is taken into account. The administrative costs imposed by the tax can, however, increase the net return demanded by foreign residents and potentially increase the government's net debt-service costs.

In a country with a withholding tax, holders eligible for a lower tax rate can apply for a rebate. As noted above, however, this process can be cumbersome. The administrative cost and uncertainty in the rebate process are real economic burdens caused by withholding taxes. To reduce this burden, rebates should be automatic and prompt.

That such costs can be substantial is illustrated by experience in New Zealand, where the authorities credit the effective elimination of withholding tax on interest payments to nonresident holders of government bonds with a significant reduction in borrowing costs. Since 1991, nonresident holders of government

bonds have been able to exempt themselves from the interest withholding tax—currently between 10 percent and 15 percent—by paying an Approved Issuer Levy (AIL) of 2 percent of the interest payment. In July 1993, the Debt Management Office (DMO) began paying the AIL on behalf of nonresident holders out of its own resources. On the night the change in policy was announced, yields on ten-year bonds declined by 30 basis points—resulting in an interest cost savings that more than outweighed the AIL payments the DMO had undertaken to make. Although other factors certainly played a role, the DMO's decision contributed to a decline of 70 basis points in the spread of ten-year government bonds versus U.S. Treasury bonds by the end of October 1993.

Despite this evidence, there are two counteracting effects through which a withholding tax may potentially lower the government's debt costs. Because taxpayers in many countries receive a tax credit for taxes paid to foreign governments, they do not bear the full burden of the withholding tax.[5] In such a case, these investors will settle for a *lower* interest rate from the withholding country, net of the withholding tax, because their tax credits mean that they do not pay the full withholding tax. The second way a withholding tax can lower debt costs is through the tax it imposes on all borrowing (private plus public); this reduces the amount of competing borrowing in the capital market and may therefore allow the government to pay a lower interest rate on its borrowing. Although both of these effects may reduce government borrowing costs, they come at the expense either of foreign governments (which must pay the tax credits) or of private borrowers (who incur higher borrowing costs).

[5] See Huizinga (1994).

---

gilt-edged market makers buy repo gilts, and they must do so through the stock exchange money brokers. The Bank of England began in January 1994 to use gilts repos as a regular open market device. This has raised expectations among observers that the Bank may soon also liberalize the use of repos among private market participants.

In some countries, enthusiasm for the establishment and growth of private repo markets is restrained by the concern that their liquidity-enhancing attributes could well be offset—or even more than offset—by a higher potential for systemic instability, generated in turn by the high leverage ratios which repos facilitate. Indeed, repos are the preferred way for hedge funds to take large, highly leveraged positions in government securities.

Hedging instruments. Liquidity and efficient price discovery have also been underpinned by the development of organized futures markets (offering interest rate futures and options on government securities, for a few benchmark maturities). Dealers

and other participants will be more inclined to hold trading portfolios if they can hedge interest rate risk. In addition, futures markets often have lower transactions costs than underlying cash markets; as such, trading volume tends to be far greater in some of the successful futures contracts than in the underlying cash markets. The when-issued market—a market in securities that have not yet been issued, with trades being settled on issue day—also allows the hedging of auction bids. Such markets now exist in most of the seven major industrial countries (Germany and Japan are the exceptions).

Withholding taxes. Withholding taxes, turnover taxes, and stamp duties are an anathema to institutional investors and traders alike. Such taxes tend to segment markets; they also reduce liquidity because they impede trading (Box 3). The trend is to eliminate these taxes altogether, or if this cannot be done for equity or political reasons, to reduce them and to rebate them to foreigners as quickly and as smoothly as possible. In New Zealand, it is reported that institutional demand for its securities increased so much in the few days after it abolished the withholding tax for nonresidents that it induced a fall in the yield large enough to more than offset lost tax revenue for the year.[45]

Investor base. Different investors have different needs. Germany, for example, just recently issued a 30–year Bund to take advantage of the needs of pension funds to have an income profile that matches the profile of expected disbursements. For much the same reason, "stripped" government securities (i.e., securities that break the principal and interest components of a bond apart and sell them as separate securities) have become very popular in the United States because different investors have different requirements for the timing of interest and principal revenues. Insurance companies, mutual funds, dealers, and banks may, in turn, each have their own preferences for maturity profile, coupon, tax status, and so on. The investor base also carries implications for liquidity. For example, because retail investors tend to be less active in trading than institutional investors, issuers in some smaller markets may be reluctant to reserve too high a share for them in view of the adverse effect on liquidity. In other circumstances, when the desire may be to increase long-term holding, retail investors could be the target group.

Large issue sizes in a few benchmark maturities. Generally, the larger the issue, the more liquid it is. By concentrating on a few benchmark or "on-the-run" issues, liquidity can be increased substantially. Transactions volume tends to be concentrated in benchmark issues, and other fixed-income securities are typically priced with reference to these benchmarks. Italy, Belgium, and Sweden have refinanced smaller issues with larger benchmark issues, yielding saving of anywhere from 5 to 15 basis points. Likewise, trading in the Japanese Government bond markets is sufficiently concentrated in the benchmark issues that the yield differential between benchmark issues and nearby issues is also often on the order of 5–15 basis points. Issue size is particularly relevant for smaller government bond markets where there may not be enough investor demand to spread across too wide a spectrum of issues. Some countries have increased the size of issues by reopening the issue of an existing security instead of issuing a different security.

---

[45]Ongoing efforts in the European Union are aimed at harmonizing withholding taxes across member countries.

A smoothly functioning clearance and settlement system. This is yet another liquid-enhancing mechanism. Where this is absent, trading will be held back by delivery problems, and systemic risk will increase as the outstanding volume of unsettled trades increases. A book-entry system for securities that is closely tied to the wholesale payments system is almost indispensable in this regard. A trade netting system can also contribute to efficiency by reducing the number of payments that brokers and dealers need to make. Links between domestic clearing systems and international clearing systems, especially Cedel and Euroclear, are likewise regarded as facilitating international transactions in a country's debt.

Global bonds. The legal separation of Euroissues and domestic issues has long operated to segment domestic and Euromarkets. Recently, an instrument known as a "global bond" has been developed in an attempt to overcome this segmentation. Global bonds are issued in a number of major financial centers simultaneously (usually, Europe, the United States, and Japan). They require bridging arrangements among different national clearing systems; when these arrangements can be put in place, global bonds can flow easily across jurisdictions, thereby enhancing liquidity by allowing buyers in different locations to react to price fluctuations. The World Bank and a variety of public issuers—Italy, Sweden, China, and Argentina, among them—have successfully used the global structure for some of their debt.

It is far from straightforward to put together a robust ranking of liquidity in the major government bond markets. For one thing, some national markets may have very high liquidity in a few benchmark issues but relatively low liquidity in all the others, whereas other markets may have somewhat lower liquidity in the benchmark issues but higher average liquidity across the whole spectrum of outstanding securities. For another, there is no single measure of liquidity that is preferred to all others and for which there is a published, long time series available for the major markets. When asked for their own ordinal rankings, a large sample of private firms indicated that they would place the U.S. Government securities market in first place by a considerable margin. The next tier would contain the benchmark issues of Japanese Government bonds, the benchmark deutsche mark bonds, and French OAT issues. The major gilt issues would be at the top of the next tier, followed in no special order by Canadian federal bonds, Italian Government bonds, Belgian linear bonds, and Spanish Government bonds.

VI

China's Emerging Capital Markets

While still in its early stages, the growth of capital markets in China will rank as one of the important financial events of the 1990s. The first recognized stock exchange was officially opened in December 1990 in Shanghai, followed in April 1991 by the Shenzhen Stock Exchange. At the end of 1993, the value of equity listed on these two exchanges was about $40 billion, similar in size to the Argentine and Turkish exchanges, and comprising roughly 3 percent of the value of all "emerging markets." Of the approximately 100 stocks listed on the Shanghai Stock Exchange (SSE), almost 90 percent are A shares (equity shares denominated in yuan and reserved for Chinese residents) and about 10 percent are B shares (equity shares denominated in foreign currency and reserved for foreigners). A shares have so far tended to be much more liquid than B shares. Seven of the most internationally well-known Chinese enterprises (Tsingtao Brewery, Shanghai Petrochemical, Maanshan Steel, and four others)—representing about $3 billion in value—have been listed on the Stock Exchange of Hong Kong (SEHK), and others will be listed later in 1994; shares listed in Hong Kong are known as H shares. In October 1993, a Chinese enterprise was listed on the New York Stock Exchange for the first time. At the same time, over 4,000 Chinese companies are reported to have issued unlisted shares that are informally traded in numerous curb markets in all the major cities. The first mutual fund was recently approved by the People's Bank of China. While enterprise bonds and equities had been issued and traded since at least the mid-1980s, trading in debt securities—mostly issued by the Central Government and state financial institutions—was officially permitted only after 1986, and promoted by the development of a national OTC market in late 1990. At least three government bonds and 27 enterprise bonds have been listed on the SSE, and futures contracts for government bonds are being actively traded on the exchange.

One of the main reasons why the development of securities markets in China is of such wide interest is that it illustrates some of the challenges faced by developing country authorities—especially those from transforming economies where private ownership has to be re-established—as they attempt to coordinate these markets into the overall reform effort.

One such challenge is to keep the pace of liberalization of capital markets under control so that it is consistent with the ongoing task of stabilization of the domestic economy. As in other areas of reform, the Chinese authorities introduced capital markets on an experimental basis, hoping to learn from experience and to ensure that change came gradually and incrementally. Securities markets were therefore first introduced in only a few regions. Despite this cautious approach, there were periods in which market developments temporarily outstripped the authorities' efforts to control such activity. This problem came to a head in the winter of 1992–93 when, against the backdrop of general overheating in the economy, speculation by Chinese investors contributed to a decline in bank deposits and to the diversion of funds from investment by state-owned enterprises to securities and real estate transactions. A decline in liquidity in the rural and state-owned enterprise sectors led authorities to respond by including, in their overall stabilization program, measures forcing the recall of all "speculative" and other unauthorized loans and the complete separation of the banking and securities industries. There had clearly been a tendency on the part of some issuers to flout official regulations. Once economic agents become initiated into the possibilities of raising funds outside the banking system and of obtaining market-determined rates of return, it can be problematic to rein in the scale of these activities or to keep them contained within officially sanctioned channels.

The authorities introduced significant improvements in the regulation of securities markets in 1993. On the institutional side, the new State Council Securities Policy Committee and its executive arm, the China Securities Regulatory Commission, which was established in October 1992, assumed its place as the chief regulator and supervisor of securities markets in the spring of 1993. Thus, the regulation of bond and equity issues and trading were centralized for the first time. This provides the basis for consistent national regulation of securities markets. As a first step, interim regulations governing A shares and bonds were introduced in March 1993, and a new companies law was passed later that year. However, national securities legislation has yet to be passed by the People's Congress.

A second challenge is how to respond to the pressures that the liberalized—or even the unauthorized—elements of the financial sector eventually place on the less liberalized elements. In this connection, the Government's response to competition for domestic savings—increasingly from high-yielding equities and enterprise bonds that outperform bank deposits or government bonds—has been instructive. Although financial sector liberalization was begun at a relatively late stage in China's reform process, when these competitive pressures emerged, the Government often opted not to clamp down on these liberalized markets but, for the most part, to instead hasten the liberalization of the controlled financial sector. Although the Central Government has sometimes sought to limit competition, for example, by restricting interest rates on nongovernment bonds and more recently by restricting access to credit by securities market participants, the more common response has been to make bank deposits and government bonds more attractive. For example, over time the Government has reduced the maturity of treasury bonds and increased their returns; in addition, the policy of distributing bonds by forced allocations to institutions and individuals was ended in 1991. In 1989 and 1990, the Government issued indexed bonds, and in 1993, when disappointing sales of treasury bonds led the Government to reinstate forced distribution, this policy was combined with an increase in interest rates and the introduction of even shorter-maturity bonds. At the same time, bank deposit rates were increased on two occasions, and a policy of partial indexation was announced.

A similar pattern emerged in the policy toward external financing. China has long relied on Hong Kong as a source of external financing, usually in the form of bank loans or direct investment. However, in the early 1990s, if not before, enterprises, particularly in the south, reportedly began purchasing controlling stakes in Hong Kong companies; they thereby obtained "backdoor" listings on the SEHK. At first the authorities in Hong Kong and China seemed to look the other way, but it soon became apparent both that there was a pressing need for foreign capital in China and that foreign investors saw investment in Chinese enterprises as an attractive opportunity. Thus, in order to regulate access to foreign equity capital, and to correct some of the improprieties that had accompanied the surreptitious access to foreign markets, the Chinese authorities introduced B shares, and then, in part to allay concerns over disclosure and market regulation, H shares. Hence, it could be argued that the unregulated backdoor listings ultimately resulted in a change in the old policy of prohibiting sales of equity abroad.[46] The Hong Kong

authorities also tightened the rules that had allowed the abuse of backdoor listings by increasing disclosure requirements and by delaying approval of new rights issues. Similarly, partly in response to unauthorized external borrowing, and partly because of inefficiencies in the old system, the practice of restricting access to international bond markets to only a few financial institutions—the "ten windows"—has recently given way to a policy of allowing a broader range of approved borrowers.

A third challenge is to use the development of securities markets as an instrument for absorbing international financial techniques and practices into the economy, and as a source of discipline for enterprise governance. The Chinese authorities are counting on securities markets—in particular, equity markets—to encourage enterprises to improve both their accountability and their operational efficiency. At the very least, the need to prepare a prospectus introduces international accounting practices and, in many cases, emphasizes the importance of profitability. Preparations for stock listings also require the rationalization of operations and the separation of nonproductive activities—such as the provision of housing—from the core production operations.

The approach adopted by the Chinese authorities toward disclosure in securities markets is especially noteworthy. Rather than settle on one absolute standard of disclosure and wait until most enterprises had met it, they opted instead for a multilevel disclosure policy. More specifically, those internationally well-known enterprises that could meet the highest disclosure standards were selected for listing on the SEHK or the New York Stock Exchange. Those enterprises that were somewhat less known outside of China and could meet only a somewhat less rigorous disclosure standard were selected for B share listings. Moving further along the disclosure spectrum were enterprises offering just A shares. Although the authorities have since improved accounting and disclosure requirements for all issuers of securities, and while all investors would presumably prefer more disclosure to less, some segments of the investor base were demonstrably willing to live with different disclosure standards from others. By drawing on demand from different investor bases, China was able to move forward on securities issuance more rapidly than if all enterprises were held to the highest standard.

Securities markets are also expected to provide an ongoing source of corporate governance and to encourage continued restructuring and improvements in efficiency. But there are several reasons why these goals are likely to be realized more over the long term than in the immediate future. In the first place, the market available only to domestic residents—A shares—seems so far to have been

---

[46]Another interpretation is that B and H shares were issued primarily to raise foreign funding for the restructuring of enterprises.

driven more by liquidity than by enterprise performance. Second, even if domestic investors were keen on monitoring enterprise operations, they are so widely dispersed that the costs of monitoring would likely outweigh any benefits that would accrue to any one individual. Third, the way takeover legislation has been written has seriously constrained the market as a source of discipline. Even foreign investors, who might be considered a more reliable source of discipline (in the short term) because they have more experience with evaluating equity markets, are hampered somewhat by questions over the information available about listed firms. Moreover, as long as foreign investors are barred from the A share market, they cannot acquire majority stakes in any of the listed enterprises.

A fourth issue in organizing domestic capital markets is whether to separate banking and securities markets, and if so, how best to delineate that separation. Here, there is a potential concern that banks may allocate an unduly large share of their assets to speculative activities and thereby expose themselves to large losses if they are permitted to participate in securities markets directly or even through subsidiaries. Another approach, which is more restrictive and which has in fact been adopted by the Chinese authorities, is to forbid banks from extending credit to participants in securities markets. In the first instance this policy, which has always been present but which was rigorously enforced under the 16–point program, ensures that funds are channeled only to their intended destinations. However, this policy also prevents bank lending from fueling a speculative bubble, which when it collapses, would involve the banks in large losses. On the other side of the ledger, however, a reduction in liquidity would probably increase the cost of transactions in the stock market because investors will have to pay the full value of their purchases up front and securities companies will have to hold greater reserves in order to protect themselves against settlement and default risk. A lack of liquidity could also increase the probability of a settlement failure, as well as knock-on failures in other institutions because the resources available to any one member of an exchange will be lower in the absence of bank credit lines. In the end, the authorities have to weigh the likely incidence and costs of these different types of risk.

A fifth issue is how to choose the firms that are to be listed on the stock exchange. Unlike most other countries, China decided to have the securities market regulators and other government agencies select the firms that will be able to list either H, B, or A shares. What makes this procedure somewhat controversial is that this selection is based, at least in part, on noneconomic considerations, such as a concern for regional equality. On the other hand,

the authorities appear to have deliberately chosen the most profitable, and often the largest, firms in the state sector. Moreover, after a long history of central planning and price controls, it may be that foreign specialists would have no comparative advantage, relative to the authorities, in picking enterprises with the best growth prospects.

Yet a sixth issue is how much to rely on securities markets as a source of finance relative to alternative sources. On the domestic side, it is well to note that compared with bank financing, securities markets have remained marginal as a source of funding in China. The value of new bank loans in 1993 was fully ten times the value of bond and equity issues. Indeed, the main reason why the authorities have pushed the need for domestic bank reform so hard is that they recognize that banks are likely to remain the primary source of outside financing for enterprises over the indefinite future.

As regards external financing, China's involvement in international securities markets has followed the pattern of other developing countries in recent years. In response to wider spreads and shorter maturities on commercial bank loans, the authorities deliberately followed a strategy of making more extensive use of international bond markets. After raising $1.3 billion in 1992, Chinese borrowers raised $2.9 billion in 1993. In raising these funds, Chinese borrowers broadened their investor base by accessing a wider range of market segments and by placing issues in a larger number of currencies. The Chinese Government has an investment-grade credit rating, reflecting the absence of debt-service problems in recent years, as well as its relatively low level of external debt. Consequently, spreads on bonds issued by Chinese borrowers were significantly narrower than on those issued by many other developing countries.

Nevertheless, equity investment by foreigners emerged as the dominant external source of financing in 1993, and foreign direct investment commitments mushroomed to over $100 billion. Most visible was portfolio investment through purchases of B and H shares and through country funds. Many individual share offerings have been oversubscribed. For retail investors, the easiest path to acquiring equity in Chinese enterprises was through investment in country funds devoted to China. There are currently some 40 funds, with total assets approaching $2 billion, that invest in "red chips" (i.e., SEHK listings of mainland firms, including both the H shares and the backdoor listings), in B shares, and in some cases, in other stock markets in the region. Most of these funds are heavily weighted toward Hong Kong "China plays" rather than B shares, because disclosure and market regulation are viewed at this stage as stronger in the former.

VII

Conclusions

1. It is not surprising that the recent surge in government bond yields across the industrial countries has attracted the close attention of policy-makers and market participants alike: the size of the increase was very large for such a short time period, it affected many countries simultaneously, and it was largely unanticipated. While the origin of the increase differed somewhat from country to country, there is by now little doubt that the main factor was a large revision of expectations about economic performance and about the future path of interest rates and exchange rates. The events triggering that revision of expectations were varied. They included a slower than expected fall in European interest rates; stronger than expected growth performance in the United States, along with new information about the timing of the long-awaited turn in U.S. monetary policy; an unexpected, episodic intensification of the U.S.-Japan trade dispute; more buoyant than expected performance of Japanese equities, in concert with larger than expected sales of Japanese Government bonds and a less pessimistic outlook for the economy as a whole; and an unexpected fall in bond and equity prices in emerging markets.

In financial markets, it is possible for such a revision of expectations—if it is shared by all market participants—to alter asset prices almost immediately; indeed, the change in asset prices can occur without any transactions even taking place. In this case, however, trading volumes soared along with the rise in bond yields, as a broad spectrum of market participants sought to undo large positions that had been built up under the projections of a continued rise of European and U.S. bond prices and a strengthening of the dollar against the yen and some European currencies. As positions were closed out, selling pressures added to the downward pressure on bond prices, especially in those smaller bond markets where liquidity was relatively limited. The same high degree of leverage that had contributed to the run-up of bond prices in 1993 now acted symmetrically on the downside to encourage a contraction. Risk management systems that incorporated marking to market of positions and explicit loss limits operated as intended to prevent firms from suffering even larger losses—but with the consequence of mandating sales into a declining market.

All the while, interest rate increases were being transmitted from one country to another by the recognition that convergence of long-term interest rates had been high in the 1990s, by the practice of cross-hedging, and by the tendency for losses in one market to generate pressure for liquidation in others. This transmission was most visible after the Federal Reserve's small increase in interest rates on February 4, 1994, but it operated at other times during the relevant two-month period as well.

To be sure, this latest bout of bond market turbulence will not be the last time that market participants take a large, one-sided bet on the evolution of economic fundamentals and then alter abruptly their view—rightly or wrongly—in response to new information. Indeed, the agility of international capital markets makes it much easier and less costly than it used to be to implement such portfolio shifts. Nor will it likely be the last time that some segment of the investment community takes on a lot of risk, guesses wrong the future path of policies, and suffers losses. The key question that needs to be asked about recent bond market turbulence is, did markets function well overall? The short answer to that question is yes.

Although the increase in bond yields was undeniably large for such a short time period, the markets did receive new information in February and March on economic performance—especially on growth rates—and on the likely future course of macroeconomic policies. Given that new information, there is no reason to presume that a slower adjustment of bond prices to the new equilibrium was to be preferred to the faster adjustment that actually took place. Perhaps with the benefit of hindsight, markets did not pay enough attention to large budgetary imbalances and to the inflationary implications of declining output gaps in driving long-term bond yields so low in 1993, and the rise in yields in the first quarter of 1994 was a correction to that earlier excessive optimism; but this is hard to document with much precision and, even if so, would not necessarily imply that the net effect on the macroeconomy was large. No doubt, during February and March 1994, there was a good deal of uncertainty and volatility in markets, and some liquidity strains were evident, particularly in the smaller cash markets. But there was no seizing-up of markets, participants made good use of greater liquidity available in the larger futures markets, and payments and settlement systems once again coped satisfactorily with the increased volumes. The disturbances in bond markets also did not spread out widely to currency markets. Some hedge funds, along with a variety of other aggressive position-takers, suffered large losses—and a few even failed. Such losses are part and parcel of the business of taking risks, and their occasional occurrence is what presumably keeps the "smart money" from getting too smart or too large. The important thing was that difficulties at individual firms did not have systemic effects. Mark-to-market accounting methods, explicit loss limits, and the taking of both marketable collateral and margin payments by banks and securities houses in their lending to the heavy position-takers, all played a helpful role in limiting systemic risk.

On the basis of developments in bond and foreign exchange markets over the past few years, it seems ill-advised to single out hedge funds for special new regulatory requirements. Where there has been turbulence, it is doubtful that it would have been avoided or significantly lessened by restricting the activities of hedge funds. There are just too many other large players in the markets who have taken a similar view of market opportunities, and who have acted on those views, to hold any single class of players responsible for what happened. Also, there will be times when hedge funds' flexibility in seeking high returns will permit them to act as a stabilizing force in markets when others—because of their external guidelines or more conservative attitudes toward risk—either cannot or choose not to do so.

But all of this does not mean that regulatory and supervisory authorities have cause to become complacent about the resiliency of the financial system. Quite the contrary. With pools of high-yield seeking capital growing rapidly, with the technology of international capital markets making it cheaper and easier to alter the asset and currency composition of portfolios at short notice, and with institutional fund managers under continuing pressure to deliver high performance, it is all the more important that systemic risk control mechanisms be up to the task of dealing with surges in transactions volumes, with occasional periods of high volatility in asset prices, and with the inevitable, sizable losses that will occur from time to time in parts of the financial services industry. The aim of these systemic risk control mechanisms is not to discourage risk-taking activity, for that activity is much needed; it is instead to ensure that risks are undertaken by those who are aware of those risks and who are able to bear the losses—without having those losses spill over broadly onto others, thereby resulting in costly disruptions of the payments and settlement system,

or in a large public sector liability, or in a weakened performance of the macroeconomy.

Toward this end, maintenance of sound risk management and exercise of vigilant supervision remain key priorities. To begin with, banks and their supervisors need to ensure that banks are setting appropriate collateral and margin requirements on their lending to hedge funds and other aggressive position-takers. Indeed, margin requirements have to reflect the fact that the collateral will decline in value whenever the borrower loses on his long position, since that position itself serves as the collateral. The large losses sustained by banks in their collateralized real estate lending over the past few years indicate that holding collateral by itself is no guarantee of repayment: the collateral must be highly marketable and its liquidation value correctly appraised. Margins too have to be set at the appropriate level and adjusted promptly when market conditions change markedly—even when the borrower is a large and important customer of the lender.

Up-to-date knowledge of the consolidated position of the borrower would be helpful in assessing the borrower's capacity to meet many margin calls simultaneously under adverse market conditions. Further protection is afforded by more general concentration and large exposure guidelines that seek to ensure that lenders do not put too many of their eggs in one basket. In terms of safeguarding the integrity of government bond markets, there is also merit in giving consideration to the passage and implementation of large position reporting and information systems throughout the industrial countries. As noted earlier, enabling legislation is now in place for such a system to be implemented in the U.S. Government securities market, but other government bond markets—particularly the smaller ones—would also benefit from the information that such a system can provide about all large trades and traders (not just those carried out by hedge funds). Finally, the impressive progress that has already been made in improving the design and functioning of payments and settlement systems needs to continue, including the introduction of real time gross settlement systems and fees for daylight overdrafts, as well as efforts to improve liquidity in the underlying bond markets themselves. When the surges in transaction volumes come, the liquidity and infrastructure of financial markets have a great deal to do with how well markets cope with it.

2. The proposals put forth by the Basle Committee on Banking Supervision for extending the 1988 Basle Capital Accord to cover market risk and to permit netting of positions are a welcome step forward in reducing potential systemic risks associated with the growing volume of off-balance sheet bank-

ing activities. So long as supervisors develop explicit criteria—preferably harmonized across the major countries—to determine whether the key assumptions embedded in banks' own risk-management models are reasonable, and so long as the burden of proof for compliance rests with the banks, there is no problem in allowing those banks who wish to do so to use their models for the purpose of figuring capital charges for market risk.[47] Other banks may decide that the Basle Committee's standardized methodology is perfectly adequate. The important thing is to put in place one method or the other so that market risk is appropriately priced in banks' portfolio decisions.

Ongoing efforts to improve accounting and disclosure standards for derivatives deserve strong support. For market discipline to operate effectively, market participants need to have adequate information on the risks they are assuming in dealing with counterparties. Derivative positions and activities are increasingly an important component of the activities of banks, securities houses, and other large players. Accurate risk assessment has up to now been hampered by a lack of transparency about these exposures. The better the quality of information available, the lower the probability of market "runs" based on false information.

Even, however, with improved measures of regulatory capital and with better accounting and disclosure standards for derivatives, the key line of defense against systemic risk in derivatives lies with firms' own risk management. A bank's trading exposure can change too fast to be protected by last quarter's balance sheet, and even a well-capitalized firm may not have sufficient capital to cover a very large trading loss after it has already occurred. The firm's risk management needs to catch an ill-conceived trading strategy or a faulty hedge before it takes place, or failing that, to at least ensure that when losses reach a prespecified limit, operations are cut back to prevent even larger losses from being sustained. Continuing efforts to improve the quality of risk management must therefore be strongly encouraged.

3. By now, it is increasingly accepted that there is not one exchange arrangement that is "best" for all countries; instead, the choice of exchange rate regime depends on the country's particular characteristics and circumstances. Much the same is true for the role of the central bank in banking supervision. In those financial centers where liquidity-intensive financial activities are most pervasive and where liquidity shocks—if not reacted to in a timely

fashion—could raise systemic risks, there is a comparative advantage in the central bank assuming a hands-on role in banking supervision. It is not that the central bank could not be effective in resolving financial crises without it—indeed, there have been cases in such economies where the central bank has been deeply involved in resolving a crisis in a sector outside its supervisory jurisdiction (e.g., insurance and nonfinancial corporations); it is instead that the central bank will likely be more effective in such situations when it has close knowledge of the links between banks and other financial institutions, when it is well acquainted (before the crisis occurs) with the exposure of individual institutions and the quality of their balance sheets, and when it knows who to contact to do what in a particular bank in a time of emergency. In those same circumstances, it is also doubtful that some other institution would do the job better.

In other economies, where the need for short-term liquidity management is somewhat less, or where a large share of banking activities are concentrated in a handful of large banks, or where financial innovation does not occur at as quite a rapid pace, there may be advantages in having some other agency act as the banking supervisor—so long as the central bank can both get the information on banks it needs at short notice and make its views on banking regulation known and listened to.[48] In those circumstances, having the central bank's money desk located close to the market and having close working relationships with banks, dealers, and other key players, may well be sufficient to absorb the information and knowledge that is useful for crisis intervention and for monetary policy implementation—without having any formal responsibility for banking supervision. This also of course frees the central bank to spend more time on its task of designing and implementing monetary policy. There can even be country circumstances (say, where there are a limited number of large banks headquartered abroad) where much of the load of banking supervision can be taken up by market forces (together with strict disclosure requirements, mandatory credit ratings, and the like). The same suit of clothes need not fit everyone. That being said, the staff is somewhat skeptical of the argument that a less hands-on role for the central bank in banking supervision will make it easier for it to resist calls for a "bailout" when a bank gets into trouble. The key consideration is size. Letting a small bank fail is one thing. But if the bank is "too large to fail," it will be difficult to resist such calls, no matter what the central bank's role, or lack of it, in supervision.

---

[47]Criteria need to be explicitly formulated to allow an objective, consistent, and cost-efficient evaluation of risk-management models.

[48]Some would argue that the central bank, as the primary guardian of overall financial stability, should receive information on all types of financial institutions—not just on banks.

4. There is no doubt that the lines of demarcation between the activities of banks and nonbanks have become blurred over the past decade. It is also apparent in some industrial countries that the muscle in financial markets has been shifting away from banks and toward institutional investors and securities houses. And indisputably, the activities of large financial institutions—banks and nonbanks alike—are becoming more international in character. The question is what do these trends imply about the appropriate way to orient supervision toward banks and nonbanks? There are two related but distinct issues here. One concerns the efficient delivery of financial services, the maintenance of a level playing field for different providers of those services, and the pressure to engage in excessive risk-taking. The second one concerns the systemic risk associated with winding down a troubled bank versus that for a troubled nonbank.

It is easy to concede that the delivery of financial services to the user would be more efficient in some industrial countries if providers of those services were free—subject to codes of conduct and overall market surveillance—to furnish whatever mix of financial services was consistent with their perceived comparative advantage—more in line with the practice in countries that have universal banking systems. It is also the case that differences in regulatory treatment (along with implicit and explicit guarantees) between banks and nonbanks—in tandem with growing similarities in the products of banks and nonbanks—has led to some significant shifts in market shares—both between banks and nonbanks within certain countries and between banks in countries with different regulatory regimes. There is a lot of empirical support for the proposition that it is precisely when banks and other depository institutions have lost market share that they are most likely to leverage off their deposit insurance (and other guarantees) to engage in excessive risk-taking (so as to increase their profitability and avoid downsizing). This is just a long way of saying that if one were starting from scratch in designing a regulatory framework for certain industrial countries, there would be a lot of merit in considering a more "functional" approach to regulation, where regulation was organized around the financial service provided, not around the provider of the services—for example, all providers of risk-hedging services would be subject to the same regulations. The difficulty of course is that we are not starting from scratch, and the existing organization of the financial services industry has not yet evolved far enough along functional lines on its own account to make such a radical change in the regulatory structure likely any time soon.

A similar argument to that outlined above might also be employed to suggest that an approach to regulation of nonbanks that focuses almost exclusively on investor protection is outmoded. As banks and nonbanks become more alike, and as nonbanks become more important, is it not true that a systemic threat is just as likely to arise in capital markets as in the banking sector? That argument ignores one powerful empirical regularity. Over the past few decades, when banks and other depository institutions (e.g., U.S. thrift institutions) have been in trouble, the systemic consequences have been substantial. Recall the huge public sector liability associated with resolving the recent banking crises in three Scandinavian countries or the cost to U.S. taxpayers of cleaning up the savings and loan problem; or recall the effects that a weakened banking sector has had on the pace of recovery from the recent recession in some industrial countries. In contrast, at least to this point, troubles at nonbanks have had much less serious systemic effects; there, it has proved easier to confine losses to those who took the risks, and those who have borne the losses have been diversified enough in their portfolios to prevent any significant feedback effects on the real economy. This difference is at the heart of the argument for why supervision of nonbanks can legitimately focus on investor protection and downplay the safety and soundness of the individual institutions themselves.

The relevant question is whether this difference in systemic risk between banks and nonbanks will persist in the future—now that there is greater similarity between bank and nonbank liabilities and assets (e.g., would runs on nonbank money market mutual funds carry the same consequences as runs on bank deposits, or would the failure of a large nonbank to settle a derivative contract carry the same consequences as the failure of a bank to settle).[49] There is no clear answer to that question—but prudence would suggest that nonbank supervisors may want to give somewhat more attention to market developments, to identifying potential systemic threats, and to international sharing and coordination of information. Some of this is already going on, as evidenced by the increase in memoranda of understanding between securities regulators in important financial centers. But perhaps it is worth considering whether nonbank supervisors from the industrial countries would profit from meeting more frequently on a regular basis to review developments in markets and to discuss problems of mutual concern. Similarly, and as noted earlier, implementation of large position reporting and information systems would help fill

---

[49]Since money market mutual funds mark assets to market continuously, a run on such a fund would not produce insolvencies, but it might nevertheless generate pressure for public support, if losses were large and if shares in these funds were viewed as being implicitly insured.

some of the gaps in understanding about the activities of large nonbanks. If an inducement were needed to get certain types of nonbanks to agree to additional reporting or supervisory requirements, granting them access to the wholesale payments system could be a possibility.

5. Private financing to developing countries has continued to mature. The volume of flows, the terms of borrowing, the width of the investor base, and the choice of financing instruments, have all improved markedly over recent years. Moreover, there are some good reasons for optimism over the longer term: many more performance-oriented investors now have direct experience with the high returns to capital available in those emerging markets that can sustain high growth rates; some more conservative investors are being induced to give emerging-market securities a closer look now that many more developing countries have a strong policy track record and now that there is more investment-grade developing country paper available; the share of institutional-investor portfolios in the largest creditor countries now devoted to emerging markets is now so small (1–2 percent) that even a moderate increase would translate into a large increase in the pool of resources going to developing countries; and larger inflows should act as an impetus for improvements in disclosure standards and in the legal and regulatory framework that, in turn, should further increase the attractiveness of these markets. So much for the good news. The bad news is that there is not yet any firm indication that the volatility that has often characterized private financial flows to developing countries is on the wane. This volatility stems from a variety of sources, including changes in the pace or scope of economic policy reform in the host countries, terms-of-trade shocks, and variations in industrial country growth, interest rates, exchange rates, and trade policies. The push that low interest rates in the industrial countries have given to these financial flows to emerging markets is a case in point: the flows have been huge, but it is difficult to know how much of it will be sustained once the recovery gains momentum in the industrial world and interest rates there return to normal levels. The fact that the investment portfolios of institutional investors are large relative to the capitalization of most stock markets in developing countries also means that sharp, one-sided shifts in foreign investor sentiment can induce large swings in local equity prices. In the end, the most effective action that host countries can take to minimize this volatility is to strive for consistency in the implementation of strong macroeconomic and structural policies and to make every effort to see that borrowed resources are wisely invested.

6. One of the more important structural changes to have taken place in international capital markets over the past decade is the trend toward increasing nonresident ownership of government debt. In effect, the largest economic entities in the industrial world have decided that participation in world capital markets confers significant enough advantages to make it worthwhile to subject themselves to the unwritten rules of the marketplace. This surveillance by global capital markets is of two types: first, the market's evaluation of national economic policies; and second, the market's evaluation of the structural characteristics of national financial markets. The more favorable is the market's evaluation on both counts, the lower will be the home country's cost of placing and servicing government debt.

While the sequencing and precise nature of reform in the government securities market inevitably differs across the industrial countries, there is a consistent enough pattern to talk of a broad consensus on what a country needs to do (macroeconomic fundamentals aside) to be attractive to international, institutional investors.

In brief, the ten commandments are (i) establish a primary dealer system to underpin liquidity, especially in the secondary market; (ii) create fungible benchmark issues in a few key maturities, as larger issues tend to be more liquid than smaller ones; (iii) have a firm issue calendar, so professionals can operate under conditions of greater predictability; (iv) opt for open auctions instead of syndications—the choice of a particular auction pricing method is less important; (v) create a safe and efficient repurchase market to facilitate the funding of positions; (vi) encourage trading in a few futures contracts on the benchmark issues, so that the market can hedge trading portfolios; (vii) establish an efficient securities settlement and clearance system, preferably in book-entry form; (viii) eliminate withholding and turnover taxes—and if that is not possible, at least reimburse these taxes to nonresidents quickly and smoothly; (ix) know the investor base, since different investors have different needs; and (x) for very large issues, consider global bonds.

The impact of this increased foreign ownership of government debt goes beyond just the potential reduction in debt-servicing costs for the borrower. Two externalities merit explicit mention. First, it seems clear that increased foreign ownership of government debt has acted as a force to dissuade countries from imposing capital controls at times of market turbulence. Any short-term gains in the room for maneuver for macroeconomic policy would have to be weighed against the long-term cost of alienating the very investors whom one wants to attract and to hold. Even when capital controls have been imposed recently during exchange market crises, they have been short-lived. Second, a common feature of many of the reforms outlined above is that they increase the liquidity of government bond markets. As noted earlier in the discussion of recent bond market turbulence, strains are more likely to occur in markets and for financial instruments that are relatively illiquid. Even the best risk management system in the world cannot get a firm out of a position without a significant loss if the market does not have the requisite liquidity. To the extent that the liquidity of government bond markets is higher today than it was ten years ago, so too is the resiliency of the system to large and sudden portfolio shifts.

7. The development of capital markets in China has to be seen in a broader context than simply as an additional source of finance; instead, it is best viewed as part of the cutting edge of the reform process itself. The development of securities markets creates a window through which international financial techniques and practices can be absorbed in China. The listing on an exchange, as well as market evaluation of an enterprise's stock, may over time provide an additional source of discipline on enterprise governance. The development of securities markets can also increase pressure for decontrolling other financial markets. Once there is a fully market-determined rate of return available to savers on some assets (such as equities), there will be pressure to liberalize the rate of return on other assets so as to limit the size of financial flows into the initially liberalized ones. These changes in capital markets need to be carefully managed so that they do not run ahead of themselves and cause problems for ongoing efforts at macroeconomic stabilization. But over the longer term, their impact is likely to be highly beneficial.

8. To sum up, international capital markets have continued to grow in size, in sophistication, and in the degree of integration. In addition to their traditional functions of channeling resources from units that are net savers to those that are net dissavers, of providing liquidity, and of allocating, pricing, and diversifying risk, international capital markets have acquired increased clout as an indicator of the credibility of the government's actual or prospective policies, as a disciplining mechanism for errant or inconsistent government policies, and as an impetus for reform of financial markets and practices in industrial and developing countries alike. But if international capital markets are to perform all these functions well—and to avoid the potential systemic risks that go along with increased size and integration—it is important that the supervisory and regulatory framework itself be sensitive and responsive to the changing structure of those markets, including their increasingly "international" dimension. Mark Twain put it succinctly: "Even if you're on the right track, you'll get run over if you just sit there."

Annex I

Government Securities Markets

Government securities are the backbone of world securities markets. Their turnover far surpasses that in any other financial market, except the global foreign exchange market. In recent years, government securities markets have undergone great changes. As many industrial countries ran sustained budget deficits in the 1980s and early 1990s, the size of government securities markets mushroomed. International competition for investors has forced governments to institute a wide range of reforms aimed at deepening liquidity in their markets and broadening their investor base. These reforms have attracted foreign institutional holders of government securities. With investors continually rebalancing their portfolios between securities of different countries, these markets have grown increasingly integrated across countries.

This annex provides an overview of major elements of government securities markets in industrial countries and of issues related to those markets. Although it focuses on the marketable obligations of central governments, obligations of other levels of government and nonmarketable claims of the central government are also discussed.

Recent Trends and Developments

The Increase in Debt Issues and Debt Outstanding

The 1980s and early 1990s have witnessed a significant rise in both the amounts of debt outstanding and in issue volumes. These increased stocks and flows have challenged the governments of industrial countries to manage their debt in a way that keeps the cost of debt service as low as possible. High real interest rates during much of this period heightened this challenge for many countries.

Table 4 shows the amount of debt outstanding in the larger industrial countries between 1980 and 1992, both in dollar terms and scaled by GDP in those countries. (Because of data limitations, the table includes debt held by the domestic central bank, and it also includes nonsecurities debt.) In most of the countries shown, debt expanded considerably as a percentage of GDP over the 1980s and early 1990s. Among the major industrial countries, U.S. debt jumped from 27 percent in 1980 to 52

Chart 2. Government Debt Outstanding in Major Industrial Countries
(In percent of GDP)

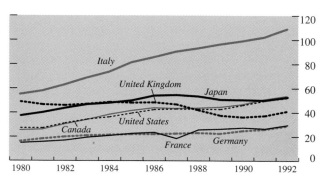

Sources: International Monetary Fund, *International Financial Statistics;* Bank of Japan, *Economic Statistics Annual* (1991) and *Economic Statistics Monthly*, various issues; Bank of Italy, *Economic Bulletin*, No. 17 (October 1993); Bank of England, *Quarterly Bulletin* (November 1993); and United Kingdom, Central Statistical Office, *Annual Abstract of Statistics 1994*.

percent in 1992, Italian debt from 55 percent in 1980 to 109 percent in 1992, and Canadian debt from 25 percent in 1980 to 54 percent in 1992. Debt also expanded in France, Germany, and Japan, although less dramatically (Chart 2). Rapid expansions of debt also took place in Belgium, the Netherlands, Spain, and Sweden.[1]

Table 5 turns from stocks to flows of debt, by reporting the volume of gross issues of securities with a maturity of more than one year. Most of the countries in the table show a strong upward trend in the dollar-equivalent volume of securities issued, but they also show considerable fluctuations from year to year. Such fluctuations can be due to variations in net financing requirements, in the volume of older securities maturing, and in variations in the proportion of medium-term and long-term securi-

---

[1]As noted in the introduction, the figures discussed here pertain only to central government debt. In some countries, the debt of other levels of government also is significant.

Table 4. Central Government Debt Outstanding

	1980	1981	1982	1983	1984	1985	1986	1987	1988	1989	1990	1991	1992
						(In billions of U.S. dollars)							
United States	738	825	988	1,174	1,373	1,598	1,813	1,954	2,097	2,244	2,548	2,845	3,142
Japan	450	433	507	611	595	911	1,267	1,584	1,562	1,323	1,587	1,736	2,121
Germany	120	123	132	127	119	162	217	282	270	293	401	449	497
France	93	87	92	93	95	141	185	185	244	281	348	348	376
Italy	229	223	250	261	275	392	566	757	776	902	1,147	1,263	1,113
United Kingdom	254	211	190	206	197	255	298	371	333	316	345	371	367
Canada	73	77	95	114	130	147	177	205	232	253	269	296	290
Spain	39	39	40	42	50	71	92	137	134	153	192	216	205
Netherlands	46	48	55	57	57	83	109	142	137	153	188	198	197
Australia	. . .	. . .	32	32	39	36	43	48	50	43	38	38	46
Sweden	38	42	45	46	51	55	74	83	82	78	84	81	110
Switzerland	18	18	17	15	14	19	24	30	26	25	31	34	38
Belgium	61	62	62	62	63	92	130	172	165	190	233	248	250
						(In percent of GDP)							
United States	27.2	27.2	31.4	34.5	36.4	39.6	42.5	43.0	42.8	42.7	46.1	49.7	52.0
Japan	37.5	40.2	43.8	46.8	48.1	50.1	54.1	54.6	53.4	50.7	50.5	50.1	52.7
Germany	16.0	18.1	19.8	20.8	21.4	21.9	21.9	22.4	23.0	22.4	24.7	25.8	28.7
France	14.9	15.8	17.0	19.5	21.0	22.7	23.6	18.5	25.7	26.4	27.5	26.6	29.6
Italy	54.9	57.7	62.8	68.5	73.4	81.1	85.4	90.0	92.7	96.0	98.8	101.9	108.6
United Kingdom	48.9	46.5	45.9	47.0	48.6	48.0	48.3	46.6	41.9	37.3	36.1	37.2	40.9
Canada	25.2	25.8	30.2	33.8	38.2	41.4	43.6	43.1	43.5	44.2	46.5	50.6	53.5
Spain	20.3	22.4	25.8	29.2	34.2	38.9	37.5	41.3	37.9	37.2	37.2	38.0	40.0
Netherlands	29.1	33.5	39.2	46.0	51.0	53.8	54.6	57.1	60.0	60.6	61.4	62.5	63.6
Australia	. . .	. . .	18.7	20.5	22.0	23.7	25.2	23.8	19.7	16.0	12.9	13.1	15.4
Sweden	30.2	36.8	43.0	49.7	52.2	55.5	56.0	52.2	46.0	42.1	37.5	36.8	42.2
Switzerland	18.6	17.1	16.9	16.4	17.2	17.2	15.9	15.2	14.6	13.2	12.9	13.7	16.3
Belgium	55.5	66.4	74.3	83.2	89.3	97.3	105.5	109.3	110.4	112.6	112.6	115.6	117.9

Sources: International Monetary Fund, *International Financial Statistics*; Bank of Japan, *Economic Statistics Annual* (1991) and *Economic Statistics Monthly*, various issues; Bank of Italy, *Economic Bulletin*, No. 17 (October 1993); Bank of England, *Quarterly Bulletin* (November 1993); United Kingdom, Central Statistical Office, *Annual Abstract of Statistics 1994*; and Treasurer of the Commonwealth of Australia, *Government Securities on Issue at 30 June 1992*.

Note: The United States, Germany, France, Italy, Canada (from 1990 onward), Spain, the Netherlands, Switzerland, and Belgium contain data for December 31; Japan, the United Kingdom, and Canada (through 1989) have data for March 31 of following year; Australia and Sweden show data for June 30.

ties relative to other debt instruments. Exchange rate fluctuations can also affect these data. A comparison of different countries shows that the greatest gross volume of new issues is in the United States and Japan, followed by Germany and Italy.

The lower half of Table 5 scales the gross issue data by GDP, and data for the major industrial countries are depicted in Chart 3. These figures give an indication of the demands that government debt issues place on the domestic financial infrastructure. Issues in most countries do not exceed 10 percent of GDP in a given year (Belgium and Italy generally are exceptions as were Japan and Spain in 1993).

Table 6 provides some data on issues of short-term securities (under one year in maturity). Chart 4 shows these data scaled by GDP for the major industrial countries. Short-term securities include treasury bills and similar products. The gross issue volume of these securities can be large because the debt stock is often rolled over several times a year.

In some countries, including Japan, such bills are issued mainly for short-term cash management. While only limited data are available for short-term issues, Table 6 shows that the United States and Japan are the largest issuers of short-term debt, as they are for longer-term debt. The volume of short-term debt issued by these countries is several times the volume of longer-term debt issued. This is also true in Italy and Canada. All of this makes it important for governments to have efficient mechanisms for issuing such debt into their money markets.

This expansion in both volumes issued and the outstanding stocks has fostered change in government securities markets through two channels. First, the rise in volumes increases the stakes associated with reform of these markets. For example, benefits from changing the method of issuing government securities are magnified as issue volumes expand. Second, the expansion in government debt outstanding tends to bring about changes in the nature of holders of the debt (see below).

Table 5. Gross Issues of Medium- and Long-Term Government Securities[1]

	1980	1981	1982	1983	1984	1985	1986	1987	1988	1989	1990	1991	1992	1993
	(In billions of U.S. dollars)													
United States	132.4	150.5	192.3	246.1	303.2	320.7	331.5	353.8	317.2	366.8	418.8	491.8	536.7	544.7
Japan[2]	61.6	71.2	63.4	91.8	79.6	90.1	141.8	185.6	196.5	185.2	264.2	287.2	346.5	461.5
Germany[3]	11.5	11.2	15.3	13.9	14.1	16.8	29.8	42.1	39.7	34.1	75.8	75.8	113.5	97.0
France[4]	9.3	4.6	6.4	6.7	10.3	11.6	21.1	13.8	16.4	14.8	21.1	20.8	33.3	63.7
Italy[5]	15.3	16.5	38.6	58.9	65.3	67.3	90.5	67.4	88.5	63.9	158.4	176.3	160.8	97.8
United Kingdom	34.9	25.8	18.5	22.0	18.6	19.5	21.8	23.5	13.3	—	—	22.7	49.6	87.3
Canada	8.9	5.2	7.0	11.0	12.6	13.1	11.2	13.3	11.5	12.8	17.0	...	...	...
Spain	1.1	1.1	2.5	1.4	1.8	2.5	14.4	8.5	10.5	15.0	14.8	30.6	25.9	61.6
Netherlands[5]	3.7	4.4	6.8	8.0	7.8	6.2	5.8	10.6	15.6	15.4	19.5	21.8	25.5	18.9
Sweden	9.2	12.9	...	...	...	...	...	...	...	...	...	...	...	...
Switzerland	0.7	0.8	0.9	1.2	0.7	0.7	0.4	0.5	0.6	0.8	0.7	0.9	4.4	6.5
Belgium[6]	6.7	5.1	5.6	10.9	8.6	12.9	9.5	18.1	19.2	15.6	16.8	27.0	...	...
	(In percent of GDP)													
United States	4.89	4.97	6.11	7.23	8.03	7.94	7.77	7.79	6.47	6.99	7.55	8.59	8.89	8.55
Japan[2]	5.81	6.09	5.84	7.74	6.29	6.71	7.14	7.70	6.78	6.45	9.01	8.58	9.44	10.92
Germany[3]	1.42	1.64	2.34	2.13	2.30	2.71	3.36	3.80	3.32	2.88	4.62	4.46	5.85	5.14
France[4]	1.39	0.79	1.16	1.27	2.06	2.22	2.89	1.55	1.71	1.53	1.77	1.74	2.52	5.09
Italy[5]	3.39	4.11	9.59	14.13	15.78	15.81	14.99	8.88	10.55	7.35	14.46	15.33	13.15	9.81
United Kingdom	6.49	5.03	3.79	4.78	4.30	4.25	3.86	3.39	1.59	—	—	2.24	4.75	9.43
Canada	3.38	1.77	2.30	3.34	3.67	3.74	3.07	3.20	2.34	2.32	2.96	...	...	...
Spain	0.52	0.59	1.39	0.90	1.18	1.52	6.23	2.90	3.04	3.93	3.00	5.81	4.53	12.98
Netherlands[5]	2.14	3.04	4.83	5.88	6.13	4.77	3.26	4.85	6.75	6.74	6.88	7.48	7.94	6.12
Sweden	7.29	11.23	...	...	...	...	...	...	...	...	...	...	...	...
Switzerland	0.72	0.86	0.93	1.21	0.79	0.70	0.30	0.29	0.32	0.45	0.29	0.41	1.84	2.78
Belgium[6]	5.54	5.18	6.48	13.22	10.95	15.77	8.26	12.64	12.43	9.97	8.53	13.73	...	...

Sources: Organization for Economic Cooperation and Development, *Financial Statistics Monthly*, various issues; and International Monetary Fund, *International Financial Statistics* and *World Economic Outlook*.

[1]Central government issues of bonds of at least one year in maturity; public issues plus private placements.

[2]From September 1991, government compensation bonds (inscribed government bonds) and subscription bonds are not included.

[3]Including German Unity Fund.

[4]Break in the comparability of data between 1985 and 1986 is mainly because the flows are recorded on the settlement date and no longer on the issue date. Issues using accounts for the Industrial Development Funds (CODEVI) are excluded.

[5]The 1993 data are for the first three quarters.

[6]The 1991 data are for the first three quarters.

The Identity of Holders of Debt

The composition of government debt holdings has changed considerably in recent years. In general, the shares of banks and individuals have fallen, while the share of foreigners has increased. To the extent that behavior differs across holders, these developments may have influenced the dynamics of government debt markets. They may also have affected other markets, notably the foreign exchange market.

Data on holders of government debt are unfortunately quite limited; more is known about holdings by financial institutions (especially banks) than about other holders. Table 7 reports data for 1980, 1986, and 1992 for those countries where this information is published; Table A1 provides more detailed data for the United States.

One trend that emerges from Table 7 is that the share of government debt held by *domestic banks* has declined since 1980. In the United States, the share of bank holdings fell from 18 percent in 1980

to 10 percent in 1992 (although bank holdings have risen in the United States since 1990; see Table A1).[2] In Germany, the share of bank holdings fell from 70 percent in 1980 to 54 percent in 1992. Marked declines are also evident in Italy and Sweden, and in France since 1986. In the United Kingdom and Canada, the shares of bank holdings have fluctuated, rising and then falling in the United Kingdom, while doing the opposite in Canada.

Insurance companies hold a small but rising proportion of government debt in the United States and in Italy. They are major holders of government debt in the United Kingdom, and this share rose considerably after 1986, so that by 1992 insurance companies held over one third of U.K. debt. Insurance companies held a moderate and declining share of government debt in Canada and Sweden.

---

[2]The recent increase in bank holdings in the United States is analyzed by Rodriguez (1993).

Table 6. Gross Issues of Short-Term Government Securities[1]

	1988	1989	1990	1991	1992	1993
	(In billions of U.S. dollars)					
United States[2]	887.2	937.5	1,132.6	1,115.0	1,484.8	1,558.9
Japan[3]	. . .	. . .	1,334.6	1,301.4	1,409.9	1,751.8
Italy[4]	320.1	371.6	471.8	489.6	553.4	364.9
Canada[3,5]	. . .	231.8	252.5	285.9	296.5	144.6
Spain[6]	56.9	73.4	95.3	87.4	105.7	96.0
Netherlands[7]	1.6	—	0.9	—	. . .	. . .
Sweden[8]	17.6	. . .	9.0	. . .	. . .	. . .
Switzerland[9]	2.4	2.2	3.8	4.2	11.5	23.8
	(In percent of GDP)					
United States[2]	18.1	17.9	20.4	19.5	24.6	24.5
Japan[3]	. . .	. . .	45.5	38.9	38.4	41.4
Italy[4]	38.2	42.7	43.1	42.6	45.3	36.6
Canada[3,5]	. . .	42.2	43.9	48.5	52.0	26.2
Spain[6]	16.5	19.3	19.3	16.6	18.4	20.2
Netherlands[7]	0.7	—	0.3	—	. . .	. . .
Sweden[8]	9.7	. . .	3.9	. . .	. . .	. . .
Switzerland[9]	1.3	1.2	1.7	1.8	4.8	10.2

Sources: Organization for Economic Cooperation and Development, *Financial Statistics Monthly*, various issues; and International Monetary Fund, *International Financial Statistics* and *World Economic Outlook*.

[1]Central government securities issued on the domestic market.
[2]Marketable bills, which have maturities up to one year.
[3]Bills.
[4]Bills plus treasury bills in ECUs. The 1993 data are for the first three quarters.
[5]The 1993 data are for the first two quarters.
[6]Bills plus notes.
[7]Treasury paper.
[8]Notes.
[9]Notes plus money market debt registered claims.

The data for *other domestic financial institutions* are sparse. Pension funds appear to have increased their shares in the United Kingdom and Canada between 1980 and 1992.

A second notable trend is that the share of government debt held directly by domestic *households* has fallen between 1980 and 1992. In the United States, their share fell sharply in the first half of the 1980s (from 19 percent in 1980 to 10 percent in 1986) and has stayed roughly constant since then. Holdings of individuals and private trusts in the United Kingdom fell from 16 percent in 1980 to 9 percent in 1992. Household holdings rose in Sweden in the first half of the 1980s, but have fallen considerably since 1986.

The third trend is the sharp increase in holdings of government debt by *foreigners*. Foreign holdings of German public debt rose from 9 percent in 1980 to 26 percent in 1992. Foreign holdings of government debt also rose sharply in France (since 1986), the United Kingdom, Canada, and Sweden.[3] In the United States, however, the share of debt held abroad has fluctuated, falling from 1980 to 1985, before rising again in the second half of the 1980s to a peak of 21 percent in 1989.

What are the implications of a relative decline in holdings by individuals and by banks and a relative increase by nonresidents? The decline in individual holdings of debt implies that institutional holdings of government debt are increasing (assuming foreign holdings are primarily institutional). Institutional holders are likely to turn over their debt positions more rapidly than households, although the effect of this on the dynamics of government securities markets is unclear. Such increased turnover could stabilize markets, since institutions probably react to small return differentials more than households do. Conversely, institutions may shift funds more rapidly from one market to the other, causing greater volatility. Institutions holding government debt are also subject to widely varying levels of supervision and regulation. Large swings in the price of government debt may lead to difficulties or even insolvency at some firms.

What about the "internationalization" of government debt holding? By opening a larger market for the debt, internationalization can potentially lower the cost of debt for a country. It has also led to pressure on governments to reform their markets

---

[3]The data for Sweden are problematic, owing to a change in the basis for reporting. The reported figure for foreign holdings for 1992 includes all debt in foreign currency plus foreign holdings of domestic currency debt, while data for earlier years are not broken down in this way.

Chart 3. Gross Issues of Medium- and Long-Term Government Securities in Major Industrial Countries
(In percent of GDP)

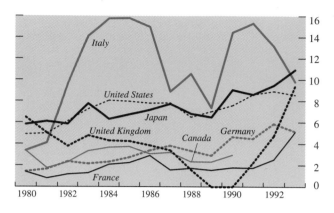

Sources: Organization for Economic Cooperation and Development, *Financial Statistics Monthly*, various issues; and International Monetary Fund, *International Financial Statistics* and *World Economic Outlook.*

Chart 4. Gross Issues of Short-Term Government Securities in Major Industrial Countries
(In percent of GDP)

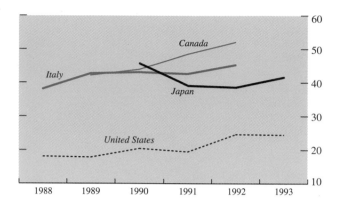

Sources: Organization for Economic Cooperation and Development, *Financial Statistics Monthly*, various issues; and International Monetary Fund, *International Financial Statistics* and *World Economic Outlook.*

to make them more attractive to international investors.

Internationalization has taken other forms for some issuers, including issuing debt on the Euromarket and in some foreign domestic markets. Such an approach has tended to be popular with smaller countries and with countries that carry relatively high debt levels. This trend has underpinned the issuance of sovereign global bonds, which can be sold simultaneously in several different markets.

Maturity and Currency Composition

Governments of the larger countries issue almost all their debt in domestic *currency*. Germany, Japan, and the United States do not issue any foreign currency debt. France has a program of issuing European currency unit (ECU) debt, but the bulk of its debt is in French francs. The United Kingdom issues the bulk of its debt in pounds sterling, but issues some ECU debt too. During the European exchange rate mechanism (ERM) crisis, it issued some debt denominated in deutsche mark on the Euromarket, in order to augment its foreign exchange reserves. Canada issues most of its debt in Canadian dollars, but issues debt in U.S. dollars to finance its foreign exchange reserves, and has issued previously in yen and deutsche mark.

Italy is alone among the seven major industrial countries in having an extensive foreign currency borrowing program. It issues Euromarket debt in a variety of currencies, and has recently issued global bonds in U.S. dollars and yen. Italy also issues domestic debt in ECU, on top of a well-developed domestic borrowing program in lira.

While data on *maturity structure* are limited, Table 8 gives a summary for six countries.[4] In the United States, maturities lengthened between 1980 and 1992, with most of this lengthening occurring before 1986. The proportion of debt of less than five-year maturity decreased from 81 percent in 1980 to 71 percent in 1992, while the proportion of debt of greater than ten-year maturity increased from 11 percent to 16 percent. For Germany, data are only available for total government debt, a broader category than central government debt. Like the United States, Germany has engineered a considerable lengthening in maturities. The proportion of debt of less than three-year maturity decreased from 44 percent in 1980 to 26 percent in 1992, while the proportion of debt longer than five years rose from 34 percent to 45 percent. In contrast to the United States, however, Germany has very little debt with maturities greater than ten years.

The maturity structure of Japanese debt shortened between 1980 and 1986. Since 1986, however, Japan has initiated a slight lengthening of maturities, especially in the very long end (more than 15 years) of the market.

The United Kingdom shows a different pattern. The proportion of debt below five years in maturity has remained roughly constant, but the proportion in the 5–15 year range has risen at the expense of longer-term debt. In March 1993, 72 percent of U.K. debt had maturities below 15 years, compared

---

[4]Data were not available for Italy, and French data were only available for 1992. The maturity of government debt is a flawed measure of the term of the debt, but better measures such as duration are generally unavailable.

with 58 percent in March 1981. Like the United Kingdom, Canada also has experienced a shortening of maturities. The proportion of debt less than three years in maturity rose from 53 percent in 1980 to 64 percent in 1992. The proportion of debt with maturities above ten years fell from 27 percent to 14 percent over the same period.

While comparable data are not available for Italy, its effective maturity structure is short relative to other major industrial countries. About 27 percent of Italian debt is in Treasury bills of maturity one year or less, with another 35 percent indexed every six months.

Governments also issue a variety of debt that is not fixed in terms of future cash flows. One type is debt indexed to inflation. Among the seven major industrial countries, the United Kingdom is an active issuer of such debt, and Canada began a program in 1991. Some governments, including Italy and Canada, also issue floating rate debt, which has the interest rate indexed to a short-term interest rate.

Interest rate swaps can also be used to adjust the maturity composition of debt. Canada has an active program of swapping its debt. The Government enters swaps in which it agrees to make floating rate payments to its counterparty, in exchange for receiving fixed rate payments that match the Government's liabilities on some of its bonds.

Another tool related to maturity management is strips. These are programs that separate a coupon bond into separate zero-coupon securities for each coupon interest payment and for the final maturity payment. Strips are arranged at the initiative of the market, rather than as a decision of the government. However, government policies can facilitate strips. While strips do not change the maturity composition of the government's debt, they do allow holders to choose more precisely the cash-flow profile of their debt portfolio, and thereby increase demand for the government's debt.

Market Structure

Primary Dealer Systems

In many countries, the authorities have designated a group of financial firms as the principal intermediaries in the government securities market. These firms receive a set of privileges in this market, in exchange for a set of obligations. The nature of these privileges varies greatly from country to country; the most common obligation is to make a secondary market in government debt. These firms sometimes operate under a special supervisory regime.[5]

The United States has long had a system of primary dealers in its government securities market. The Federal Reserve Bank of New York designates these firms, which currently number 39. In the wake of the Salomon scandal in 1991, U.S. authorities reduced the extent of both the privileges and the obligations of primary dealers[6]—in part to increase the competitiveness of government securities markets.[7]

Primary dealers in the United States are required to be active in both the primary and secondary markets for government securities. They must make reasonable bids in every Treasury auction. The Federal Reserve Bank of New York used to require each primary dealer to account for at least 1 percent of the total transactions of all primary dealers with customers, but it abandoned this rule in January 1992. The rule reportedly had forced some smaller primary dealers to offer steep commission discounts to their customers. Primary dealers, however, still must maintain a presence in the secondary market, because the Bank requires them to "make reasonably good markets in their trading relationships with its trading desk and provide the trading desk with market information and analysis that may be useful to the Federal Reserve in the formulation and implementation of monetary policy."[8]

In October 1991, the U.S. Department of Treasury eliminated two privileges that primary dealers had enjoyed. One was the exclusive right to place bids for customers in Treasury auctions. The other was exclusive access to Treasury announcements of its borrowing plans, which the Treasury now disseminates to the entire market.

Primary dealers enjoy two remaining privileges. They have exclusive access to some of the interdealer broker screens, although this exclusivity also is eroding.[9] They also serve as the Federal Reserve Bank of New York's counterparties in its open market operations. Primary dealers thus are the main conduit through which the Federal Reserve conducts its monetary policy. It is sometimes argued that such a position gives primary dealers knowledge of monetary policy that other market participants do not have.

Japan does not have a primary dealer system along the U.S. lines. However, it does bestow a special role in the government securities market to a large group of firms. These firms make up the issuing syndicate for Japanese Government bonds (JGBs). Over 900 firms are members of the syndicate, including banks, securities firms, and insurance companies. Additionally, a much smaller

---

[5]In addition to the countries discussed in this section, other countries, including Italy, Canada, Spain, and Finland, have primary dealer systems in place.

[6]See Goldstein, Folkerts-Landau, and others (1992).
[7]See Mullins (1992).
[8]Federal Reserve Bank of New York (1992).
[9]See section on Liquidity in the Secondary Market for a discussion of interdealer brokers.

Table 7. Holders of Central Government Debt in Selected Industrial Countries[1]

(In percent of total debt outstanding)

	1980	1986	1992
United States[2]			
Domestic banks	18.19	12.33	10.35
Domestic money market funds	0.57	1.79	2.81
Domestic insurance companies	3.89	6.34	6.95
Domestic individuals[3]	19.00	10.16	10.18
Other domestic holders	37.31	52.95	50.34
Foreign and international	21.04	16.44	19.36
Germany[4,5]			
Domestic banks	69.66	59.45	54.31
Other domestic holders[6]	21.20	20.32	19.41
Foreign	9.14	20.22	26.28
France[7]			
Domestic banks	. . .	19.57	8.17
Other domestic holders	. . .	79.59	49.22
Foreign	. . .	0.84	42.61
Italy[8,9]			
Domestic banks	41.32	28.13	17.03
Domestic investment funds	. . .	6.81	2.72
Domestic insurance companies	1.30	1.88	4.21
Other domestic financial institutions[10]	3.96	4.02	2.31
Private sector and foreign	53.42	59.16	73.73
United Kingdom[11]			
Domestic banks	4.89	6.73	3.83
Domestic insurance companies	30.36	30.15	36.62
Domestic pension funds	16.82	23.43	21.67
Domestic investment and unit trusts	0.53	0.76	0.64
Other domestic financial institutions[12]	12.29	8.93	2.34
Domestic individuals and private trusts	16.34	12.01	8.94
Other domestic holders[13]	9.88	8.20	8.51
Foreign	8.89	9.78	17.43
Canada[14]			
Domestic banks	16.37	8.77	11.48
Domestic investment and closed-end funds	0.47	1.49	5.46
Domestic insurance companies[15]	9.76	8.80	7.89
Domestic trusteed pension funds	7.71	9.75	10.63
Other domestic financial institutions[16]	5.75	5.51	5.78
Other domestic holders[17]	46.07	48.06	34.25
Foreign	13.87	17.61	24.51

group of about 35 firms negotiates the terms of syndicated government bond issues with the Ministry of Finance. In contrast to the U.S. system, the syndicate has a special role only in the primary market, but not in the secondary market or in central bank monetary operations.

The primary obligation of syndicate members is to accept their allocation of bonds. Forty percent of the biggest Japanese issue, the ten-year bond, is syndicated, although most other bonds—and the rest of the ten-year bonds—are auctioned. The syndicated bonds are sold at the weighted-average price from the auction.[10] In exchange for accepting

their share of syndicated bonds, syndicate members enjoy two benefits. First, they have exclusive access to auctions for government bonds. Second, they receive a commission from both the syndicated and auctioned portions of the ten-year bond.

Germany sells its bonds through a consortium of 109 members. Most long-term bonds in Germany are sold through a combination of a syndicated distribution through the consortium with an auction and subsequent tap sales by the Bundesbank.[11] In contrast to primary dealer systems in other countries, membership in the bond consortium appears to carry no significant costs. The primary role of consortium members is to accept their share of syn-

---

[10]Since the Japanese Government pays a commission on both the auctioned and the syndicated share, the commission does not result in the price on the syndicated tranche being higher than on the auctioned tranche. See Kroszner (1993) for details of the syndication process.

---

[11]For the ten-year Bund, about 30 percent each is sold through the syndicate and the tap and 40 percent is sold at auction. Kroszner (1993) contains details on the German bond consortium and the issuance of government bonds in Germany.

Table 7 *(concluded)*

	1980	1986	1992
Sweden[18]			
Domestic banks[19]	32.04	9.28	3.97
Domestic insurance companies	12.96	12.71	10.38
Other domestic financial institutions[20]	2.93	9.39	2.82
Domestic households	22.76	26.11	17.84
Other domestic holders[21]	1.33	14.56	19.24
Foreign[22]	27.97	28.00	45.75

Sources: Bank of Canada, *Bank of Canada Review* (Winter 1992–93 and Winter 1993–94), Table G5; Bank of England, *Statistical Abstract: Part 1* (1993), Table 17.3; Bank of Italy, *Ordinary General Meeting of Shareholders Report*, various issues; Bank of France, *Statistiques Monétaires et Financières Annuelles* (1987) and *Statistiques Monétaires et Financières Trimestrielles* (May 1993); Deutsche Bundesbank, *Monthly Report of the Deutsche Bundesbank*, various issues; France, Directorate of the Treasury; Sweden, Central Bureau of Statistics, *Statistical Abstract of Sweden* (1984 and 1988) and *Statistical Yearbook of Sweden 1994*; United States, Department of Treasury, *Treasury Bulletin* (March 1988 and December 1993), Table OFS-2; and IMF staff estimates.

[1]Data are as of March 31 for the United Kingdom; end-year data for all other countries.

[2]Securities valued at par; some savings bonds are included at current redemption value.

[3]Includes savings bonds and other securities.

[4]Of Federal Government, Equalization of Burdens Fund, ERP Special Fund, Länder governments, and local authorities (for 1980 and 1986); of Federal Government, German Unity Fund, Debt-Processing Fund, ERP Special Fund, west German Länder governments, east German Länder governments, west German local authorities, and east German local authorities (for 1992).

[5]Excluding public authorities' mutual indebtedness; and holdings of Bundesbank.

[6]Social security funds plus other.

[7]Of central government securities; excludes Bank of France holdings.

[8]1981 data are presented for 1980.

[9]Total marketable central government debt excluding the holdings of Bank of Italy and Ufficio Italiano dei Cambi.

[10]Deposits and loans fund, special credit institutions, and social security institutions.

[11]Total market holdings of gilts.

[12]Including building societies and other U.K. institutional investors.

[13]U.K. public sector, industrial and commercial companies, public trustees and various noncorporate bodies, and other (including residual).

[14]Government of Canada direct securities and loans (underlying outstanding amounts are in par value); excludes the holdings of securities by the Bank of Canada and in Government of Canada accounts.

[15]Life insurance companies plus other insurance companies; IMF estimates for other insurance companies in 1992.

[16]Trust and mortgage loan companies, investment dealers, local and central credit unions and caisses populaires, and other financial institutions.

[17]Nonfinancial corporations, provincial governments, municipal governments, all other holdings of market issues by Canadian residents (residual), and Canada savings bonds; IMF estimates for all other holdings of market issues by Canadian residents (residual) in 1992.

[18]Holdings of national debt excluding the holdings of Riksbank, other state institutions and funds, and the National Pension Insurance Fund.

[19]Includes cooperative banks in 1992.

[20]Savings banks, cooperative banks, and other financial institutions.

[21]Local governments, joint-stock companies and economic associations, enterprises, other associations, private companies, and so on.

[22]Holders abroad (1980 and 1986); and external debt in Swedish kronor and debt in foreign currency (1992).

dicated bonds at the price determined by authorities, but there is no automatic mechanism to ensure that this price is close to the auction price. Since a selling commission is paid on these bonds (but not on those allocated through the auction or tap), these shares are probably more a privilege than an obligation. Shares are decided by the Bundesbank. In addition to their syndication shares, consortium members enjoy other privileges: they have exclusive access to government bond auctions; they hold a regular meeting, at which they exchange market information; and they have special access to Bundesbank repurchase agreement (repo) operations in order to finance their government security purchases.

The French Treasury adopted in 1987 a system of primary dealers known as Spécialistes en Valeurs du Trésor (SVTs). These firms were assigned duties in both the primary and secondary markets; SVTs, however, have no special role in central bank monetary operations. The Bank of France carries out monetary operations through a different, separately designated group of firms, although some firms are members of both groups.

The 18 current SVTs have specific, quantitative obligations in the government security auctions and in the secondary market. During the course of a year, each SVT must purchase 2 percent of the total amounts auctioned of each of the three principal types of securities: BTFs (short-term), BTANs

Table 8. Remaining Maturity of Domestic Currency Debt[1]
(As cumulative percent of total value of outstanding issues)

United States[2]	0–1 year	0–5 years	0–10 years	0–20 years	All
End-1980	48.69	81.11	89.47	95.01	100.00
End-1986	36.80	71.50	85.72	90.81	100.00
End-1992	34.65	71.24	83.62	87.38	100.00

Japan[3]	0–5 years	0–10 years	0–15 years	0–20 years	0–25 years	All
FY 1980	28.85	100.00	100.00	100.00	100.00	100.00
FY 1986	48.01	93.73	98.61	100.00	100.00	100.00
FY 1992	47.78	92.40	96.41	99.98	99.98	100.00

Germany[4]	0–1 year	0–3 years	0–5 years	0–10 years	0–15 years	0–20 years	All
End-1980	17.73	43.68	66.38	98.15	100.00	100.00	100.00
End-1986	9.76	28.87	54.88	94.34	99.40	99.40	100.00
End-1992	6.75	25.53	54.71	97.99	99.68	99.68	100.00

France[5]	0–1 year	0–5 years	0–10 years	0–15 years	All
End-1992	28.72	63.74	84.41	89.86	100.00

United Kingdom[6]	0–5 years	0–15 years	All
End-March 1981	27.74	57.69	100.00
End-March 1987	28.91	70.61	100.00
End-March 1993	27.65	72.20	100.00

Canada[7]	0–3 years	0–5 years	10 years	All
End-1980	53.21	67.50	72.60	100.00
End-1986	55.00	64.08	81.75	100.00
End-1992	64.01	71.72	85.71	100.00

Sources: Bank of Canada, *Bank of Canada Review*, various issues; Deutsche Bundesbank, *Capital Market Statistics* (February 1993) and *Statistical Supplement to the Monthly Reports of the Deutsche Bundesbank—Series 2: Securities Statistics* (February 1981 and February 1987); France, Directorate of the Treasury; Japan, Ministry of Finance; United Kingdom, Central Statistical Office, *Annual Abstract of Statistics*, various issues; and United States, Department of Treasury, *Treasury Bulletin*, various issues.

[1]All debt valued at nominal values, not current market value.

[2]Marketable central government debt held by private investors.

[3]Domestic central government bonds excluding financing bills and grant-in-aid bonds.

[4]Public bonds including bonds issued by the Federal Government, and of German Unity Fund, Currency Conversion Equalization Fund, ERP Special Fund, Treuhand privatization agency, Länder governments, local authorities, Federal and east German Railways, and Federal Post Office.

[5]Marketable central government debt.

[6]Market holdings of central government and government-guaranteed marketable securities.

[7]Marketable unmatured central government securities, including government-guaranteed securities.

(medium-term), and OATs (long-term).[12] SVTs must be considerably stronger than this threshold in at least one of these types of securities, because the average of their annual shares in the three types of securities must exceed 3 percent. In the secondary market, each SVT must account for at least 3 percent of the transaction volume in each type of security. SVTs must also provide quotes upon request for any government security and post continuous screen quotes for the most active issues. In addition to these auction and market-making requirements, the Treasury requires SVTs to work to place securities with final investors, both in France and abroad.

In exchange for these obligations, SVTs enjoy two specific privileges. One, which is unique to the French system, is a provision for submitting non-competitive bids. SVTs are permitted to purchase additional amounts of an auctioned security at the weighted-average auction price for up to one day after the auction. The amount an SVT may buy at this price is proportional to its average purchases in the last three auctions for the same type of security, subject to a ceiling for all SVTs of 15 percent of the issue. The second privilege is that SVTs have sole access to an interdealer broker. SVTs are also expected to advise the Treasury on market conditions and issuance policy. Such a relationship with the Treasury is likely to benefit the SVTs as well as the Treasury.

In the United Kingdom, the primary-dealer equivalent is the gilt-edged market makers (GEMMs). The GEMM system has operated since the Big Bang in 1986. In exchange for a variety of special privileges, GEMMs are required to make markets for gilts—essentially all marketable medium- and long-term U.K. Government securities. GEMMs do not have any special role in the market for short-term U.K. Treasury bills, and their role in Bank of England monetary operations is limited.

---

[12]BTFs denote Bons du Trésor à taux fixe; BTANs, Bons du Trésor à taux annuel; and OATs, Obligations Assimilables du Trésor.

The principal obligation of GEMMs is to make continuous markets in gilts. Each GEMM must make a market in the full range of gilts, including index-linked gilts, which tend to have lower transaction volume than conventional gilts. They are also expected to participate regularly in gilt auctions, though this requirement receives less emphasis than the market-making requirement. The Bank of England does not measure the GEMMs' secondary and primary market conduct against any explicit numerical standards.

GEMMs receive a package of privileges in exchange for their market-making activities. They have the exclusive right to deal in gilts with the Bank of England, and they may borrow from the Bank. They also have the exclusive right to borrow gilts, which they do through special stock exchange money brokers. These gilts are lent by other GEMMs, as well as by investors. Finally, GEMMs have exclusive use of special interdealer brokers. GEMMs do not have any special privileges relating to gilt auctions, except that only they may submit bids by telephone, which may give them some advantage in reacting to late-breaking market developments.

Primary dealer systems such as those described in this section clearly involve constraints on the workings of markets. These systems restrict entry of firms into parts of the government securities market and tie the participation of firms in some parts of the market to participation in other aspects of the market. Their justification is that the obligations of primary dealers satisfy public goals that would otherwise not be met. The most prominent of these goals is to maintain the liquidity of secondary markets, which arguably is increased by requirements that primary dealers make continuous markets. Such an arrangement resembles that in other financial markets, such as stock markets, where agents are charged with making markets in return for some privileges.[13] Another justification for primary dealer systems is that such systems serve as devices for authorities to regulate and supervise the firms that are the major players in the domestic government securities market and which play an important role in other domestic financial markets as well.

Issuance Techniques

The methods used by many countries for issuing government securities have changed in recent years; in brief, more securities are being auctioned and fewer are being issued through syndicates. Different auction techniques have also been under consideration, especially in the United States.

Most debt securities are issued by one of four methods: auctions, direct syndications, tap issues, and underwritten syndications. The last of these methods is used for Euromarket and global issues, while the other three are used for domestic issues. Tap issues by the central bank are often used to sell parts of issues that are also sold through auctions or syndications.[14] Table 9 lists the methods used by governments of the major industrial countries to sell their domestically issued government securities. Of these countries, only Italy is a regular issuer on international markets. Smaller industrial countries use techniques similar to those used by the major industrial countries. Several of these smaller countries are active borrowers on Euromarkets and other international markets and use underwritten syndications for these issues.

Auctions are used for the bulk of government debt issued worldwide. There is a variety of types of auctions. Auctions for government securities usually are sealed bid, where the government receives all bids in a single batch before the auction. With improvements in communication and information processing, however, it may also be possible to conduct interactive auctions, in which the government gradually raises prices, soliciting bids at ascending prices, until supply equals demand. U.S. policymakers have considered implementing such a system. Among sealed-bid systems, the big choice is between uniform-price and discriminatory (multiple-price) systems.[15] In a uniform-price system, all units of the security are sold for the same price, generally the price of the lowest successful bidder. In a discriminatory system, each bidder pays the price bid.

For their auctioned debt, Canada, France, and Germany exclusively use discriminatory auctions, while the other major industrial countries use a mix of auction techniques. In the United States, the authorities have begun to use uniform-price auctions for sales of some Treasury notes on an experimental basis, after some incidents of manipulation in discriminatory auctions. Initially, this was a one-year experiment from September 1992 through August 1993, but the experiment has been extended for an additional year. Discriminatory auctions are also the more common auction technique in countries other than the major industrial countries.

---

[13]On the New York Stock Exchange, for example, designated specialists in particular stocks are charged with maintaining continuous and orderly markets. In return for this, these specialists have privileged access to the order flow in the stocks.

[14]In addition to formal tap sales, in many cases central banks purchase part of the debt issued by the government and subsequently sell debt in the secondary market. Such operations bear some resemblance to tap sales, although central banks often segregate securities used for open market operations from those held for investment.

[15]Uniform-price and discriminatory systems have a variety of other names. The terminology of Bikhchandani and Huang (1993) is followed here.

Table 9. Techniques for Issuing Domestic Government Securities in Major Industrial Countries

	Methods of issuance
Canada	Syndicate (indexed bonds) Discriminatory auction (all other securities)
France	Discriminatory auction (all securities, except occasional syndicates)
Germany	Combination of syndicate, discriminatory auction, and tap sales by central bank (Bundesanleihen) Discriminatory auction (various securities) Tap sales by central bank (various securities)
Italy	Discriminatory auction (Treasury bills) Uniform-price auction (longer maturities)
Japan	Combination of discriminatory auction and syndicate (ten-year Japanese Government bond) Syndicate (five-year Japanese Government bond) Discriminatory auction (various securities) Uniform-price auction (financing bills)
United Kingdom	Discriminatory auction (Treasury bills and some gilts) Uniform-price auction with minimum price (some gilts, infrequently) Tap sales by central bank (some gilts)
United States	Discriminatory auction (all maturities) Uniform-price auction (two- and five-year notes, on an experimental basis)

Sources: Bank of England; Italy, Ministry of the Treasury; and Bröker (1993).

Auctions often embody incentives to encourage bidding. In Germany, shares in the syndicate for issuing bonds are adjusted periodically, with the amounts syndicate members have purchased in auctions influencing their syndicate shares. Some incentives result in options conferred on some bidders. The noncompetitive bids available to SVTs in France are an example of such an option.

Germany and Japan have made the most prominent use of syndicates for domestic bond issues (see section on Primary Dealer Systems above). Other countries, including Canada and France, have virtually ceased using syndicates in recent years.[16]

Some researchers have criticized the use of discriminatory auctions and have recommended the use of uniform-price auctions instead. Although the former appears to increase revenue through price discrimination, critics argue that these auctions exacerbate the winners' curse phenomenon, in which successful bidders suffer from having overestimated the value of the securities, and therefore, that bidders reduce their bids accordingly. It is unclear whether this reduction outweighs the increased proceeds from price discrimination, and therefore it is unclear which technique yields higher proceeds for the government. However, another consideration is that uniform-price auctions do appear to reduce risk faced by bidders. There has also been considerable debate in the United States as to which technique is less prone to manipulation,

such as market cornering and collusion among bidders.[17]

A broader question concerns the advantages of auctions compared with other techniques. This issue has not received as much attention as the debate on auction techniques. At first blush, auctions appear to be a more efficient mechanism to elicit market demand than other techniques. However, the risk inherent in the winners' curse problem may reduce this efficiency, although the asymmetric information between buyers that drives winners' curse in auctions must still operate in other systems and may cause other inefficiencies.

Organization of When-Issued Markets

A when-issued market is a market in securities not yet issued. Settlement normally occurs on the same date that deliveries are made in the primary market. In the United States, for example, when-issued trading begins when an auction is announced, up to ten days before the auction.[18] The primary economic role of the market is price discovery. The when-issued market provides information on market demand to participants in an auction for a security. The market also plays a risk-shifting role; investors with a demand for the particular security can lock in the yield on this security in advance of the auction, and the risk of interest rate

---

[16]Canada, however, uses syndicates for its inflation-indexed Real Return Bonds, which it began to issue in 1991.

[17]These issues are discussed in Bikhchandani and Huang (1993) and in Feldman and Mehra (1993).

[18]See Pirrong (1993) for some background on the U.S. when-issued market.

movements is shifted to their counterparties in the when-issued market. These counterparties, who have a short position in the when-issued market, are often bidders in the auction.

A when-issued market exists in all the major industrial countries other than Germany and Japan. Trading starts in these markets when the particulars of an auction are announced, including the amount to be issued and the maturity. This period ranges from as much as ten days before the auction (in the United States) to as little as two days (in France). Settlement of when-issued trades occurs when the auctioned securities are distributed. This post-auction settlement period ranges from one day (in the United Kingdom) up to over three weeks (in France).

Activity on these markets varies considerably from country to country. While volume statistics are not available, the U.S. market appears to be the most active. The when-issued security in the United States becomes the "on-the-run" (i.e., the benchmark) issue. This security is the most recently issued of its maturity range and is the most heavily traded and liquid issue. The when-issued market is also reported to be heavily used for gilts in the United Kingdom and for government securities in Canada. The Italian when-issued market, on the other hand, does not experience heavy trading.

The when-issued market came under scrutiny in the United States because of several incidents of manipulation in 1991. The market was manipulated when one dealer amassed a dominant position in the auctioned security and forced those dealers with short positions in the when-issued market to pay abnormally high prices to cover these positions. This is one example of what is known as a "short-squeeze." In the U.S. case, rules on the amount one dealer may purchase at an auction were circumvented in order to accomplish this squeeze. The possibility of such squeezes raises risks to participants in the when-issued market and therefore reduces the liquidity and efficiency of the market, in turn reducing the information available to bidders in the primary market. This reduced information may increase the likelihood of winners' curse and increase debt costs of the government.

There are two important unresolved questions regarding when-issued markets. The first is what are the benefits to the price discovery process of the when-issued market. Preauction trading in the when-issued market permits at least the partial aggregation of private information on the value of the issue. This reduces the asymmetry of information at the auction and therefore reduces the likelihood of winners' curse. In turn, that is likely to make bidders bid more aggressively and increase proceeds to the government. However, the when-issued market may simply shift risk from auction participants to when-issued participants. The when-issued market may serve to reallocate risk among market participants rather than reduce it, although it will reduce the amount to which the government must compensate auction participants with lower issue prices.

The second question surrounding the when-issued market is how susceptible is it to manipulation, as discussed above. Because of the long settlement periods relative to the cash market, when-issued positions can be taken at lower cost, and it is therefore less expensive to build up market power in such a market. One possible solution to such a risk of manipulation might be to build alternative delivery options into the contract, so that if a particular security were scarce, those with short positions in when-issued securities could deliver either cash or some alternative security.[19] Improved reporting of price and trade information also might reduce manipulation, as might improved supervision of the market.

Liquidity in the Secondary Market

The function of a secondary market is to provide liquidity. It is particularly important that markets are able to provide liquidity in times of stress, when buy or sell orders increase. A variety of features in secondary markets contribute to liquidity.

One rough gauge of the liquidity of secondary markets is the volume of transactions in the market. The higher this volume, the more market-makers are compensated for the fixed costs of serving their role. This in turn is likely to increase the financial resources these market-makers have at their disposal, while also drawing additional firms into the market.

Table 10 reports *transaction volume* in cash government securities markets for five major industrial countries.[20] Generally, transaction volume in these markets is very large and has grown tremendously since 1980. The volume of transactions involving primary dealers in the United States grew from an average of $14 billion a day in 1980 to $120 billion in 1993. Volume in the Japanese market has grown even more sharply, from $1.4 billion a day in 1980 to $58 billion in 1993. Volume in the U.K. market is considerably smaller, but has also risen substantially since 1980, especially after the Big Bang in 1986. Using 1992 figures, 3 percent of U.S. debt

---

[19]See Pirrong (1993).

[20]The table involves a number of distortions. The U.S. data exclude transactions not involving primary dealers. The German data exclude OTC and offshore transactions, which are substantially more than half—perhaps 80–90 percent—of trading volume. The French data include repurchase agreements.

Table 10. Transaction Volume in Government Securities Market[1]
(Daily average in billions of U.S. dollars)

	1980	1981	1982	1983	1984	1985	1986	1987	1988	1989	1990	1991	1992	1993
United States[2]	13.78	18.09	23.54	30.34	38.51	55.53	68.82	77.07	70.70	77.88	76.72	88.11	105.22	119.56
Japan														
Over-the-counter market in Tokyo	1.38	1.63	1.77	2.30	4.84	17.21	29.13	73.90	62.06	49.48	44.11	38.47	44.24	57.62
Transactions in stock exchanges[3]	0.03	0.07	0.08	0.23	0.45	0.80	1.50	1.39	1.15	0.97	0.92	0.53	0.20	0.19
Germany[4]	...	...	...	...	...	...	...	2.32	3.67	3.65	3.93	4.25	6.15	9.67
France[5]														
Short- and medium-term securities	...	...	...	...	...	...	0.24	1.18	2.12	2.45	2.88	3.65	7.56	13.73
Treasury bonds (OATs)	...	...	...	...	...	...	...	...	...	...	...	...	8.16	14.42
United Kingdom[6]	1.39	1.16	1.40	1.27	1.42	1.33	2.46	7.42	7.94	6.33	6.75	7.76	8.53	9.48

Sources: Bank of Japan, *Economic Statistics Annual* and *Economic Statistics Monthly*; Board of Governors of the Federal Reserve System, *Federal Reserve Bulletin*; Deutsche Bundesbank, *Capital Market Statistics* (November 1993); France, Directorate of the Treasury; International Monetary Fund, *International Financial Statistics*; Japan, Ministry of Finance; and United Kingdom, Central Statistical Office, *Financial Statistics*.

[1]Data adjusted for double counting. Daily transactions volume for Japan, Germany, and France are estimated by the IMF staff from the annual volume data.

[2]Primary dealers transactions of Treasury securities.

[3]Data through 1989 from eight domestic stock exchanges; since 1990, from Tokyo Stock Exchange.

[4]Stock exchange turnover for bonds of the Federal Government, Federal Railways, and Federal Post Office.

[5]Secondary market transactions in central government securities, including repurchase agreements.

[6]Stock exchange transactions of U.K. Government securities.

was traded on an average trading day, compared with 2 percent for both Japan and the United Kingdom.

Transaction volume in most markets tends to be concentrated in *benchmark* securities. In most countries, a benchmark is the most recently issued security of a particular maturity. Usually the list of benchmarks in different countries includes a ten-year bond, which forms the basis for international comparisons of yields. Nonbenchmark securities are traded less frequently than benchmarks and are more likely to be held in the portfolios of longer-term investors. Because benchmarks are traded frequently in liquid markets, market yield information is more reliable and up to date than for other securities. For this reason, markets use benchmarks to price other fixed-income securities. For example, a ten-year corporate bond in U.S. dollars might be priced at, say, a 100 basis point spread to the ten-year Treasury bond with the same maturity, or a French franc bond at a spread above the French Government bond (known as the OAT). Typically, benchmarks also carry a somewhat lower yield than similar nonbenchmark securities; this difference in yield can be thought of as the market price of the greater liquidity of benchmark issues.

In Japan, trading is heavily concentrated in the benchmark Japanese Government bond (JGB). While this benchmark is a JGB with an original maturity of ten years, the benchmark is often not the most recently issued JGB. Instead, the benchmark bond is chosen by securities dealers. Requirements

for benchmark status are that the bond have a sufficient volume outstanding, between eight and ten years remaining to maturity, and a price near par (which means that the coupon rate is close to the yield to maturity). Trading in JGBs is heavily concentrated in the benchmark, with about 80 percent of total trading concentrated in this security. Bid-ask spreads are also considerably narrower for benchmarks than for nonbenchmarks, which is a sign of the greater liquidity of the benchmarks.[21]

Many governments have adopted a practice known as "*fungibility*," which involves reopening an existing security, instead of issuing a new security. By increasing the amount outstanding of particular issues, markets have available a larger inventory of the security to trade, which increases liquidity. This practice is particularly common in France, which since the mid-1980s has followed a policy of adding frequently to existing securities, while issuing new securities less often. For example, France issues a new ten-year bond only once a year, but auctions additional tranches of this bond every month. Belgium makes heavy use of this technique for its "linear bonds," and Canada, Germany, Japan, the Netherlands, and the United Kingdom also reopen issues.[22]

---

[21]See Kroszner (1993) for more information on the JGB benchmark.

[22]In some cases, the new tranche of the reopened security is not identical to the existing security until after the first coupon has been paid.

The bulk of volume in government securities is traded *over the counter* (OTC), rather than on exchanges. This is true in all the major industrial countries except the United Kingdom. This exception is perhaps due to the different nature of the U.K. stock exchange, which relies on dealers' posting quotes, rather than the order-matching processes more common in exchanges. In most countries, government securities are listed on exchanges, partly because some institutional investors are required to buy on exchanges, even though the bulk of volume occurs off the exchanges. Significant German trading takes place both on the domestic stock exchanges and OTC.

In many markets, *interdealer brokers* play an important role. They specialize in gathering price quotes from government securities dealers and posting them on an anonymous basis on screens to which all the dealers have access. When dealers trade, interdealer brokers do one of two things. Some interpose themselves between each side of a trade, so each counterparty actually trades with the interdealer broker. In this case, the identity of the counterparties is never revealed. Other interdealer brokers reveal the names of each counterparty to the other, and then the two counterparties complete the trade themselves. In most markets where interdealer brokers operate, the bulk of interdealer trades go through them. Interdealer brokers are also active in the offshore market based in London.

Offshore markets can be an important source of liquidity for government securities markets. This market is particularly active in London, where a considerable share of the volume of trading in French and German Government securities takes place.

Futures markets also contribute to the liquidity of government securities markets. Exchange-based futures contracts on government bonds from all the major industrial countries are actively traded. There also are contracts on short-term government securities from several countries. Additionally, options on many of these futures or on the underlying bonds are traded through the same exchanges. Table A2 lists contracts that are traded. In terms of contracts traded, the U.S. Treasury bond futures on the Chicago Board of Trade are the most active of all financial futures listed. Futures on U.S. Treasury bonds also are traded in Tokyo and London, although in much lower volume, making this market a 24-hour market.

Futures and options markets provide a method for market participants to adjust their exposure to government securities markets. Such markets contribute to liquidity in the underlying cash markets in two ways. First, they permit market-makers to hedge cash positions and to adjust those hedges

relatively quickly. Some of this liquidity may be illusory, however, since futures markets involve two opposite positions, and the short position may be hedged or arbitraged in the cash market. However, this leads to the second way futures markets contribute to liquidity: futures markets generate trading volume in the cash market, through this arbitraging and hedging. This additional trading volume helps attract additional market-makers in the cash market. Futures markets also enhance market transparency, as contracts are traded on exchanges with published, real-time volume and trade information.

Countries vary in their systems for *clearing and settling* government securities transactions. Of the major industrial countries, only the United Kingdom and the United States settle transactions in long-term government securities (bonds) as quickly as the next day; other countries exhibit longer delays, although some clear short-term securities more quickly. In the United States, some Treasury bill transactions settle on the same day as the trade. Most government securities in major countries are held in a computerized book-entry system, so that there is no cumbersome physical delivery. In the United States, most government securities transactions are routed through the Government Securities Clearing Corporation (GSCC). The GSCC nets trades, and net payments and securities transfers are made through the wholesale bank payments system, Fedwire, which is connected to the book-entry system run by the Federal Reserve. This netting reduces the volume of payments made over Fedwire.

The time between trade execution and settlement exposes participants to the risk of nondelivery of securities or cash. Having a book-entry system for securities can make settlement considerably more efficient and reduces risk by facilitating delivery-versus-payment settlement. A trade netting system can also contribute to efficiency, by reducing the number of payments brokers and dealers need to make. Links between domestic clearing systems and international clearing systems, especially Cedel and Euroclear, facilitate international transactions in a country's debt.

Markets vary according to the degree to which information on the market is disseminated. Government securities typically have a lower degree of transparency than stock markets, where real-time price and trade information is available to the public. Since most government securities transactions occur OTC, there is no exchange through which to disseminate information. In many government securities markets, market-makers post quotes and transact through interdealer broker screens. Typically, only market-makers have access to these screens. Thus, agents outside the circle of market-makers have less information about the market than insiders do.

Organization of Repurchase Agreement and Securities Lending Markets

Repurchase agreements (repos) facilitate leveraged long and short positions in securities. A portfolio of long positions in securities can be financed in part by executing repos on some of the securities in the portfolio. The trader that held the original portfolio and executed the repos remains exposed to price movements on the securities used in the repos. Conversely, a trader executing a reverse repo can immediately sell the security acquired through the reverse repo, thereby creating a short position which it must cover in the future to complete the repo.[23] The ability to engage in these transactions can facilitate inventory management by securities dealers, and thus reduce the cost of market-making and increase liquidity in cash markets. Securities lending is a somewhat more generalized term than repo. Repos are essentially a way to lend a security with the cash lent serving as collateral, but securities may also be lent either with other securities as collateral or without any collateral.

Repo and securities lending facilities are often cited as a key element in a liquid bond market. They allow dealers to take long and short positions in a flexible manner, buying and selling according to customer demand on a relatively small base of capital. Both repo and securities lending facilities allow dealers to acquire specific securities demanded by customers, without having to find another customer willing to sell the bonds. These transactions are often facilitated by brokers who specialize in these markets. Repos also contribute to liquidity by allowing nondealer investors to take positions in securities without putting up much capital. The market can therefore react to any price movements in securities markets, keeping prices close to their equilibrium.

In the United States, the repo market for government securities is very large. As of October 20, 1993, primary dealers had open repo contracts in government securities outstanding of $852 billion. This figure includes repos both in Treasury securities and agency securities, including mortgage-backed securities. This was equivalent to 29 percent of U.S. marketable debt outstanding at the end of the third quarter of 1993. Overnight and continuing repos ($466 billion) were more common than longer-term repos ($386 billion).[24] The primary dealers also had $670 billion in reverse repos outstanding. Securities lending by primary dealers was smaller, with a total of $184 billion borrowed and $5 billion lent.[25]

In the mid-1980s, several government securities dealers in the United States failed. These failures resulted in the failure of several savings and loans, and precipitated the collapse of the Ohio state deposit insurance company. A factor in the failure of these dealers was that the dealers had executed repos with customers, but had failed to place the securities involved in their customers' accounts. Instead the dealers used the same securities to execute multiple repos. These secondary dealers had been unregulated and unsupervised, since their sole business was government securities. In response to these events, the Government Securities Act of 1986 became law, placing government securities dealers under the regulation of the U.S. Treasury and the supervision of the Securities and Exchange Commission (SEC).

Repo markets in other large countries are substantially smaller than the U.S. market. In many countries, repo and securities lending markets are inhibited by regulatory restrictions or taxes. In Japan, repo transactions are known as gensaki. The market for gensaki on short-term government securities is active and accounts for a reported 28 percent of transaction volume in government securities. The main borrowers of funds in this market are securities firms. Gensaki in longer-term securities are less common, however. The reason for this is that these repos are considered bond transactions and therefore are subject to Japan's tax on securities transactions. This transactions tax also tends to lengthen the maturity of gensaki relative to U.S. repos.[26] In contrast to most U.S. repo transactions, gensaki do not permit the borrower of funds to substitute one security for another as collateral. Total repo contracts outstanding in Japan (including those on nongovernment securities) totaled ¥10.6 trillion ($101 billion) at the end of September 1993, which was 9.8 percent of total Japanese Government debt outstanding.[27] While these numbers are substantial, they show less use of repo transactions than in the U.S. market. Bond lending was authorized in Japan in 1989. This type of transaction is not subject to the transaction tax, so it has become an active market and a source of market liquidity in the bond market. Bond lending can be as short as

---

[23]A reverse repo is the other side of a repo. It entails purchasing a security and agreeing to resell it in the future.

[24]Continuing repo contracts are contracts that can be terminated at any time by either party.

[25]Data from the Board of Governors of the Federal Reserve System (1994a), Tables 1.41 and 1.43.

[26]The tax rate paid by the seller of the bond is 0.01 percent of the transfer price for financial institutions and 0.03 percent for other sellers. The transaction tax is applied at both ends of the Gensaki, both on the sale and on the subsequent repurchase.

[27]Data from Bank of Japan (1993), pp. 83, 171. Government debt outstanding excludes debt held by the Government and the Bank of Japan.

overnight, in contrast to Gensakis, for which the transaction tax makes such a short-term transaction prohibitively expensive.

In Germany, banks borrowing funds through repo transactions face a reserve requirement on these borrowed funds. As a result, a domestic repo market essentially does not exist. In contrast, a repo market in German Government securities flourishes in London, with most of the volume concentrated on the long-term bonds (Bunds). German firms reportedly are active in this market, which is linked to trading in futures contracts on German Government securities.

French Government securities repos are executed both in the domestic market and offshore. There are no tax impediments, although legal uncertainties have hampered the development of the domestic market; the French Government passed a new law intended to eliminate these uncertainties at the end of 1993. As of December 1993, there were about F 200 billion in domestic repos outstanding, and about twice that amount in international repos. Italy also has an active domestic market in repos, especially in longer-term government securities. At the end of 1993, there were Lit 92 trillion in repos outstanding, excluding interbank repos.

In the United Kingdom, a market for repos in gilts between private parties does not exist, and there is only a limited market in gilt borrowing. Only gilt-edged market-makers may borrow gilts, and they must do so through the stock exchange money brokers. The Bank of England began in January 1994 to use gilts repos as a regular open market device. In Canada, there is an active repo market in government bonds. This market has grown rapidly since 1992, after the elimination of a tax on cross-border repos. U.S. investors reportedly are active in the market and have driven much of the growth of the market.

A variety of issues arise in these markets. One is that the legal validity of repurchase contracts has been in question in some jurisdictions. This makes the status of repos uncertain under bankruptcy; while repos have the features of a collateralized loan, bankruptcy procedures may not recognize this. The tax treatment of repos can also be an issue. Such problems stem from the fact that repos combine short-term collateralized lending with a loan of a security, but not formally as a loan, but rather as a sale with a future contract to reverse the sale. Issues related to the transfer of the title to the security can also come up, especially when a dealer conducting a repo holds the security in custody for its counterparty.

Another technical issue concerns the settlement of repo and securities lending transactions. In principle, these transactions can use the same clearing and settlement facilities as regular cash transactions in securities. However, the complexity of these transactions complicates matters.

Finally, these transactions raise potential systemic concerns. Repos in particular are used by some parties, including hedge funds, to take large, leveraged positions in government securities. Dealers essentially lend to these funds using the repo as a collateralized loan. Repos typically are relatively short term (under a week), with the initial market value of the underlying security exceeding the amount of cash loan by small margin. This margin protects the dealer from fluctuations in the value of underlying security. If, however, the volatility of market prices unexpectedly increases, dealers could be left with insufficiently collateralized positions against borrowers.

International Debt Markets

The Distinctions Between Domestic Debt and Eurodebt

Governments tend to issue the bulk of their debt on their own domestic market, but many also issue on Euromarkets. In addition, some governments issue on the domestic markets of foreign countries, although less frequently. Countries normally use international markets for their foreign currency issues, while issuing domestic currency debt at home. In most major currencies, regulatory barriers generally separate the Euromarket from the domestic market. The result is that domestic residents of a country tend to hold more of domestic debt issued in that country, while nonresidents hold more of the Eurodebt. Eurodebt is typically issued in bearer, nonregistered form, which makes it difficult for the authorities to monitor and tax the holders of the debt.

While many countries auction their domestic government debt, Eurodebt normally is issued through an underwriting syndicate. Countries issuing in the domestic market of another country (most often in the United States) also use a syndicate. The nature of the syndicate varies across markets. Euro-syndicates include sellers able to place the debt internationally, while syndicates for domestic issues place more domestically. This distinction typically dictates the nationalities of members of the syndicates.

Although a Eurobond usually is listed on some exchange, most transactions occur OTC. The settlement of Eurobonds typically takes place through two international clearing agencies, Euroclear and Cedel. Domestic bonds most often clear through their domestic clearers, although international trades of these bonds sometimes use international clearers.

In the United States, SEC rules serve to differentiate bonds issued on the domestic market from

Eurobonds. Bonds issued in the United States must be registered with the SEC.[28] Eurobonds are exempt from SEC restrictions, but consequently they may not be sold to U.S. investors on the primary market. The SEC imposes a seasoning period of 40 days from the date of issue of a Eurobond, during which time the bonds may not be sold in the United States. Although U.S. investors may purchase Eurobonds after the seasoning period is over, the bulk of Eurobonds tend to be held outside the United States.

There are no significant regulatory barriers between deutsche mark bonds issued by foreigners on the domestic German market and Euro-deutsche mark bonds. Bonds that are sold internationally are designated Eurobonds, while others are considered domestic issues. The Bundesbank requires all deutsche mark bonds to clear through the domestic German clearing system, although international trades in Euro-deutsche mark bonds may also clear through international clearers. Euro-deutsche mark bonds arose in the 1960s as a result of a withholding tax imposed on domestic deutsche mark bonds held by foreigners, but this withholding tax has since been abolished.[29]

Global Bonds

As noted above, there is some separation between the Eurobond market and domestic bond markets. An issuer normally must choose on which market to issue. Demand for the bond is then constrained by the barriers between the markets. In the last few years, an instrument known as the global bond has been developed to overcome this segmentation.

The World Bank issued the first such bonds in 1989 and still remains the leading issuer of global bonds. It has issued in U.S. dollars, Japanese yen, and deutsche mark. Its first global bond issue in 1989 was in dollars, and it continues to issue regularly in dollars. It has made four issues in yen and has ¥ 900 billion in yen global bonds outstanding. Most recently, the Bank pioneered the deutsche mark global bond with a DM 3 billion issue in October 1993.

A number of sovereigns have also issued global bonds. Among the Group of Ten countries, Italy and Sweden have used this technique. Sweden issued a $2 billion U.S. dollar global bond in February 1993. More recently, Italy issued $5.5 billion in U.S. dollar global bonds in September 1993 and a ¥ 300 billion yen global bond in January 1994.

Global bonds combine SEC registration and U.S. clearing arrangements with separate clearing on the Euromarket. In some cases, there is also registration and clearing in other domestic markets, particularly in Germany and Japan for deutsche mark and yen issues. These bonds require arrangements for bridges between different clearing systems, so that the quantities of bonds in different markets can shift according to demand. If these bridges work smoothly, bonds can flow across jurisdictions easily. This enhances liquidity in the market, by allowing buyers from different jurisdictions to react to price fluctuations.

By allowing issuers to solicit demand for a variety of markets and to offer greater liquidity to investors, global bonds have the potential to reduce borrowing costs. While there does not appear to be systematic evidence on this, the World Bank has reported that the use of global bonds has reduced its interest cost of borrowing in U.S. dollars by about 18 basis points relative to the interest rates paid by agencies sponsored by the U.S. Government.[30] This cost saving does not, however, take into account the fixed costs of borrowing through the global format, such as registration and clearing arrangements. These costs are presumably higher than for comparable Euro-issues, which do not require registration. For a global bond, SEC registration fees are proportional to the amount of the issue placed in the United States.

Administration and Supervision

Debt Management

In most industrial countries, the finance ministry carries out debt management. In doing so, the ministry normally consults with the central bank. In some countries, debt authority is somewhat decentralized in that other agencies can issue debt backed by the central government. In all large industrial countries, the objectives of debt management are cast only in general terms. For example, both U.S. and Japanese authorities maintain that they attempt to minimize debt costs, but they need follow no formal guidelines on the maturity structure of their issues.

In contrast, Ireland and New Zealand have recently reorganized their debt management operations. They have sought to increase the independence of these operations, while also giving debt management more clearly defined goals. Since 1988, debt management in *New Zealand* has been placed in a division of the Treasury that has a degree of autonomy from the rest of the government. The Debt Management Office (DMO) is responsible for increasing the Crown's net worth and minimizing the risk to this net worth. New Zea-

---

[28]Bonds issued by foreign issuers in the U.S. domestic market are known as "Yankee bonds."

[29]See Box 3 for a discussion of withholding taxes and their effect on borrowing costs.

[30]See Evans (1993).

land has developed a set of financial statements for the government, including a balance sheet. The goals of the DMO resemble those of a treasurer's office for a corporation. It essentially attempts to reduce financial risk while maximizing return. To this end, the DMO adopted the practice of marking its liabilities to market on daily basis.

The DMO is now considering implementing a system of minimizing the risk to the Crown's balance sheet. Under such a system, the DMO would set the duration and currency profile of its liabilities to match that of its assets. Since most of its assets consist of payments in New Zealand dollars, this strategy would entail reducing its foreign currency liabilities well below the current 45 percent of total liabilities. It would also entail a lengthening of the duration of liabilities. A rigorous matching of asset and liability risk would also call for indexing liabilities to inflation, but the DMO has said that it is unlikely to issue indexed debt.

Like New Zealand, *Ireland* has organized its debt management in order to provide clear performance objectives and a degree of autonomy from other government objectives. The National Treasury Management Agency (NTMA) began operations in Ireland in December 1990. It took over both the debt management operations from the Irish Department of Finance and the gilt (domestic government bond) market operations of the central bank.

The debt management objective of the NTMA is cast with reference to a benchmark portfolio. The main objective is to fund the Government's debt at a lower cost than that of the benchmark portfolio. The benchmark consists of debt of a collection of specified maturities, with new debt issued at preset dates. The NTMA attempts to beat the benchmark both by funding at different dates than the benchmark, in order to take advantage of favorable market opportunities, and by issuing at different maturities than the maturities of the benchmark. The NTMA chooses its maturities subject to a limit on the amount of debt it is permitted to issue with maturities less than five years, and subject to guidelines on the proportions of foreign currency and floating rate debt.

Both Ireland and New Zealand have structured debt management to provide the debt manager with a degree of autonomy from the rest of the government and with explicit performance objectives. Such defined performance objectives facilitate the recruitment of personnel with the know-how to attain these objectives.

The Irish NTMA has a clear objective, which is to beat the benchmark. New Zealand's DMO has a less clearly defined, but more comprehensive, objective, which is to optimize in a risk-return framework the Crown's net worth. The advantage of a narrow Irish-type objective is that the task of the debt manager is clear and its performance easy to evaluate. Such a narrow objective, however, may fail to take into account other objectives, such as risk (although risk is limited by constraints on the maturity structure of the debt). A broader objective such as in New Zealand runs less risk of omitting such important considerations, but it may also be less clear operationally, and it may be more difficult to evaluate the performance of the debt manager.

Both countries offer an example of providing a government agency with a defined objective against which the performance of the agency can, at least in theory, be evaluated. Among government functions, debt management appears particularly well suited for such an approach, since its goals can be expressed in financial terms for which market prices can be used to determine results. Nonetheless, as discussed above, there is a trade-off between concreteness and comprehensiveness in the objectives. Countries not following this alternative may prefer their more comprehensive, although less concrete, approach.

The goals of debt management are easy to define in general terms, but are more difficult when specifics are examined. Typically a government seeks to minimize the costs of financing itself, perhaps with some allowance made for risk. Such a goal is, however, very difficult to implement in a coherent manner. Ex ante, only imprecise estimates can be made of the ultimate costs of different maturity and currency profiles of debt. Even if one could wait until the debt has matured, when the cost of the profile of debt chosen by the government can be determined and compared to the realized cost on other hypothetical profiles, no account can be taken of the risk of different portfolios. Debt management can also address other goals, such as providing instruments attractive to domestic savers, improving the depth and efficiency of domestic capital markets, and subsidizing and taxing various domestic and foreign entities.

The case for an independent debt management office is not clear-cut. In contrast to the interaction of monetary policy with other short-term policy objectives, such objectives do not conflict so obviously with debt management. Debt managers do not face a time consistency problem similar to that faced by monetary policymakers. However, a case for the independence of debt management is sometimes made on two grounds. First, if the debt management office is independent, its goals can be clearly defined and it can be organized to achieve those goals. Second, the human resources needed to operate a professional debt management operation are also in high demand in the private financial sector. If the debt management office is independent, it can offer salaries and career paths that can attract skilled personnel who might be unwilling to work under the conditions of ordinary government employment.

Finally, there is the interaction of debt management with other government policies. Of particular interest is the interaction of debt management with monetary policy. In theory, central banks may be tempted to manipulate financial markets to reduce the interest rates at which government debt is issued. However, the market will presumably learn about such behavior over time and demand compensation in the form of higher interest rates. Thus, the interests of policy are better served if the central bank does not engage in such manipulation. Central banks may also be tempted to inflate away some of the value of nominal debt, to which the market is also likely to react by demanding a higher interest rate. If the central bank does act in this way, the maturity and currency structure can start conveying information to the market about the central bank's future monetary policy. Although these two considerations might suggest that monetary policy and debt management should be separate, arguments can be advanced for why coordination between the two functions is necessary. Day-to-day debt management operations affect the demand for liquidity in the economy, to which the central bank must react in order to manage liquidity in the economy. Moreover, many central banks use government securities to conduct their open market operations, and liquid government securities markets are essential for this.

Currency and Maturity Decisions

One of the basic decisions a debt administrator faces is the currency and maturity structure of its debt. The administrator has related options as well, such as issuing floating rate debt or debt indexed to inflation, and some countries also use derivative transactions to adjust their debt exposures. Countries have made very different choices both in the maturity and the currency of the debt, as well as in related matters. Market conditions in different countries, including clientele effects, are among the factors that influence such policies.

Observing that the yield curve has tended to be positively sloped over the postwar period, authorities in the United States in 1993 embarked on a policy of shortening the maturity structure of the debt. To implement this, they have reduced the volume issued of 30-year bonds, which have been the longest maturity securities issued by the U.S. Government. They have also stopped issuing seven-year notes and will compensate by issuing more Treasury bills (one-year maturity or less) and Treasury notes of three-year maturity and less.

Germany and Japan both issue most of their debt in medium-term maturity. The bulk of Japanese Government securities are the ten-year bonds, although Japan also issues a range of other maturities. Most German issues are five-year and ten-year securities. German officials have until recently followed a policy of not issuing liquid short-term issues. This policy has changed incrementally in recent years with the issue of commercial paper by the government-guaranteed Treuhandanstalt and the issue of bills by the Bundesbank.[31] German authorities also have embarked on a policy of issuing longer-term debt; they issued a 30-year bond in December 1993, for the first time since 1986, and reportedly plan to issue such bonds regularly. German policy has therefore focused on expanding the range of maturities issued, but the impact of this expansion on average maturity seems uncertain.

France and the United Kingdom follow a policy of not using short-term issues (one-year maturity or less) to finance their budget deficits. In these countries, short-term securities are largely issued in order to provide a liquid instrument in the domestic money market; this is especially true in the United Kingdom, where operations in Treasury bills are the main monetary policy tool of the Bank of England. In 1993, however, the U.K. authorities suspended a full-funding rule that required the deficit to be financed by medium-term and long-term liabilities held outside the banking sector. French debt policy is to finance the deficit with BTANs and OATs, which carry maturities of two years and up.

Adjustment of a government's maturity and currency profile of debt can reduce the cost of its debt services. Whether this has an economic impact is related to whether government deficits matter, which in turn depends on whether markets are complete.[32] Long-term debt often carries a return premium that appears to be in excess of expected future short-term rates. If this term premium is in fact a risk premium, a government could reduce its expected debt costs by issuing short-term debt instead of long-term debt. In a world where debt policy did not matter, future taxes would become riskier to compensate for such a policy, and in an ideal world there might be no economic impact. However, if reducing debt costs is an independent objective, such a term shortening could still be desirable.

An active theoretical literature covers the maturity and currency structure of government debt from a different angle. In terms of maturity structure, there are two contradictory lessons of this literature. The first is that a government with short-term debt will have less of an incentive to choose an inflationary policy than will a government with long-term debt. The reason for this is that a perma-

---

[31]These bills are issued by the Bundesbank for monetary policy purposes and not to finance the federal deficit.
[32]See Sargent (1993).

nent increase in the inflation rate will reduce the value of long-term debt by more than it will reduce the value of short-term debt. It follows from this that a government may in theory be able to enhance the credibility of its monetary policy by reducing the average maturity of its debt. For this to work, however, the value of the debt must be an objective of monetary policy.

On the other hand, short-term debt exposes the government to greater risk of a crisis of confidence.[33] A government that is exposed to a speculative attack on its currency can defend its currency by raising domestic interest rates. If the government has to roll over its domestic currency debt during this period, however, it will have to pay the higher domestic interest rates, which will make it less willing to raise interest rates to defend the currency, thus making a successful speculative attack more likely. The solution is for the government to minimize the amount of domestic currency debt coming due at any single time, by lengthening maturities and smoothing the maturity dates over time. This smoothing of maturity dates goes against the desirability of bunching of maturity dates in order to build the size of individual issues and enhance secondary market liquidity.

This literature has a less ambiguous message about debt in foreign currency or indexed to inflation. Such debt is beneficial, because the government cannot affect its real value by changing the rate of inflation. Despite this argument, however, most countries continue to issue most of their debt in their own currency and to avoid indexation. The literature suggests that perhaps this is because nominal debt has an insurance role; if a country encounters a bad shock, it can use inflation as a means of taxing debt holders, some of whom are foreign, thereby spreading the effects of the shock. Knowing this, however, holders of nominal debt may demand a higher expected return.

Supervision of the Secondary Market

Authorities supervise the secondary market in government securities for several different reasons. One goal of supervision is to prevent systemic risk that might arise from the failure of firms operating in the market. A second goal is the protection of investors in the market from deceptive or unfair practices. Authorities may also wish to ensure that the market is liquid.

In the *United States*, supervision of most major firms involved in the secondary market for government securities is accomplished as part of the overall supervision of these entities. One of the federal banking supervisors (usually the Comptroller of the

Currency or the Federal Reserve) supervises the banks involved in the market, which include a number of primary dealers. The main focus of this supervision is to ensure these banks' financial soundness. Securities firms involved in the market fall under the purview of the SEC. This supervision focuses on both financial soundness and customer protection, although it does not extend to subsidiaries of the registered broker-dealers, which in some cases are unsupervised.

Entities that served as only brokers or dealers for government securities used to be exempted from regulation and supervision. After a series of failures of secondary government securities dealers in the early and mid-1980s, this regulatory gap was plugged by the Government Securities Act of 1986, which took effect in 1987. This act gave authority to regulate these brokers and dealers to the Treasury Department. The act also required them to join a self-regulatory organization, in practice, the National Association of Securities Dealers, which would conduct supervision.

The U.S. system of supervision therefore covers all entities engaged in brokering or dealing U.S. Government securities in the United States. However, firms involved in the market but not brokering or dealing may be exempt from supervision. Firms operating in the U.S. Government securities market outside the United States are also not covered by this supervisory regime. Although Treasury securities are listed on the New York Stock Exchange (NYSE), secondary market trading in U.S. Government securities is almost exclusively an OTC dealer market. This market is subject to little direct regulation or supervision. There are no daily price limits or circuit breakers in place.

Publication of quote, price, and trade information is incomplete. The bulk of secondary market trading occurs between primary dealers through the seven interdealer brokers. Primary dealers have access to broker screens, which contain the quotes and transactions data that give the best picture of the market. Only one of these brokers makes its screen public. A limited amount of information from some of the other brokers began to be made public in 1991 through the GOVPX service. The information available through GOVPX consists of real-time price and quote information for all Treasury securities, although there is no information on strips of Treasury securities (separate trading of interest and principal as zero-coupon issues) and the quote information does not contain quote sizes. Dissemination of market data has also been increased by the expansion of the customer bases of some of the interdealer brokers, which have expanded their customer bases to all netting members of the Government Securities Clearing Corporation, a status for which approximately 75 firms are eligible.

---

[33]See Giavazzi and Pagano (1990).

In the last two years, the Federal Reserve Bank of New York has developed a system of market surveillance. It examines price data in an attempt to detect anomalies that may be associated with market manipulation. U.S. authorities recently received authorization to request reports of large positions in securities where a pricing anomaly exists.

In *Japan*, banks and securities firms acting as market-makers for government bonds must receive permission to do so from the Ministry of Finance. The Ministry examines a firm's capital level and management before granting this license. The Ministry also authorizes brokers in the market. Trading in government securities can take place either OTC or on the Tokyo Stock Exchange, where all government bonds are listed, although most trading occurs OTC. The transaction tax applies to all domestic bonds, including government securities (except short-term bills), and tends to reduce trading volume. Trades involving two foreign counterparties are exempt from the transaction tax.

Most dealers and brokers in securities markets in *Germany* are banks. In contrast to the United States and Japan, there is no legal distinction in Germany between securities firms and commercial banks. Banks are licensed and supervised by the Federal Banking Supervisory Office. Some brokers, however, fall outside this supervisory system and normally are licensed and supervised by one of the eight regional stock exchanges. The implementation of a new regime with a federal securities supervisor is under way, with the new supervisor likely to commence operations in 1994. Trading in German Government securities takes place both on the stock exchanges and OTC, in addition to substantial offshore trading. Most domestic trading is in the OTC market, although there is a daily fixing on the stock exchange at which the price of government bonds is set. Most exchange trading occurs at this price, and the Bundesbank sometimes intervenes at this fixing to counteract price pressure. Market activity both on the exchange and OTC is subject to little supervision; the stock exchanges have nominal authority, but their power is limited.[34] Some German trading restrictions have loosened recently. The Government eliminated taxes on securities transactions in 1991 and 1992. It also abolished in 1990 a special commission that inhibited the resale of bonds in the first year following issue.

In *France*, the secondary market in government securities is open to a broad spectrum of participants. The main group of participants consists of the eighteen SVTs. The French Treasury requires these entities to participate in both the primary and

secondary markets for these securities, in exchange for certain privileges (see section on Primary Dealer Systems above). Members of the Paris Bourse and other financial intermediaries may also participate in the market; market participants are supervised by the Société des Bourses Françaises. Trading is permitted both on the Bourse and OTC, with most trading OTC. In addition, a substantial portion of the secondary market, especially in OATs, takes place offshore. In general, France has no capital restrictions that apply separately to government securities. SVTs, however, must satisfy a minimum capital requirement of F 300 million. SVTs are supervised by the Commission Bancaire; they must also submit weekly activity reports to the Treasury. Other participants in the market do not appear to face separate supervision or reporting requirements for their government securities operations.

The market for government securities in the *United Kingdom* centers on the GEMMs (see section on Primary Dealer Systems above). These are firms approved by the Bank of England, which also supervises the firms' market-making activities in gilts. Through the same system, the Bank authorizes and supervises two special types of institutions, the interdealer brokers and the stock exchange money brokers, which do business with the GEMMs. Other participants in the gilts market fall under general U.K. investment business regulation, and must generally be authorized by the Securities and Investment Board (SIB) and join a self-regulatory organization. This authorization does not apply to firms operating offshore, although it does apply to foreign firms operating in the United Kingdom. It also does not apply to investors in gilts and other securities.

Firms operating in the market for Treasury bills fall under the money markets' supervision system. Firms conducting wholesale transactions in the sterling money market or in the foreign exchange or bullion market must be "listed" by the Bank of England under its wholesale markets supervision regime. This listing entails a series of checks on the firms' management, reputation, and financial position. Firms conducting nonwholesale money market transactions fall under the general securities regulation and supervision of the SIB and its self-regulatory organizations.

GEMMs are under stringent capital adequacy rules. Other participants in government securities markets face capital requirements set by the Bank of England for banks and money market firms or by the SIB or a self-regulatory organization for securities firms. Banks with significant securities business may also face the SIB's securities capital rules. These rules, as well as those of the Bank's money markets regulation, focus on market risk as opposed to credit risk.

---

[34]"Financial Centre Germany: Underlying Conditions and Recent Development," *Monthly Report of the Deutsche Bundesbank*, March 1992, pp. 23–31.

U.K. authorities conduct intensive monitoring of market participants. GEMMs submit daily electronic reports of their position in each gilt issue to the Bank of England. For money market firms, the Bank requires fortnightly reports on risk exposures and capital positions, except for pure brokers, which must submit reports only monthly. The Bank can also carry out spot checks of these firms at other times to ensure continuous compliance with its capital requirements.

U.K. securities firms also are subject to detailed investor protection rules. Most securities firms, including GEMMs, are subject to the rules of the Securities and Futures Authority (SFA), one of the self-regulatory organizations under the SIB. Wholesale money market firms are subject to a lighter regulatory system under the Bank of England. For GEMMs, the Bank also solicits feedback from investors to verify that the GEMMs are providing adequate investor services.

There are no formal circuit breakers for the gilts market. However, procedures are in place for the Bank of England to intervene in the market. The Bank has the authority to enter the market to react to price anomalies for particular issues. The Bank's tap mechanism is also designed to react to market conditions. The guiding principle is for the Bank not to sell additional amounts of an issue into a falling market.

In *Italy*, the domestic secondary market in government securities is divided in three parts, two of them closely supervised. The bulk of trading volume occurs on the screen-based Mercato Telematico Secondario (MTS). A variety of financial firms can join the market; over 330 have signed up to be dealers on the MTS. A small proportion of Government securities transactions, mostly retail, pass through the Milan Stock Exchange. All Government securities except Treasury bills are listed on the exchange. There is also an informal OTC market that is more loosely regulated. In addition, some trading of domestic issues of Italian Government securities occurs in foreign countries. Until recently, there was a stamp tax on government securities transactions. The Government abolished this tax at the end of 1993, in part to entice trading back from offshore centers.

Primary dealers on the MTS are required to post continuous two-way quotes in a subset of Government securities issues. These quotes must be for a minimum size of Lit 5 billion, which is also the minimum trade size on the MTS. Other dealers on the MTS face no market-making requirements. There also are no market-making requirements on the OTC market.

Primary dealer status is open to both banks and nonbanks incorporated in *Canada*. These entities are known as "primary distributors," with a more active subset known as "jobbers."[35] Jobbers are required to make markets in government securities. Both primary distributors and jobbers must submit weekly statistical reports on their trading activities to the Bank of Canada. The domestic market in Canadian Government securities is exclusively an OTC market, but trading also occurs internationally. Since August 1993, information from interdealer broker screens has been made available to the public. Before then, information was only available to those dealing on the screens.

---

[35]See "Administrative Arrangements Regarding the Auction of Government of Canada Securities," *Bank of Canada Review* (Summer 1993), pp. 71–76.

Annex II

Developments in the Regulation of International Banking

The impetus for recent regulatory initiatives in international banking has come from the growth of derivatives markets and the increasing involvement of wholesale banks in these markets.[1] The debate over the regulation of derivatives markets has led to a redoubling of the long-standing efforts by bank regulators to improve the capital cover for risk positions entered into by international banks, without unduly distorting incentives.[2] This effort resulted in the publication of three proposals in April 1993 that recommended a capital requirement against market risk, a broader recognition of netting as a means of reducing credit risk, and disclosure of interest rate risk.

Recent trends in the markets for derivative instruments are described first, followed by a discussion of the proposed extensions of the Basle capital requirements.

Growth of the OTC Derivatives Markets

The notional principal amount of exchange-traded derivative instruments increased by 69 percent in 1993, reaching $7.8 trillion, which was more than 12 times the total in 1986 (Table A3).[3] Interest rate futures and options together had a notional principal value of $7.3 trillion in 1993, while currency futures and options accounted for $111 billion and stock index futures and options for $406 billion. Turnover of these contracts on organized exchanges rose by 22 percent in 1993, reaching a combined total of 774 million contracts (Table A4).[4] Trading was boosted in both 1992 and

1993 by the turmoil in the European exchange rate mechanism.[5]

While comparisons between the markets are difficult, activity on the OTC market appears to have grown more rapidly than has activity on the exchanges. At the end of 1992, the notional principal value of outstanding interest rate swaps and currency swaps was $4.7 trillion (Table A5). This was 22 percent higher than the end-1991 notional principal and more than five times the end-1987 figure. In the second half of 1992 alone, the notional principal of new interest rate swaps was $1.5 trillion, and new currency swaps reached $146 billion (Table A6).

In more specific terms, the growth of the markets is characterized by increasing globalization, increasing involvement by banks, and increasing complexity of products.[6] At the end of 1987, 79 percent of all outstanding interest rate swaps by notional value were denominated in U.S. dollars (Table A7). However, by the end of 1992, U.S. dollar interest rate swaps represented only 46 percent of outstanding interest rate swaps. Similarly, the proportion of U.S. dollar currency swaps has declined from 44 percent of the outstanding notional value in 1987 to 36 percent in 1992. A parallel trend is observed in the distribution of notional principal and turnover of exchange-traded instruments between the United States, Europe, and Japan (Tables A3 and A4).

Swaps are used to reduce funding costs and to transfer payment characteristics and interest rate or currency risk exposures. Thus, for example, an issuer of a straight bond might swap the proceeds into an obligation to pay a floating rate, or a U.S. corporation might issue a deutsche mark bond and swap the proceeds into dollars, thereby eliminating exchange rate risk. The counterparty data on interest rate swaps show that by far the most important

---

[1]There are also concerns about the involvement of nonbanks in the derivative markets; see section on Strengthening Capital Requirements, below.

[2]These efforts are discussed in Goldstein, Folkerts-Landau, and others (1992); and Goldstein, Folkerts-Landau, and others (1993b).

[3]The notional principal value refers to the face value of the instruments underlying the derivative contract. This is used to calculate payments under the contract and is not a measure of the exposure of the institutions holding these contracts. The latter is provided by the replacement cost of the contract, which is estimated at approximately 2 percent of the notional value for interest rate swaps and 5 percent for currency swaps.

[4]The measure of turnover used in Table A4 is the number of contracts traded. Comparisons over time are complicated, since

contracts representing different amounts of the underlying instruments are traded on different exchanges and new contracts are frequently introduced.

[5]See Goldstein, Folkerts-Landau, and others (1993a) for a discussion of the impact of the exchange rate crisis in September 1992 on derivatives trading.

[6]These complex products have names such as swaptions, forward swaps, knockouts, step-up recovery floaters, index-amortizing notes, and lookback options.

participants in these markets are financial institutions, which held 76 percent of the outstanding contracts by notional principal value of interest rate swaps in 1992 (Table A5). In the market for currency swaps, however, financial institutions accounted for only 54 percent of the outstanding positions at the end of 1992.

The involvement of banks in the OTC markets has motivated much of the regulatory examination of derivatives. The notional value of financial derivatives (including forwards) held by U.S. bank holding companies was $5.1 trillion in June 1992, which was 27 percent higher than the notional value in September 1990.[7] In June 1992, bank holding companies with less than $10 billion in capital held about $34 billion in interest rate swaps and $153 million in currency swaps. These were, respectively, more than 47 percent and 186 percent higher than the corresponding figures in September 1990. Many regional banks in the United States have started to sell derivative products to clients in addition to using derivatives as a financing and risk management tool for themselves. Many mutual funds have used derivatives to manage risk or enhance returns.[8]

The use of interest rate and currency swaps by nonfinancial institutions has also increased substantially.[9] The amount of interest rate swaps used by governments and international institutions has increased from $47.6 billion at the end of 1987 to more than $242 billion at the end of 1992 (Table A5). The use of interest rate swaps by corporations has also increased significantly, from about $129 billion in 1987 to about $666 billion at the end of 1992. In the same five-year period, currency swaps used by governments and international institutions rose from $33.9 billion to $110.6 billion, and currency swaps used by corporations increased from $51.6 billion to $282.2 billion.

Outstanding notional principal in the sophisticated OTC products such as caps, collars, and floors increased from $468 billion at the end of 1991 to $507 billion at the end of 1992. The notional principal value of outstanding swaptions rose from $109 billion at the end of 1991 to $127 billion at the end of 1992.

Many reasons have been cited as explanations for the rapid expansion of the OTC market. These include (i) a rise in the demand for hedging instruments owing to increases in the volatility of exchange rates and interest rates; (ii) an increase in the demand for sophisticated instruments to profit from relatively large interest rate differentials across borders and across different investor groups; (iii) a rise in the demand for sophisticated products to unbundle risk and to alter the risk characteristics of portfolios in a rapidly changing investment environment; (iv) a reduction in the cost of providing OTC derivatives securities owing to advances in technology (including computing and information processing facilities); (v) a growing demand by banks to seek new business as the profitability of their traditional lending business has declined; and (vi) worldwide deregulation and financial market liberalization.

Strengthening Capital Requirements

The Basle Committee proposed a capital adequacy standard in July 1988 that provided an explicit approach by which the minimum capital requirement to cover credit risk for both on- and off-balance sheet positions could be computed. In addition, it provided guidelines on what could be counted as capital. In 1989, the Council of the European Community issued an Own Funds Directive (OFD) and a Solvency Ratio Directive (SRD) for similar purposes.

While the 1988 accord was well received, it has been long recognized that its focus on credit risk alone was too narrow. Other risk factors, such as interest rate risk and exchange rate risk, might be very important, especially for positions that are held for relatively short periods of time. Furthermore, banks might have an incentive to seek a higher return on capital by substituting interest rate or exchange rate risk for credit risk when designing their portfolios if capital requirements apply only to credit risk. Market participants have also expressed concern that the definition of capital is too restrictive. That definition was chosen to cover banks' traditional loan positions, which tend to be held for long horizons. However, as banks' "trading books"—which are composed of relatively short-term positions—become more important, a more flexible definition might be appropriate.

It is also widely recognized that the 1988 accord was too stringent in its treatment of netting. Under that accord, only netting by novation was recognized for the purposes of calculating the capital requirement. The 1990 Lamfalussy Report suggested that any legally enforceable form of bilateral netting should be recognized, since netting can improve the efficiency and the stability of the banking system by reducing credit exposure, liquidity risk, and transaction costs.[10]

---

[7]See Board of Governors of the Federal Reserve System and others (1993).

[8]While many mutual funds are barred by their investment guidelines from participating in the swaps markets, some are bypassing the restriction by investing in structured notes.

[9]With this increased use of derivatives have come more frequent reports of losses as in the cases of, among others, Metallgesellschaft, Codelco, Rockefeller Center Properties, Procter and Gamble, and Gibson Greetings (see Box 1).

[10]Bank for International Settlements and Group of Ten (1990).

The 1993 Basle Proposals

In response to these concerns, the Basle Committee released in April 1993 a set of three consultative papers that contains proposals to revise the 1988 accord. The papers consider: (i) the recognition of netting for the capital requirements for credit risk; (ii) the reporting of, and capital requirements for, market risk and foreign exchange risk; and (iii) the measurement and reporting of interest rate risk. Furthermore, a new tier of capital, called tier 3 capital, was also defined.

The 1993 Basle proposals are similar in many ways to the Capital Adequacy Directive (CAD) issued by the EC Council to modify and supplement its 1989 directives, which had been criticized for the same reasons as the 1988 Basle accord.[11] The CAD and the new proposals follow the same approach in measuring interest rate risk and have the same duration-based market risk weights. Furthermore, for debt securities, the two share the same structure for aggregating market and specific risk and have the same risk weights for specific risks. However, the two differ significantly in the treatment of foreign exchange risk and position risk in equities. In those respects, the Basle proposal is more stringent than the CAD. On the other hand, the CAD applies to both banks and securities houses while the Basle proposals apply only to banks.

Capital Adequacy Standards

The proposed framework. The main conceptual breakthroughs of the proposals on the computation of capital requirements are (i) the recognition of a need to treat items in the loan book and the trading book of banks differently when setting minimum capital requirements; (ii) the recognition of a need to account for market risk and specific risk differently; and (iii) the calculation of capital requirements for general market risk from a portfolio perspective.

The trading book is composed of (i) proprietary positions in financial instruments; (ii) exposures due to unsettled transactions; and (iii) positions taken in order to hedge other elements of the trading book. Because these positions are usually held for only a short time, risks arising from adverse movements in interest rates, exchanges rates, or other prices can be very important relative to credit risk. This suggests that positions in the bank's trading book and loan book should be treated differently. Under the new proposals, the capital requirement for items in the loan book is calculated in the same way as specified in the 1988 accord, with only some changes to reflect the more general recognition of bilateral netting. However, the capital requirement for items in the

trading book is calculated based on a new framework.

In this new framework, risk exposure is separated into specific risk and a general market risk. The key distinction between the two is that the specific risk exposures of different positions are generally unrelated, which is not true for market risk. The specific risk exposure of the entire trading book can be computed simply as the sum of the specific risk exposures of each position in the book. However, since the market risk of different positions is related, the proposals suggest a portfolio approach that permits some offsets between long and short positions in the calculation of the general market risk exposure. Thus, the total capital requirement is computed as the sum of a specific risk charge (applied to the gross position of the portfolio) and a general market risk charge (applied to the net position of the portfolio). This is the so-called building block approach in the proposals.

Furthermore, since the nature of the specific risk and market risk varies across types of instruments, the Basle proposals classify positions into debt securities positions, equity positions, and foreign exchange positions and use different approaches for calculating the specific risk and general market risk charges for these groups of instruments. Under the proposed framework, a bank's minimum capital requirement is computed as the aggregate of capital charges for the specific and market risks for each of its debt and equities positions, plus charges against foreign exchange risk and credit risk arising from its loan book.

It is important to note that, in general, the various components of general market risk are neither uncorrelated nor perfectly correlated. In simply adding the capital charges for general market risk of debt securities to the capital charge for foreign exchange risk and to the capital charge for general market risk of equity positions, the Basle Committee implicitly assumed that the market risk elements are perfectly correlated. This approach is a conservative one, as the standard deviation of portfolio value computed in this way is always at least as high as the actual standard deviation of the portfolio value under less than perfect correlations among the risk factors. The approach has the merit of being easy to implement since time-varying relationships among the many risk factors are ignored. Furthermore, the capital requirement for each individual risk factor can be set separately.

Specific risk of debt securities. As in the 1988 accord, debt securities are classified into a number of broad categories by issuer; then a different risk weight for each category is assigned to capture differences in the probability of default or credit rating change for different groups of issuers. There are five such categories under the 1993 proposals: (1) government (with no risk weight); (2) qualifying securities (basically investment grade) with residual maturity of six months or less (with a risk weight of 0.25 percent);

---

[11] See European Community (1993).

(3) qualifying securities with residual maturity between 6 and 24 months (with a risk weight of 1 percent); (4) qualifying securities with residual maturity exceeding 24 months (with a risk weight of 1.6 percent); and (5) other securities (with a risk weight of 8 percent).[12] The CAD has the same definition of these categories and assigns the same risk weights.[13]

The definition of "qualifying" as investment grade is an important improvement over the 1988 accord in which the classification of counterparties was dependent not on credit rating but on whether they were Organization for Economic Cooperation and Development (OECD) country institutions. For example, under the 1988 accord, loans to OECD official borrowers carry a zero risk weight; claims on banks incorporated in OECD countries carry a 20 percent weight; residential mortgages have a 50 percent weight; and foreign currency loans to non-OECD governments and loans to private companies carry a 100 percent weight.[14] Since the weighted exposures are multiplied by 8 percent to yield the capital requirement, the effective percentages for comparison with the risk weights in the 1993 proposal are 0 percent, 1.6 percent, 4 percent, and 8 percent, respectively. Under the 1988 accord, an interest rate contract with less than six months to maturity to a private firm, in a non-OECD country, that is rated AAA or equivalent by approved rating agencies, would carry capital charge equal to 8 percent of the marked-to-market value under the so-called current exposure approach. Under the new proposal, the capital charge would be 0.25 percent of the marked-to-market value of the position.

General market risk of debt securities. The general market risk of debt securities is mostly interest rate risk. Unlike credit risk, which is counterparty-specific (and hence position-specific), interest rate changes can affect many positions in the book simultaneously. The approach taken in the 1988 accord, which computes the total capital charge as the sum of capital reserves for individual positions, is perceived to be inappropriate by many market participants who have argued that interest rate risk should be accounted for from a portfolio perspective in which offsets at least between long and short positions should be allowed.

The interest rate risk exposure of a portfolio of debt securities is determined by the sensitivity of the value of the portfolio to interest rate changes and by the volatility of interest rates. The sensitivity of a portfolio of debt securities and derivatives to changes in interest rates can be constructed from the duration measures of the debt instruments and the deltas of the derivative instruments, which can be calculated from pricing models or from simulation techniques.[15] The volatility of interest rates can be implied from options prices or calculated from historical data. However, for relatively small institutions that lack sophisticated risk management systems, these computations can be prohibitively difficult when their trading books contain a large number of positions. Hence, the Basle Committee has developed a "standard" approach, which is a compromise to facilitate implementation.

This standard "maturity ladder" approach involves setting (i) a manageable number of maturity bands (instead of a continuum of maturities); (ii) a representative duration measure for each band (instead of a duration measure for each instrument); and (iii) a representative interest rate change for each band (instead of a different change for every interest rate maturity within each band).

Under this approach, each position is converted into a combination of simple debt instruments that are then classified into 15 maturity bands. For example, a ten-year interest rate swap under which a firm is receiving floating rate interest and paying fixed is treated as a long position in a floating rate instrument of maturity equivalent to the period until the next interest fixing date (often six months) and a short position in a ten-year fixed rate bond. A long position in a three-month interest rate future maturing in one month is reported as a long position in a government security with a maturity of four months and a short position in a government security with a maturity of one month. An option on a debt instrument is treated as if it is a position equal in value to the amount of the underlying instrument, multiplied by the delta of the option determined by an approved option pricing model.

Each converted position is then assigned a risk weight, which is the product of the representative modified duration measure for the maturity band and an assumed interest rate change for the particular maturity band.[16] The capital requirement is then calculated as the sum of the weighted positions (where long and short positions can offset each other).

However, positive and negative positions in the same maturity band might not be perfect hedges for each other because of the size of each maturity band and the existence of gap risk and spread risk. As an example of spread risk, a long position in a three-

---

[12]Different risk weights are proposed for qualifying issues with different residual maturity because uncertainty about creditworthiness increases with the life of the security.

[13]See Basle Committee on Banking Supervision (1993), pp. 14–16; and European Community (1993), Annex I.14.

[14]For precise definitions of the different categories, see Bank for International Settlements (1988), Part II.

[15]Delta measures the sensitivity of the price of a derivative security with respect to a change in the price of the underlying security.

[16]The representative duration measure for a particular maturity band is computed as the modified duration of a bond with a maturity equal to the mid-point of the time band, assuming an 8 percent interest rate and an 8 percent coupon. Furthermore, the assumed interest rate change is designed to cover about two standard deviations of one month's yield volatility in most major markets.

month U.S. Treasury bill is not a perfect hedge for a short position in a three-month Eurodollar bond since the three-month Treasury bill rate and the three-month LIBOR or Eurodollar rate are not perfectly correlated. The variation in this spread is a risk factor that should be taken into consideration. Another example is gap risk: a long position in a three-month Treasury bill is not a perfect hedge for a short position in a four-month Treasury bill (even though they are classified in the same maturity band) because the three-month yield and the four-month yield are not perfectly correlated.

To provide for such imperfections in the mutual hedging of instruments in the same maturity band, the Basle Committee proposed to impose a vertical disallowance. This disallowance is added to the net capital charge in the computation of the capital requirement for debt securities. A vertical disallowance for each maturity band is calculated as 10 percent of the smaller of the total capital charge for long positions within the band and the total capital charge for short positions within the band. The total vertical disallowance is then computed by summing the vertical disallowances across maturity bands. Without the vertical disallowance, the pairs of positions in the above examples will be treated as perfect offsets as if there is no risk at all.

Similarly, positive and negative positions in different maturity bands are not perfect hedges for each other since the yield curves need not move in a parallel fashion. In order to account for such imperfect offsets, the Basle Committee also proposed the imposition of horizontal disallowances. Since positions from distant maturity bands are the worst offsets, the capital charge should be increased appropriately. For this purpose, the Committee has proposed to group the maturity bands into three different maturity zones. Within-zone horizontal disallowances are smaller than across-zones disallowances. Also, adjacent-zones disallowances are smaller than nonadjacent-zones disallowances.

While the CAD does not explicitly mention these disallowances, the computation of capital requirements is essentially equivalent to the imposition of such disallowances, since matched and unmatched positions within and across maturity bands are assigned different weights that take into account the risk from hedging with nonidentical instruments.

The Basle Committee also proposed to allow banks with more sophisticated risk management systems to use an alternative method under which the duration of each position is computed separately. However, this is permitted only if the alternative method produces results that are consistently equivalent with the standard method.

Specific risk of equity securities. The specific risk of an equity security is the risk of an unexpected change in the price of the security that is unrelated to the general movement of the stock market. The Committee has proposed that the specific risk charge for an institution be computed as 8 percent of its gross equity position—the aggregate value of all equity positions without any offset between long and short positions. However, at the discretion of national regulators, a 4 percent weight can be applied if the equity portfolio is liquid and diversified. Under the CAD, the specific risk charge is 4 percent of the overall gross equity position instead of 8 percent. Furthermore, if the portfolio is liquid and diversified, a 2 percent weight can be allowed.

General market risk of equity securities. Since general market risk is common to all equity securities, the market risks of long and short positions can offset each other. Thus, the actual risk exposure depends on the overall net equity position rather than the gross position. Under the 1993 proposal, the capital charge for the general market risk of an equity portfolio is computed as 8 percent of the overall net position of the portfolio. The CAD follows the same approach and has the same 8 percent weight.

Foreign exchange risk. Foreign exchange risk is the risk of loss owing to fluctuations in exchange rates. The exchange rate risk exposure of a portfolio is determined by (i) the sensitivity of the value of the portfolio to changes in exchange rates; (ii) exchange rate volatilities; and (iii) correlations between exchange rates. Computing the sensitivity of the portfolio to exchange rate changes can be difficult because the values of foreign exchange derivatives are often complicated functions of the exchange rate. Strictly speaking, to determine the foreign exchange risk exposure, the behavior of all exchange rates on which the contracts depend has to be modeled, correlations need to be taken into consideration, and the future profits or losses of the entire portfolio should be simulated. However, such modeling and computation can be too complicated and expensive for smaller banks. Hence, the Basle Committee proposed a shorthand method for measuring foreign exchange risk.[17]

The Basle Committee also proposed that institutions with the necessary expertise, computer systems, and data could, if permitted by their national supervisors, use an alternative method based on simulations. However, an additional 3 percent charge is added to the capital charge obtained from the simulation. Consequently, the minimum capital charge can never be less than 3 percent of the overall net foreign exchange position.

The CAD is more lenient than the Basle proposal in that under a similar standard method, the capital charge is computed as 8 percent of the amount by which the overall net foreign exchange position exceeds 2 percent of the institution's own funds. Fur-

---

[17]See Section III for a description of how the shorthand method is applied to foreign exchange exposures.

thermore, under the simulation method, the CAD requires only that the capital charge be larger than 2 percent of the overall net foreign exchange position.

Netting

In the 1988 accord, only netting by novation was recognized for the purpose of calculating capital requirements. Netting by novation entails a bilateral contract between two counterparties under which a new obligation to pay or receive a given currency is automatically amalgamated with all previous obligations in the same currency, thereby creating a single legally binding net position that replaces the larger number of gross obligations. The 1993 proposals extend the recognition of netting for capital requirement purposes to include any bilateral netting agreement that is legally binding in the jurisdictions of both parties and meets the minimum standards recommended by the 1990 Lamfalussy Report.

The more general recognition of bilateral netting for the computation of capital requirement is facilitated by recent legal developments on the enforceability of close-out netting. A close-out netting arrangement can eliminate cherry-picking behavior at the time of bankruptcy, and its enforceability is usually regarded as the legal basis for bilateral netting for capital adequacy purpose. In the United States, legal developments facilitate the recognition of bilateral netting.

Under the new Basle proposal, for banks using the so-called current exposure method in the 1988 Basle accord, the credit exposure on bilaterally netted forward transactions is calculated as the sum of the net marked-to-market replacement cost, if positive, plus an add-on based on the notional underlying principal. For banks now using the so-called original exposure method under the 1988 Basle accord, a reduction in the credit conversion factors applying to bilaterally netted transactions is permitted temporarily until the market risk related capital requirements are implemented. The original exposure method, which computes capital charges as percentages of notional values, will ultimately be abandoned for netted transactions, as it does not account for current and potential future exposures separately and hence is not entirely compatible with the idea of netting.

Industry Responses to the 1993 Basle Proposals

Regarding the treatment of market risk and interest rate risk, a frequent comment from market participants has been that the proposals may increase capital requirements for the affected institutions. An increase in capital requirement would be due to the size of the vertical disallowance and the computation of total capital charge as the simple sum of the capital charges for individual general market risk elements. There is also a concern that the proposals do not create incentives for banks to adopt more advanced risk measurement systems. Instead, most banks would have to maintain two risk reporting systems (one for the computation of capital requirement under the Basle proposals and a more complicated one for everyday risk management). This is financially inefficient and can reduce banks' competitiveness relative to nonbanks. Furthermore, there is also a general feeling that the distinction between the trading book and the loan book should be clearly defined. Leaving the definition to the discretion of national authorities can potentially create unfair competition among banks in different nations.

The banking industry generally welcomed the recognition of bilateral netting since this can reduce capital requirements, which in turn will allow banks to take on more business than they are currently able to accept. The Bank for International Settlements (BIS) estimated that this proposal may reduce capital requirements for swap dealers by between 25 and 40 percent. The International Swaps and Derivatives Association (ISDA) estimated that the recognition of bilateral netting could reduce capital requirements by as much as 48 percent.

Some market participants have argued that a 10 percent vertical disallowance is too large, particularly for an institution that has a lot of interest rate swaps and short-term debt instruments. Since a floating rate instrument is at par immediately after a payment set date, the value of the floating rate side of a swap is treated as a debt instrument with maturity date equal to the next payment set date and with a principal amount equal to the notional value of the swap, which can be a huge number. As a result, a 10 percent charge can be a substantial burden.

Some participants have also expressed concern that simply adding the capital charges for individual risk elements can result in an overestimation of the amount of capital required. At the heart of the criticism is the implicit assumption of perfect correlation among the risk factors. Participants have argued that the correlation between two risk factors should be taken into account when aggregating the capital charges. If risk factors are imperfectly correlated, then less capital should be needed. In addition, the proposed aggregation approach might distort banks' activities since risk factors having low correlations are overcharged relative to risk factors having high correlations. Some market participants have therefore recommended that actual correlations estimated from historical data should be used.

A remaining criticism deals with the calculation of add-ons and the way they are included in the computation of capital charges. The Committee's decision to retain the rules in the 1988 accord on add-ons has been criticized as being inconsistent with the idea of netting. Under the 1988 accord, add-ons are computed as a percentage of the gross notional principal. That is, netting is allowed for potential future exposure. The Committee's explanation is that there is no guarantee that there will be offsets of exposures in the future, so it might be prudent to keep the current scheme. Critics, on the other hand, tend to argue that this is too conservative. They have complained also that computing credit exposure as the sum of the add-ons and the higher of the net replacement value and zero might overstate the actual capital requirement needed. The argument is that under the proposed rule, a financial institution will be required to hold capital equal to the add-on regardless of its net replacement value. That is, the institution is even required to hold capital to safeguard a liability. The position of the Basle Committee is that the purpose of the add-ons is to cover potential future exposure; there is no reason to expect that there would be no future exposure just because the current exposure is zero.

Under the recent proposals, derivatives positions are converted into equivalent positions in the underlying instruments based on the deltas of the derivatives. However, delta can change as the price of the underlying security changes. There is therefore an additional risk element—gamma risk—related to the sensitivity of the delta with respect to the price of the underlying security. This gamma risk can be substantial. Furthermore, related to the gamma risk is the risk of changes in volatility—vega risk. Given the highly volatile nature of exchange rates and the rapid changes in volatility, many market participants have essentially taken derivatives positions to bet on volatility changes. These positions are typically created to have zero delta. As such, no capital charge is attached, yet these can be highly risky positions. The failure of the Basle proposals to cover gamma risk and vega risk can potentially lead to distortion in the banks' activities in which these uncharged risks are substituted for those covered by the proposals in order to reduce the capital requirement.

Some practitioners have complained that the 3 percent foreign exchange risk add-on that would be added to the capital requirements obtained from simulation methods is arbitrary and can be a severe penalty for banks using a sophisticated and probably more accurate approach to risk management. This can discourage the adoption of advances in risk management technology, which goes against the spirit of the exercise.

Recommendations from Regulators

In the United States, the 1988 Basle accord was adopted by all bank regulators. In a joint report, the Federal Reserve, the Federal Deposit Insurance Corporation (FDIC), and the Office of the Comptroller of Currency (OCC) discussed the importance of the market risk component of the derivatives activities of commercial banks and argued for a portfolio-based evaluation of this risk.[18]

The importance of interest rate risk has also been noted by these agencies. In September 1993, they issued a proposal on measuring banks' interest rate risk and establishing a related capital requirement.[19] Under this proposal, a bank's interest rate risk exposure can be measured by a supervisory model similar to the interest rate risk measurement model proposed by the Basle Committee in April 1993 or by the bank's own risk management system if it is approved by the regulator. Two alternative methods were proposed for setting minimum capital requirement. Under a so-called minimum capital standard approach, an explicit capital charge based on the amount of interest rate exposure in excess of a supervisory threshold would be imposed. Under the so-called risk assessment approach, the capital requirement would be assessed on a case-by-case basis, dependent on the bank's interest rate risk exposure, internal risk controls, and financial condition.

Bank regulators also recognized the importance of netting arrangements. In a circular issued in October 1993, the OCC recommended that each national bank should use master close-out netting agreements with its counterparties to the broadest extent possible as long as those agreements are legally enforceable. The OCC also proposed that for positions collateralized by cash or government securities, the risk weight used in the computation of risk-based capital requirement should be reduced to reflect the minimal credit risk of these positions.

Harmonization of Standards for Banks and Securities Firms

In some countries, securities houses are subject to capital requirements by securities and exchange regulators. For example, in the United States, securities houses are subjected to SEC capital requirements that utilize a different approach from that of the Basle Committee. The "Net Capital Rule" of the SEC requires a minimum level of liquid net worth after some deductions—the "haircuts"—to account for market and credit risks. The haircut for unrealized profit associated with OTC derivatives positions is 100 percent, which is viewed by many market participants as too stringent. The SEC is considering modifying the Net Capital Rule to better capture the credit and market risks of derivative products. In May 1993, it issued a proposal in

---

[18]See Board of Governors of the Federal Reserve System and others (1993).

[19]See *Federal Register* (1993).

which the calculation of the market risk exposure of interest rate swaps was considered. Two alternative approaches to dealing with interest rate swaps were suggested. Under the first approach, a swap book is treated as a portfolio of debt securities with the same interest rate sensitivity. These "converted" debt securities are then treated as simple bond positions in the net capital calculation. Under the second approach, swaps are assigned to maturity bands currently used by government securities, and then a capital charge of 0 percent to 6 percent of the notional value, depending on the maturity, is applied to each swap. The capital charges for long and short positions in swaps are allowed to offset each other depending on the relative maturities of the swaps. In March 1994, the SEC issued a proposal to modify the capital requirements for brokers or dealers by allowing them to use a theoretical pricing model developed by the Options Clearing Corporation when calculating capital charges for listed options and related positions.

The Commodity Futures Trading Commission (CFTC) follows a similar haircut approach to setting capital requirements for brokers and dealers engaged in commodity futures transactions. The approaches used by the SEC and the CFTC are in contrast to the "risk-weighted capital approach" in the 1988 Basle accord for banks and the recently proposed "building-block approach" by the Basle Committee. Generally, there are also differences in the definition of capital between bank and securities firm regulators.

In order to promote harmonization of regulations applied to securities companies in different countries, the International Organization of Securities Commissions has devoted substantial effort to setting up global capital standards. To date, the effort has not been brought to completion because of disagreements within its Technical Committee.

Accounting and Disclosure

As a result of the complicated nature of the regulatory structure for the OTC derivative markets, data on OTC derivative market activities are collected by a large number of regulators and concerned parties under different regulatory and accounting regimes in many countries. However, given the lack of uniformity of reporting documents and the discrepancies in reporting requirements, it is very difficult to aggregate all the information to give a clear picture of the market situation. This is further complicated by the fact that OTC derivative positions are generally off-balance sheet items and are not readily available from institutions' financial statements.

Given that all major securities houses in the United States are engaged in OTC derivatives activities, either directly or through subsidiaries, information on the risk exposure of these companies from the derivatives activities of their subsidiaries is needed. To this end, both the SEC and the CFTC have required brokers and dealers with affiliates engaging in OTC derivatives trading to report on the portfolios of these units. In February 1994, the CFTC proposed a set of rules to further improve disclosure. These rules require a company unit that engages in swaps transactions to file quarterly and annual reports on its financial situation and to provide information on how it monitors and controls the risks related to swap trading. Some regulators have emphasized the importance of identifying the source of revenue for market participants, especially dealers. The concern is that the current lack of information has made it impossible for the regulators to tell whether the many profitable dealers are serving a financial intermediation function or not—or if most of their profits are from proprietary trading or speculation.

To improve the international coordination of disclosure requirements, the SEC, the CFTC, and the Securities and Investment Board in the United Kingdom announced in March 1994 that they will share their information on the OTC derivative markets.

The broad range of OTC derivatives products and the ease with which new tailor-made OTC products can be created has significantly complicated the application of existing instrument-specific accounting standards, many of which were issued well before many OTC derivative products were created. Furthermore, the accounting method used can be affected by whether or not the transaction is used for hedging purposes. Under the so-called hedge accounting approach, hedges are reported as related to the position being hedged and are not marked to market. The issue is complicated if the hedge is imperfect.

Efforts are under way to write new accounting rules for OTC derivative transactions. In the United States, the Financial Accounting Standards Board (FASB) has introduced Financial Accounting Standard (FAS) numbers 105 and 107, and Interpretation number 39. FAS 105 requires that the notional amount of OTC derivative positions be reported in the firm's financial statement or in the accompanying notes together with their nature and terms. It also requires that information on the concentration of credit risk to groups of counterparties be reported. FAS 107 requires the disclosure of the fair value of related on- and off-balance sheet derivative instruments. FASB Interpretation 39 allows the offsetting of derivatives positions with the same counterparty under a master netting arrangement. The FASB is still working on improving the accounting and disclosure of OTC derivative transactions.

In its July 1993 report, the Group of Thirty recommended that the agencies that set national accounting standards should (i) provide comprehensive guidance on the accounting and reporting of transactions in derivatives and (ii) work toward international harmonization of standards.[20] The Group also suggested that firms should disclose the following information: (i) management's attitude toward financial risks; (ii) how instruments are used; (iii) how risk is monitored and controlled; (iv) accounting policies; (v) analysis of credit risk; and (vi) the extent of dealers' activities in financial instruments.

The Group of Thirty further recommended that dealers should regularly perform simulations to determine the market risk of their portfolio. It is important for the market participants to have a risk management unit, which is independent of the trading units, to monitor transactions, develop risk limits, identify various risk components, and review the pricing models and valuation systems used by the traders.[21]

In its study of the OTC derivatives markets, the Group of Thirty proposed that regulators should recognize netting arrangements to the extent that they are legally enforceable. The Group also recommended that dealers and end-users should be encouraged to use a common master agreement with all counterparties to document existing and future derivatives transactions, including foreign exchange forwards and options.

---

[20]Global Derivatives Study Group (1993).

[21]The importance of managerial oversight of risk management operations is exemplified by the recent losses incurred by Codelco and Metallgesellschaft discussed in Box 1.

Annex III

Developments in International Financial Markets

This annex discusses recent developments in international financial markets, beginning with the markets for fixed-income securities. The first section chronicles the decline in yields in 1993 and the remarkable growth in the market. The second section discusses developments in the international equity market, where activity reached record nominal levels. The third section discusses international banking activity in 1993, including the market for syndicated loans. The annex concludes with an update of developments in the banking sectors of some of the Nordic countries and of Japan.

International Bond Market Developments in 1993

A continued decline in long-term interest rates, exchange rate turmoil in Europe, and increased demand for official financing contributed to a record increase in bond issues in 1993. Yields on ten-year government bonds issued by the major industrial countries ended the year lower than their opening levels (Chart 5), as monetary authorities in each of these countries attempted to reverse a general slowdown in growth through declines in policy interest rates. In the United States, the federal funds rate did not decline further in 1993 but remained at a low level of 3.0 percent. Yields on U.S. bonds declined by 102 basis points from December 1992 to December 1993, while those on French Government bonds fell by 245 basis points and Italian yields fell by 504 basis points. These interest rate declines were reflected in the international bond markets. Yields on deutsche mark Eurobonds fell by 140 basis points from the end of 1992 to the end of 1993, while yields on dollar Eurobonds fell by 110 basis points (Table 11).

Overall, gross bond issues increased for the third consecutive year in 1993, reaching a record $481 billion, an increase of 44 percent over the previous record in 1992 (Table 11). Since redemptions and early repayments increased by only 27 percent over the 1992 level, net issues of bonds increased by 78 percent to $198 billion. Among total bond issues, straight (fixed rate) bonds accounted for a record $369 billion, a 77 percent share, compared with $265 billion in 1992, as borrowers took advantage

Chart 5. Long-Term Government Bond Yield for Seven Major Industrial Countries, January 1990–March 1994[1]
(In percent)

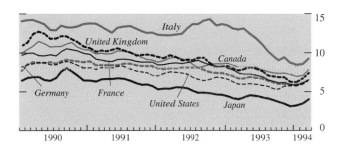

Source: International Monetary Fund, *World Economic Outlook*.
[1]United States: 10-year treasury bond. Japan: Before January 6, 1992, refers to over-the-counter 10-year government bonds with longest residual maturity; thereafter, refers to benchmark 10-year government bond. Germany: Government bonds with maturities of 9–10 years. France: Long-term (7–10 year) government bond (Emprunts d'Etat à long terme). Italy: Before June 1991, refers to government bonds with 2–4 years' residual maturities; thereafter, refers to 10-year government bonds. United Kingdom: Medium-dated (10 year) government stock. Canada: Government bonds with residual maturities of over 10 years.

of the low interest rates (Table 12). A sharp decline in amortization resulted in an increase of more than 200 percent in net issues of such bonds.

The *floating rate note (FRN)* sector saw even more impressive growth in 1993, with gross issues rising 60 percent to $70 billion and net issues increasing by approximately 270 percent. Particularly during the latter part of the year, the anticipation of an increase in official interest rates in the United States provided an incentive for lenders to avoid committing to fixed rates. The FRN sector also saw an increased use of structured issues such as "collars"—in which the lender is assured of receiving a minimum interest rate while the borrower is protected by a ceiling on the rate it would pay in the event of large increases in the reference rate. Other variants on the structured-note theme included "corridors" or "range floaters" and SURFs (step-up recovery floaters), in which the coupon is linked to the Constant Maturity Treasuries index rather than the shorter-term LIBOR.

Table 11. Developments in International Bond Markets

	1986	1987	1988	1989	1990	1991	1992	1993
	(In billions of U.S. dollars)							
Total gross international bonds	227.1	180.8	227.1	255.8	229.9	308.7	333.7	481.0
Amortization	64.0	76.0	82.9	89.2	107.9	149.3	222.5	283.0
Net issues[1]	163.1	104.8	144.2	166.6	122.0	159.4	111.2	198.0
By residence of borrower								
Industrial countries	201.2	156.3	198.3	224.4	190.2	255.9	265.0	368.5
Developing countries[2]	3.9	3.2	5.2	3.6	4.9	10.2	17.5	43.3
Offshore centers[3]	0.6	0.2	0.3	0.2	0.2	0.1	—	6.2
Countries in transition	0.3	0.6	1.4	2.2	1.7	1.5	1.3	5.8
Other, including international organizations	21.1	20.6	22.0	25.3	32.9	40.9	49.9	57.3
By category of borrower								
Governments	40.8	23.8	24.7	20.2	24.5	44.4	63.6	104.3
Public enterprises	23.9	21.3	32.1	32.1	41.0	48.3	52.8	65.1
Banks	65.3	38.8	61.8	62.1	56.0	55.9	67.3	110.1
Private corporations	79.3	78.0	88.8	119.8	79.0	123.7	108.7	153.6
International organizations	18.8	18.8	19.7	21.6	29.4	36.4	41.3	47.9
By currency of denomination	*(In percent)*							
U.S. dollar	55.0	36.2	37.2	49.6	34.8	31.1	37.9	38.1
Japanese yen	10.4	14.7	10.0	9.3	13.4	13.4	12.3	12.4
Deutsche mark	7.5	8.3	10.4	6.4	8.0	6.6	10.1	11.4
Swiss franc	10.2	13.4	11.6	7.3	10.1	6.5	5.4	5.6
Pounds sterling	4.8	8.3	10.5	7.7	9.2	8.4	7.0	8.9
ECU[4]	3.1	4.1	4.9	4.9	7.8	10.6	6.4	1.5
Other	8.9	14.9	15.3	14.8	16.9	23.4	20.9	22.2
Interest rates	*(In percent a year)*							
Eurodollar deposits[5]	6.3	7.9	9.4	8.4	7.8	4.5	3.6	3.3
Dollar Eurobonds[6]	8.6	10.2	9.7	8.7	9.1	7.9	7.3	6.2
Deutsche mark international bonds[6]	6.6	6.5	6.2	7.9	9.6	8.6	7.8	6.4
Memorandum items	*(In billions of U.S. dollars)*							
Net issues of medium-term notes or Euronotes	. . .	23.3	19.5	6.9	32.0	32.5	37.5	72.7
Bonds purchased or issued by banks	76.0	53.0	67.0	78.1	80.1	40.4	74.7	121.5

Sources: Bank for International Settlements, *International Banking and Financial Market Developments*; Organization for Economic Cooperation and Development, *Financial Market Trends* and *Financial Statistics Monthly*; and IMF staff estimates.

[1]Gross issues less scheduled repayments and early redemption.
[2]All developing countries except the seven offshore centers (listed in footnote 3).
[3]The Bahamas, Bahrain, the Cayman Islands, Hong Kong, the Netherlands Antilles, Panama, and Singapore.
[4]European currency unit.
[5]Three-month deposits, at end of period.
[6]Bonds with remaining maturity of 7–15 years, at end of period.

SURFs provide higher returns to investors as long as the yield curve is upward-sloping and getting steeper. As interest rate uncertainty increased, FRN issues grew in popularity at the expense of straight bonds. This development was particularly pronounced in the first quarter of 1994 as straight bond issues reportedly declined by 30 percent while FRN issues expanded by 130 percent.

The search for higher yields contributed to a modest recovery in the *equity-related bond* market. Such bonds were popular with Japanese borrowers in the mid- to late-1980s, but the decline in the Japanese stock market in 1990 and the ensuing recession in Japan resulted in a decline in activity in that segment of the bond market. The increase in equity returns in some of the industrial countries in 1993 provided an opportunity for this vehicle to expand (Chart 6). Gross issues of convertible bonds and bonds with warrants increased by 85 percent to $39 billion in 1993. However, a bunching of redemptions resulted in a net decline of $58 billion in outstanding issues.

With long-term interest rates falling sharply and yield curves in the United States and the United Kingdom flattening out during the second half of the year (Chart 7), borrowers sought to lock in the low interest rates for a longer period of time. Indeed, one of the notable achievements of the bond markets in 1993 was a *lengthening of maturities*. While, previously, Eurobond issues of longer than 10 years had been relatively uncommon, bonds with maturities as long as 30 years were very successfully issued in 1993. This development was most pronounced in the U.S. domestic market,

Table 12. Sources of International Capital Markets Financing

	1987	1988	1989	1990	1991	1992	1993
	(Gross issues in billions of U.S. dollars)						
Syndicated loans	91.7	125.5	121.1	124.5	116.0	117.9	130.1
Euronotes	102.2	93.2	81.6	73.2	87.9	134.6	158.7
Of which:							
Euro-commercial paper	55.8	57.1	54.1	48.3	35.9	28.9	36.6
Euro-medium-term notes	8.0	12.6	15.5	16.0	43.2	97.9	113.5
Bonds	180.8	227.1	255.7	229.9	308.7	333.7	481.0
Straight bonds	121.3	160.2	154.6	158.9	242.7	265.4	369.1
Floating rate bonds	13.0	22.3	17.8	37.1	18.3	43.6	69.8
Convertible bonds	18.2	11.3	14.1	10.6	10.1	5.2	18.1
Bonds with warrants attached	24.8	29.7	66.2	21.2	31.6	15.7	20.6
Other bonds	3.5	3.6	3.0	2.1	6.0	3.8	3.4
International equity offerings	20.2	9.0	16.9	14.0	23.8	25.3	36.6
Of which:							
Depository receipts (ADRs/GDRs/Rule 144A)	4.6	1.3	2.6	1.7	4.6	5.3	9.5
Total	394.9	454.8	475.3	441.6	536.4	611.5	806.4
Memorandum items							
Global bonds	—	—	1.5	9.6	15.4	25.1	34.4
Cross-border equity trading[1]							
Gross equity flows	1,377.8	1,166.7	1,562.6	1,390.9	1,322.5	1,400.0	2,000.0
Cross-exchange trading	508.6	342.6	582.9	873.9	779.1	980.0	1,600.0
Net equity flows	16.4	32.9	86.6	3.2	100.6	53.2	159.2
Cross-border mergers and acquisitions	70.8	109.6	117.5	128.4	81.1	80.9	...
	(In percent of total)						
Syndicated loans	23.22	27.60	25.48	28.19	21.63	19.28	16.13
Euronotes	25.88	20.49	17.17	16.58	16.39	22.01	19.68
Of which:							
Euro-commercial paper	14.13	12.56	11.38	10.94	6.69	4.73	4.54
Euro-medium-term notes	2.03	2.77	3.26	3.62	8.05	16.01	14.07
Bonds	45.79	49.94	53.80	52.06	57.55	54.57	59.65
Straight bonds	30.72	35.23	32.53	35.98	45.25	43.40	45.77
Floating rate bonds	3.29	4.90	3.75	8.40	3.41	7.13	8.66
Convertible bonds	4.61	2.48	2.97	2.40	1.88	0.85	2.24
Bonds with warrants attached	6.28	6.53	13.93	4.80	5.89	2.57	2.55
Other bonds	0.89	0.79	0.63	0.48	1.12	0.62	0.42
International equity offerings	5.11	1.98	3.56	3.17	4.44	4.14	4.54
Of which:							
Depository receipts (ADRs/GDRs/Rule 144A)	1.16	0.28	0.55	0.39	0.86	0.86	1.18
Total	100.00	100.00	100.00	100.00	100.00	100.00	100.00

Sources: Bank of New York; Baring Securities; and Organization for Economic Cooperation and Development, *Financial Market Trends*, various issues.

[1]Data for 1993 are estimates.

which saw three issues of 100-year bonds. Long-term bonds benefited from strong demand from prudential institutions, which were keen to improve the maturity match between their assets and liabilities. Even narrow spreads above government securities were sufficient to attract this type of investor.

The turmoil in European currency markets in September 1992 gave rise to a significant increase in sovereign borrowing on the international market as the countries that had defended their currencies attempted to replenish their foreign exchange reserves. To this source of demand was added a cyclical demand arising from weakening fiscal positions. Sovereign borrowers raised $104 billion in international bonds in 1993, up from $64 billion in 1992, and increased their share of gross bond issues to 22 percent from 19 percent (Table 11). Banks also increased their share of total issues by raising $110 billion in the bond markets in 1993, compared with $67 billion in 1992.

Another broad characteristic of the market in 1993 was the ease with which very large issues were marketed. Liquidity concerns have plagued the international bond market since its early days, and in 1993 some issuers took action to try to improve the liquidity of their bonds—and thereby capture the liquidity premium investors appear willing to pay—by issuing larger bonds and by offering

Chart 6. Major Industrial Countries: Changes in Stock Market Indices, January 1990–May 1994

(Twelve-month changes, in percent)

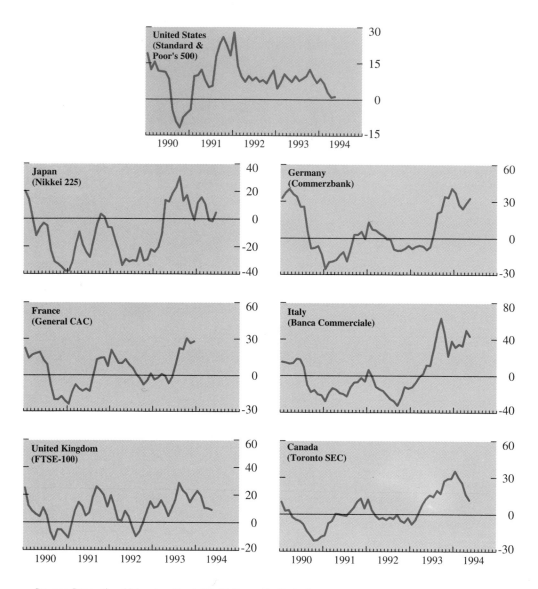

Source: International Monetary Fund, *World Economic Outlook.*

to provide a secondary market. Much as governments have discovered that they can lower their borrowing costs in domestic markets by providing large benchmark issues rather than issuing a larger number of smaller-sized bonds with different characteristics, issuers in the international bond market have increasingly turned to "jumbo" bonds. Whereas only a couple of years ago most bonds were in the $50–100 million range, in 1993 bonds exceeding $1 billion were common in the international market, and there were some very large individual issues. For example, the World Bank issued

a DM 3 billion global bond and Italy issued $5.5 billion in 10- and 30-year global bonds together. The World Bank deutsche mark global bond can be traded on both the German and U.S. markets despite their very different clearing systems. Some issuers deliberately created new benchmarks out of existing outstanding stocks—Italy, for example, offered to exchange all its outstanding straight bonds for new FRNs with a common maturity— while others attempted to provide a secondary market. The World Bank, for example, has required the seven underwriters of its $5 billion European

Chart 7. Major Industrial Countries: Yield Differentials, January 1990–April 1994[1]
(In percent)

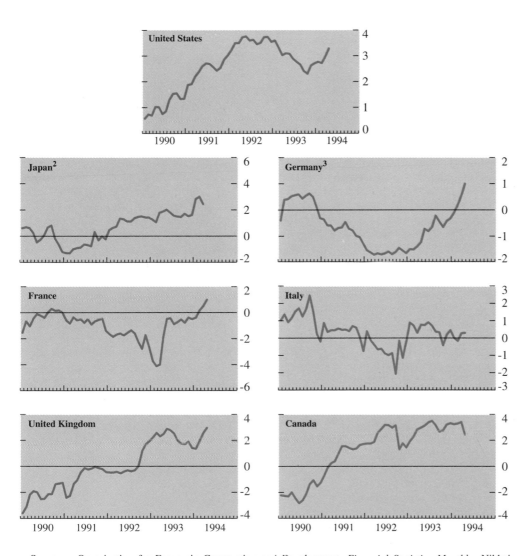

Sources: Organization for Economic Cooperation and Development, *Financial Statistics Monthly;* Nikkei Telecom; and IMF staff estimates.

[1]Government bond yield minus three-month treasury bill rate, except for Germany and Japan.

[2]Government bond yield minus three-month Gensaki rate.

[3]Government bond yield minus three-month FIBOR rate.

medium-term notes (EMTNs) to post public bid prices.

Turnover on the secondary market increased significantly in 1993, exceeding the rate of increase in net bonds outstanding. Eurobond trading through Euroclear and Cedel increased by 11 percent to $4,426 billion in 1993, while the net outstanding stock of bonds increased by 9 percent to $1,850 billion.

Another important development in 1993 was the globalization of the bond market both in terms of investor base and currency of denomination. The market for global bonds—bonds registered with the SEC and marketed and traded in North America, Europe, and Asia—grew markedly in 1993, with new issues raising $34 billion—including the first sovereign FRN global bond—compared with approximately $25 billion raised in 1992 and $15 billion in 1991.[1] Formerly the preserve of industrial country governments and agencies and supranational borrowers, the global bond market opened up

[1]For further discussion on global bonds, see Annex I.

to private issuers and to issuers from developing countries—including Argentina and China—in 1993. The attraction for this vehicle has continued in 1994, with over $10 billion in new issues in the first two months alone. Somewhat paradoxically perhaps, 1993 also witnessed the coming of age of regional bond markets in which borrowers seek to tap a local rather than global market. The Dragon bond market in particular saw an increase in activity with issues totaling $3.2 billion.

With the emphasis on long-term issues both from issuers and investors, the shorter end of the market registered less impressive growth in 1993, with gross Euronote issues increasing by 18 percent to $159 billion.[2] The most dynamic segment of this market continued to be the EMTN facilities, gross issues of which increased to a record $113 billion. Since 1991, the EMTN sector has rapidly overtaken the Euro-commercial paper (ECP) market. Since EMTNs are generally relatively short-term, small issues, they provide an attractive point of entry into the international bond market for new borrowers. The key to the success of the EMTN market is its highly flexible structure provided by the ability to register facilities without having to specify exactly how the issues will be structured. Thus, once the program is registered, it can be accessed very quickly in a wide range of currencies and maturities and with a seemingly unlimited range of credit enhancements. This flexibility has given rise to substantial "reverse enquiry" issues in which investors will communicate their preferences for maturity, currency of denomination, and embedded derivatives to issuers through their program managers. Thus, notes can be designed to fit precisely the requirements of particular investors and then placed directly with them. In 1993 between 50 percent and 60 percent of EMTN issues are believed to have included some kind of structure allowing investors to take positions in other markets. The use of structured issues—which link the return on the bond to prices of other assets such as equity or commodities—is used to provide more attractive returns to investors seeking to combine some minimum yield with a play on a particular market. At the same time, the increased use of underwriting methods to distribute EMTNs with sizes and maturities similar to those of Eurobonds means that the expansion of the EMTN market is increasingly at the expense of both the commercial paper and the bond markets.

As in previous years, the U.S. dollar was the most frequent currency of denomination for bonds in 1993. However, with the expansion of currency swap markets, the importance of this statistic is less

clear, since many dollar issues are swapped into other currencies. With the virtual collapse of the ECU bond market in the last quarter of 1992 following the first ERM crisis, issues of bonds denominated in ECU declined from 6.4 percent of total gross issues in 1992 to only 1.5 percent in 1993. The share of issues in deutsche mark increased as European governments restored their foreign exchange reserves and German regional governments increased their use of international bond markets. The share of bonds issued in pounds sterling also rose as U.K. interest rates fell after sterling's suspension from the ERM. The main development in terms of currency distribution of new issues, however, was the increased use of currencies other than the dollar, the yen, the deutsche mark, and the pound sterling. The expansion of issues into a broader range of currencies was facilitated by deregulation in a number of markets. For example, the French Government approved the use of the franc in the EMTN market; the Italian Government eliminated the stamp tax on government bond trading on regulated exchanges and introduced a more efficient system of withholding tax reimbursements for investors from countries with double taxation agreements with Italy; and Portugal abolished withholding taxes on foreign investors in government bonds. The most significant liberalization, however, was implemented in Japan, where financial deregulation has proceeded rapidly in recent years. The Japanese Government eliminated the 90-day "lockup" on Euro-yen bonds issued by governments and international institutions and reduced the credit rating requirements for corporate issuers in the domestic and foreign markets.

International Equity Market Developments

Reflecting the greater recourse to securities markets as an alternative to bank financing—and benefiting from price rises on most exchanges—cross-border equity issues increased by 45 percent in 1993 to $37 billion (Table 12). Of this total, the United States alone accounted for approximately $10 billion in 1993, while the developing countries issued $11 billion in new equity, up from about $7 billion in 1992. An increasingly important segment of the international equity market is the market for depository receipts. Total net issues of these instruments by all countries reached $9.5 billion in 1993, an increase of 81 percent over $5.3 billion in 1992 (Table 12).

Privatization has played an important role in expanding the international primary market for equity. In 1993, an estimated $8.9 billion in privatized equity was sold to foreign investors. The central governments of OECD countries alone have

---

[2]The Euronote category comprises Euro-commercial paper and EMTN in addition to note-issuance facilities and other short- and medium-term borrowing facilities.

Table 13. Net Cross-Border Equity Flows[1]

(In billions of U.S. dollars)

	1986	1987	1988	1989	1990	1991	1992	1993
Investor from								
North America	3.68	−2.18	4.03	21.04	12.03	48.25	46.39	70.90
United States	2.61	−2.68	1.95	19.00	10.26	43.31	41.99	66.40
Canada	1.07	0.50	2.08	2.04	1.77	4.94	4.40	4.50
Japan	8.15	16.87	2.99	17.89	6.26	3.63	−2.73	15.30
Europe	21.32	9.42	14.29	38.40	4.58	39.55	7.56	45.20
Of which:								
United Kingdom	8.85	3.77	9.66	24.16	−0.88	25.84	−2.96	24.20
Emerging markets	1.48	−5.73	1.47	0.79	−5.47	6.58	2.57	21.50
Pacific rim	0.79	−5.39	1.31	−0.61	−5.79	5.49	−3.78	12.50
Latin America	0.47	−0.42	0.09	1.49	0.30	0.53	6.33	7.50
Other[2]	0.22	0.08	0.07	−0.09	0.02	0.56	0.02	1.50
Rest of world	7.35	−1.95	10.07	8.48	−14.22	2.62	−0.62	6.30
Australia	0.60	0.92	1.44	2.08	−1.31	2.71	−0.59	1.50
Other	6.75	−2.87	8.63	6.40	−12.91	−0.09	−0.03	4.80
Equity from								
North America	19.82	20.26	−3.69	13.80	−15.89	9.60	−3.95	28.60
United States	19.11	16.47	−1.39	11.42	−14.61	11.02	−4.20	21.10
Canada	0.71	3.79	−2.30	2.38	−1.28	−1.42	0.25	7.50
Japan	−15.76	−42.84	6.81	7.00	−13.28	46.83	8.96	20.00
Europe	33.38	29.67	22.75	47.11	15.29	23.35	24.83	56.10
Of which:								
United Kingdom	7.83	19.50	9.72	11.24	5.35	5.84	10.08	19.60
Emerging markets	3.34	5.88	3.47	10.07	13.16	15.78	22.45	52.00
Pacific rim	3.43	6.03	2.45	3.36	3.89	4.73	10.95	30.00
Latin America	0.20	0.43	0.72	6.98	9.89	11.15	9.64	20.00
Other[2]	−0.29	−0.58	0.30	−0.27	−0.62	−0.10	1.86	2.00
Rest of world	1.20	3.46	3.51	8.63	3.90	5.06	0.87	2.50
Australia	0.76	2.16	3.76	0.96	1.48	1.86	0.15	2.00
Other	0.44	1.30	−0.25	7.67	2.42	3.20	0.72	0.50
Total	41.98	16.43	32.85	86.60	3.18	100.63	53.17	159.20

Sources: Baring Securities; and Howell and others (1993).

[1]Data for 1993 are estimates.

[2]Africa, Middle East, and Eastern Europe.

announced approximately $196 billion in privatizations to be completed by the end of the century.

More important perhaps than the expansion in the international primary market, the significant price increases on stock exchanges worldwide—particularly those of the emerging market economies—increased the attractiveness of international portfolio investment.[3] For a U.S.-based investor, for example, investment in foreign markets proved highly lucrative in 1993. All of the emerging stock markets tracked by the International Finance Corporation (IFC), except for China, Nigeria, and Venezuela, outperformed the Standard and Poor's (S&P) 500 index in dollar terms. In addition, many of the European markets performed relatively well; however, the highest returns were found in the emerging markets. As discussed in Annex IV, the proliferation of country funds has greatly facilitated access by retail investors in industrial countries to foreign markets, especially the emerging markets.

[3]For further discussion on emerging markets, see Annex IV.

In the United States in particular, the search for higher returns on savings than have been offered by banks led individuals increasingly to invest in mutual funds and, among them, country funds.

Net international equity trading reached an estimated $159 billion in 1993, up sharply from $53 billion in 1992, and by far the highest volume of cross-border trading estimated since 1986 (Table 13). U.S. investors once again provided most of the demand, investing an unprecedented $66 billion in foreign equity while benefiting from inward investment of only $21 billion. Although European investors showed the largest annual increase in investment outflows, from $7.6 billion in 1992 to $45.2 billion in 1993, the European markets again benefited the most from international portfolio flows, with sales to foreign investors rising from $25 billion in 1992 to $56 billion in 1993.

It was, however, the scale of investment in the emerging markets that attracted the most attention in 1993. Sales of equity to nonresidents more than doubled in 1993 to $52 billion. The increase was greatest among the Asian markets, which recorded net equity sales of $30 billion, up from $11 billion in 1992. Latin American markets also more than doubled their sales of equity to foreign investors. Emerging market investors ventured abroad on a greater scale in 1993 than they had previously. Investors in these markets spent $21 billion on equities listed on the exchanges of the more developed markets.

International Banking Activity

Banks' cross-border activities continued to expand slowly in 1993—as they did in 1992—after having contracted sharply in 1991.[4] The aggregate figures, however, conceal markedly different experiences between different types of counterparties in 1993. Lending to nonbank borrowers increased by the second largest margin since 1982, while interbank lending rose by the smallest amount in any year other than 1991 (when the interbank market contracted sharply). A feature common to both market segments since 1990 is the slowdown in deposit growth relative to the experience of the mid- to late-1980s. This difference between lending to banks and nonbanks was observed for industrial countries, but not for developing countries, where lending to nonbanks rose by a much smaller amount than in 1992. Reporting banks continued to reduce their net exposure to all counterparties in the countries in transition.

Aggregate cross-border bank lending increased by $257 billion in 1993, down slightly from an increase of $262 billion in 1992 and well below the increases achieved in the years since 1985 (Table 14). Lending to industrial country counterparties increased by $190 billion, more than in 1992 but still considerably lower than the increases observed in the late 1980s, while claims on developing country borrowers increased by $38 billion, which was $7 billion less than in 1992. With cross-border liabilities increasing by $195 billion in 1993, net claims actually increased by $63 billion, compared with an increase of $95 billion a year earlier.

While the overall figures suggest a declining importance for international bank lending, in fact lending to nonbank borrowers has been fairly robust during the 1990s. Net international claims on nonbanks rose by $147 billion in 1993, almost twice the increase in 1992 and the largest increase since data

became available in 1983 (Table A8). This expansion in net claims was due both to a rapid rise in gross claims and a slowdown in liabilities. Total lending rose by $191 billion, more than in any year since 1982 except 1990. The increase in lending was most visible in the U.S., German, and U.K. banks. Cross-border lending by Japanese banks, on the other hand, fell in the second half of the year as these institutions continued their retrenchment from international lending in response to domestic balance sheet difficulties.

On the other side of the balance sheet, nonbanks' cross-border deposits grew by only $43 billion in 1993, compared with an increase of $65 billion in 1992. Liabilities of nonbanks in Japan and the United States, in particular, declined for the third consecutive year. Banks in France also saw a decline in cross-border nonbank liabilities. The decline in cross-border deposits by nonbanks parallels the recent trend toward weaker deposit bases for banks in their domestic markets. In the United States, for example, there has been a tendency for nonbanks, including households, to look for higher returns on their savings in nonbank financial institutions such as mutual funds (see Box 2). Part of the explanation for the coexistence of a slowdown in deposits and an expansion in credit lies in the significant increase in banks' purchases of international corporate bonds. Hence, banks are increasingly extending credit not through loans but through the securities markets.[5]

In sharp contrast to the experience of the nonbank sector, gross interbank claims rose by a modest $67 billion in 1993. Industrial countries accounted for most of the slowdown, with cross-border lending growing by only $31 billion, less than one tenth of the increases observed during 1986–90 (Table A9). Lending to developing country banks actually picked up slightly, increasing by $34 billion compared with $22 billion in 1992. A sharp rise in interbank liabilities—particularly to industrial countries—resulted in a strong contraction in net cross-border interbank claims of $85 billion in 1993 after a $20 billion increase in 1992. This reversal was due mostly to a decline of $73 billion in net lending to industrial country banks, although net claims on developing country banks fell by $10 billion, continuing the series of annual decreases dating back to 1987.

Developments in the interbank market in 1993 reflected a number of influences. The large buildup of cross-border interbank claims within Europe during the attack on the European ERM in September 1992—which saw intra-European interbank claims rise by $146 billion—was partially reversed during the subsequent three quarters. The unwinding of

---

[4]The following centers report activity for the international banking statistics: Australia, Austria, The Bahamas, Bahrain, Belgium, Canada, the Cayman Islands, Chile, Denmark, Finland, France, Germany, Hong Kong, Ireland, Italy, Japan, Korea, Luxembourg, the Netherlands, the Netherlands Antilles, Norway, Panama, Portugal, Saudi Arabia, Singapore, Spain, Sweden, Switzerland, the United Arab Emirates, the United Kingdom, and the United States.

[5]See Bank for International Settlements (1994).

Table 14. Changes in Banks' Cross-Border Claims and Liabilities[1]

(In billions of U.S. dollars)

	1986	1987	1988	1989	1990	1991	1992	1993
Total changes in claims on[2]	531	799	565	833	732	−70	262	257
Industrial countries	405	543	483	563	563	−67	171	190
Of which:								
United States	93	106	108	93	73	−7	74	83
Japan	154	223	203	172	101	−89	−108	−18
Developing countries[3]	2	22	−4	13	3	34	45	38
Offshore centers[4]	86	164	85	181	135	−5	26	5
Countries in transition	4	1	5	7	−5	3	4	−4
Of which:								
Former U.S.S.R.	4	1	5	8	−6	4	6	−2
Other transactors	−11	17	2	26	−17	−12	38	3
Unidentified nonbank borrowers[5]	44	52	−6	44	53	−22	−20	25
Total changes in liabilities to[6]	588	764	518	823	668	−100	168	195
Industrial countries	423	494	371	574	490	−122	87	138
Of which:								
United States	82	57	84	67	24	−4	−42	−56
Japan	114	146	148	138	55	−47	−71	−42
Developing countries[3]	−5	47	33	69	80	20	26	31
Offshore centers[4]	130	144	100	148	51	−29	−14	—
Countries in transition	−1	−1	4	4	−5	1	11	5
Of which:								
Former U.S.S.R.	1	−2	2	−1	−7	—	6	2
Other transactors	−7	19	4	13	−13	−6	32	2
Unidentified nonbank depositors[5]	47	61	6	14	64	35	25	19
Total changes in net claims on[7]	−57	35	47	11	64	31	95	63
Industrial countries	−18	49	113	−12	73	55	84	52
Of which:								
United States	12	49	24	26	48	−3	115	139
Japan	40	77	55	34	46	−42	−37	24
Developing countries[3]	7	−25	−37	−57	−77	14	18	8
Offshore centers[4]	−44	20	−16	33	84	24	40	4
Countries in transition	5	2	1	3	−1	2	−7	−9
Of which:								
Former U.S.S.R.	3	2	4	8	1	4	—	−4
Other transactors	−3	−3	−2	13	−5	−6	6	1
Inidentified nonbank borrowers[5]	−2	−9	−12	31	−10	−58	−45	6

Sources: Bank for International Settlements, data reported to the IMF on currency distribution of banks' external accounts; International Monetary Fund, *International Financial Statistics*; and IMF staff estimates.

[1]Data on changes in claims and liabilities are derived from stock data on the reporting countries' assets and liabilities and are net of changes due to exchange rate movements.

[2]As measured by changes in the outstanding liabilities of borrowing countries defined as cross-border interbank accounts by residence of borrowing bank plus international bank credit to nonbanks by residence of borrower.

[3]Excluding offshore centers. Data include some accumulation of interest arrears and reduction in bank claims resulting from debt conversions, sales, and write-offs.

[4]The Bahamas, Bahrain, the Cayman Islands, Hong Kong, the Netherlands Antilles, Panama, and Singapore.

[5]The difference between the amount that countries report as their banks' positions with nonresident nonbanks in their monetary statistics and the amount that all banks in major financial centers report as their positions with nonbanks in each country.

[6]As measured by changes in the outstanding assets of depositing countries, defined as cross-border interbank accounts by residence of lending bank, plus cross-border bank deposits of nonbanks by residence of depositor.

[7]Change in claims minus change in liabilities.

such positions in the first quarter also resulted in a large fall in net claims of U.S. banks. However, renewed tensions in the foreign exchange market led to a further accumulation of cross-border claims within Europe in the third quarter of 1993. Interbank activity within Europe was also buoyed by an increase in securities transactions and large currency transfers in the fourth quarter. For example, German banks' net claims on other, mostly

European, banks increased strongly in the fourth quarter, as a result of the decision to apply withholding tax to interest earned on foreign mutual funds. German residents responded by liquidating investments in offshore funds. The Japanese banking industry continued its retrenchment from the international interbank market, with the third consecutive year-on-year decline in total claims. Finally, the favorable borrowing conditions avail-

Box 4. New Episodes of Stress in Banking Systems

A banking crisis emerged in Venezuela in early 1994. The liberalization of interest rates in 1989 led to intense competition among banks for market share in deposits. In the anticipation of further reforms that would introduce universal banking and open up the sector to foreign competition, many banks attempted to increase their share of the deposit and loan markets. The most aggressive competitor was *Banco Latino*, which had become the second-largest bank in Venezuela by the end of 1993. By offering higher interest rates than the other banks, Banco Latino nearly doubled its deposits in 1991 alone. This strategy contributed to operating losses in 1992, since it resulted in narrower interest margins. On the other side of the balance sheet, the rapid expansion of lending—including to other members of the same financial group and to bank insiders—led to increasing loan losses. By the end of 1992, 7 percent of the bank's loans were nonperforming, a much higher ratio than for other banks. Liquidity problems emerged in December 1993, which led to a run on deposits. On January 13, 1994, the central bank announced that Banco Latino had a deficit of Bs 26.5 billion in the check-clearing system. The bank was placed under receivership by the Superintendent of Banks and Other Financial Institutions.

Problems at eight smaller Venezuelan banks developed in the ensuing weeks as a result of a flight to quality by depositors. The deposit guarantee agency, FOGADE, responded by providing Bs 446 billion in low-interest loans in exchange for at least 51 percent of the capital of these banks. This amount is in addition to the Bs 313 billion lent to Banco Latino prior to its reopening on April 4, 1994.[1] The Bs 759 billion ($6.4 billion) total represents approximately 14 percent of Venezuela's 1993 GDP. To try to limit the political, monetary, and fiscal impacts of this rescue operation, the Government has increased deposit insurance coverage to Bs 4 million (effectively covering almost all of Banco Latino's deposits), issued zero-coupon bonds to soak up the extra liquidity, and imposed a 0.75 percent tax on bank withdrawals. The authorities have proposed that the eight banks, which are now effectively state owned, will be liquidated or merged with stronger banks.

Serious problems also surfaced at two of the largest banks in Europe. On December 28, 1993, the Bank of Spain announced that it was intervening to support *Banco Español de Credito* (Banesto), the fourth largest bank in Spain. After two years of very rapid expansion, the bank's problem loans grew too large to be covered by investment income; at the end of 1993, approximately 20 percent of the bank's loans were nonperforming. This news came only six months after the bank had successfully raised in June 1993 Ptas 95 billion in capital, at which time nonperforming loans were an estimated 9 percent of total loans. The interim management of Banesto, installed in December 1993, estimated that provisions and write-offs totaling Ptas 605 billion (approximately $4.3 billion) were needed. Under an agreement with the Bank of Spain, Banesto assumed Ptas 320 billion of the loss, wiping out its reserves and almost half its share capital. The Bank of Spain and the other commercial banks shared equally in Ptas 285 billion in losses. In addition, Ptas 600 billion in problem loans with an estimated market value of Ptas 315 billion was transferred to the Deposit Guarantee Fund. On April 25, 1994, Banesto was sold at auction to Banco Santander for Ptas 313 billion, making the latter the largest Spanish bank with total assets of Ptas 17.1 trillion.

Difficulties at *Crédit Lyonnais*, the largest banking group in Europe, became more widely known in February 1994, although the replacement of its executive chairman in November 1993 had signaled that the bank was in trouble. Here again, the problem appears to have stemmed from a rapid expansion of lending in the late 1980s and early 1990s, a downturn in the economy, and a decline in prices for commercial property used as collateral for loans. In early 1994, the bank reported a loss of F 6.9 billion for 1993 and a significant shortfall in capital was recognized. In March 1994, an agreement was reached that called for a capital injection of F 4.9 billion ($850 million) from the French Government and two state-owned companies, the transfer of F 40 billion in doubtful real estate loans—partially guaranteed by the Government—to the Treasury, and asset sales of over F 35 billion over two years. Once again, problems appear to have come to a head relatively quickly. At the end of June 1993, problem loans were reported to be only F 24 billion.

---

[1]Banco Latino also benefited from Bs 48 billion in loans from other banks to resolve its liquidity problems in January 1994.

---

able on international securities markets caused banks to rely less on the interbank market. Bond issues by banks reached record levels in 1993, increasing by 64 percent to $110 billion (Table 11).

Reflecting the weakening of overall international bank lending, the syndicated loan market continued a trend of declining net issues that began in 1991. Although the total value of syndicated loans signed in 1993 rose by 10 percent to $130 billion, an increase in redemptions resulted in a 20 percent decline in net new lending to $70 billion. This development is attributable to the reduction in long-term bond rates, which made such issues more attractive and increased concern for credit quality among lending banks. New lending in the first quarter of 1994 reportedly declined by 25 percent over the same period in 1993, owing in part to increased uncertainty over interest rates.

Banking Developments in Three Nordic Countries and in Japan

As discussed in last year's report, *International Capital Markets: Part II*, rapid financial liberalization in some industrial countries had led banks in the 1980s to enter into new activities, as well as to increase their exposure to real estate. A decline in asset prices at the end of the decade and in the early 1990s reduced both borrowers' ability to repay loans and the value of loan collateral, resulting in significant losses on bank balance sheets. This section provides a brief update on efforts undertaken since the first quarter of 1993 to resolve these difficulties in the banking sectors in three Nordic countries and in Japan. This year, Venezuelan banks have encountered severe difficulties, while some individual large banks in France and Spain have also registered large losses (Box 4 discusses these events).

Developments in Nordic Banking

In three Nordic countries—Finland, Norway, and Sweden—a rapid increase in credit and the expansion of bank activities into riskier, less familiar markets—such as real estate lending—was accompanied by the liberalization of the financial sectors in the early to mid-1980s.[6] There, as in Japan, a

decline in real estate prices, combined with other country-specific factors, triggered the emergence of substantial stocks of nonperforming loans. In these three countries, the Governments declared their willingness to provide the necessary support for the banking system. In Finland and Sweden, unlike in Norway and Japan, the Governments responded with explicit guarantees of the banks' liabilities and, in many cases, with equity injections, which have resulted in governments becoming majority shareholders in a number of institutions.

The crises that afflicted the banking industries in Finland, Norway, and Sweden appeared to have eased significantly in 1993, as declining interest rates and exchange rate depreciation contributed to increased profits, which allowed many banks to raise capital on domestic and international markets.[7] These crises have been costly. The Governments of Finland, Norway, and Sweden have together committed about $20 billion in capital injections and guarantees in support of their banks since the onset of the crisis.[8] The individual country amounts represent 8.2 percent of 1992 GDP in Finland, 4.0 percent in Norway, and 6.4 percent in Sweden; in each case, the commitments have exceeded the value of equity in the banking system when the crisis emerged.

In late 1992 and into early 1993, interest rates in these three Nordic countries fell sharply, in part following a global trend, but partly also because of a change in policy away from defending fixed exchange rates. The lower rates resulted in a widening of interest margins, which directly led to an improvement in operating profits. In addition, lower interest rates translated into capital gains on banks' bond and equity portfolios, which in turn provided additional income. Finally, securities trading commissions in some banks were favorably

---

[6]The Danish banking industry, while also suffering from high loan losses, has not required government support on anything like the scale of the other Nordic countries. The four major Danish banks—Den Danske Bank, Unibank, Sparekassen Bikuben, and Jyske Bank—reported operating results in 1992 not unlike those in Finland, Norway, or Sweden. High loan-loss provisions and large valuation losses on securities holdings contributed to a combined pretax loss of DKr 8.2 billion in 1992 (compared with DKr 338 million in 1991). Despite continued high loan-loss provisions, the banks' pretax profits turned sharply upward in 1993, owing in large part to gains on bond holdings (which are carried at market value). At year-end, the banks' combined pretax profit was DKr 5.5 billion.

While all of the Danish banks have incurred substantial loan losses in recent years, problems at the eighth largest bank, Varde Bank, had grown so serious in November 1992 that the central bank arranged a consortium of the seven larger banks to provide a DKr 750 million guarantee fund. Despite some balance sheet restructuring, the central bank determined in 1993 that the bank was about to fail. Consequently, it was decided in December 1993 to transfer the DKr 7 billion in performing assets to Sydbank Sonderjylland and to retain the DKr 4 billion in nonperforming assets in Varde Bank, which will be wound down over the next few years by the central bank with the support of a government guarantee. This is another example of the "good bank/bad bank" model for resolving banking difficulties.

However, the Danish banking situation differed in at least two important respects from those in the other three Nordic

countries. First, Danish banks have always been well capitalized. Even at the end of 1992, the major banks had capital/asset ratios in excess of 11 percent. Second, banks are required to report the current market value of their securities holdings and must set aside loan-loss provisions at the first hint of problems rather than waiting for arrears to accumulate. As a result, bank profitability will be affected by a downturn in the economy earlier than otherwise, but banks will be better equipped to deal with any problems that emerge.

[7]Earlier exchange rate depreciation had actually contributed to problems in the Finnish banking sector. The corporate sector had relied heavily on foreign-currency-denominated bank loans and many of these became nonperforming in 1991–92 when the depreciation of the markka led to significantly higher debt-service costs.

[8]The estimated gross amounts committed, with attribution, are SKr 92 billion in Sweden (Bank Support Authority), Fmk 39 billion in Finland (IBCA Limited), and NKr 28.2 billion in Norway (IBCA Limited).

Table 15. Nordic Countries: Performance of Major Banks[1]

(In billions of local currency)

	1990	1991	1992	1993
Finland				
Net interest income	. . .	6.89	7.66	9.01
Net operating revenue	. . .	0.98	2.06	4.56
Loan-loss provisions	. . .	5.96	12.47	11.66
Operating profit	. . .	−4.98	−10.41	−7.10
Net income	. . .	−8.77	−9.87	. . .
Net nonperforming loans	. . .	21.40	28.67	26.33
Loans	. . .	307.40	304.55	309.87
Norway				
Net interest income	12.24	11.15	11.48	12.74
Net operating revenue	4.28	−0.42	4.77	9.92
Loan-loss provisions	9.11	16.24	9.79	6.26
Operating profit	−4.83	−16.67	−5.02	3.66
Net income	−1.98	−16.30	−5.42	3.55
Net nonperforming loans	. . .	22.73	23.29	19.14
Loans	346.93	352.11	321.24	303.05
Sweden				
Net interest income	. . .	41.80	39.04	40.88
Net operating revenue	. . .	25.26	20.44	33.68
Loan-loss provisions	. . .	32.30	57.41	45.44
Operating profit	. . .	−7.05	−36.98	−12.53
Net income	. . .	−1.65	−12.06	−13.80
Net nonperforming loans	. . .	. . .	107.07	53.11
Loans	. . .	1,292.75	1,313.56	1,170.00

Sources: IBCA Limited; and IMF staff estimates.

[1]Includes the following banks: for Finland, Kansallis-Osake-Pankki, Okobank, Postipankki, Skopbank, and Union Bank of Finland; for Norway, Christiania Bank, Den norske Bank, Fokus Bank, and Union Bank of Norway; and for Sweden, Gota Bank (data not yet available for 1993; preliminary estimates have net interest income of SKr 1.7 billion and operating profit of SKr −13.57 billion), Nordbanken, Skandinaviska Enskilda Banken, Swedbank, and Svenska Handelsbanken (Securum and Retriva are not included).

affected both by the European exchange rate turmoil in late 1992 and early 1993, and by a general increase in securities trading activity (as bond and share prices rose).

Table 15 shows the improvement in Nordic banks' income statements in 1993. With one exception, all of the major banks in these countries recorded increases in operating profits—or declines in losses—in 1993. In most instances, the most important source of increased income was the securities trading account. For example, in Norway, securities trading earned profits of NKr 1.4 billion in 1993, after a NKr 600 million loss in 1992—accompanied by modest increases in net interest income. The turnaround in profits is most noticeable in Norway where net income increased by NKr 9 billion. The 1993 results for Sweden are not directly comparable to the 1992 results because of the substantial restructuring of the banking system in that country. Both Nordbanken and Gota Bank had most of their nonperforming loans removed from their balance sheets and received large capital injections from the Bank Support Authority (BSA). With the exception of Gota Bank, all of the major Swedish banks enjoyed improved profits in 1993. In Finland, although only one of the major banks,

Okobank, was profitable, losses at the other institutions declined considerably—by more than 40 percent at Postipankki and Skopbank.

In Finland, the increase in profits made it unnecessary for some banks to seek government assistance. The largest Finnish bank, Kansallis-Osake-Pankki (KOP), announced in February 1993 a Fmk 3 billion capital restructuring proposal. This involved cutting the nominal value of existing shares in half, and then issuing bonus shares and a rights issue with a combined value equal to the new value of old equity. In October 1993, after the parliament's decision to adopt the "good bank/bad bank" model, KOP announced that its investment banking operations were to be spun off into a new unit, called Prospectus. KOP raised a total of Fmk 4.5 billion in new equity in 1993—38 percent of its end-1992 capital—through sales of shares to the Government, rights issues, and international offerings. The Union Bank of Finland also announced an ambitious capital raising campaign in August 1993 that involved a Fmk 1.158 billion rights issue, a Fmk 300 million direct offering, and finally the sale of Fmk 1 billion in new shares.

On the other hand, the first bank taken over by the Finnish Government, Skopbank, continued to require government support in 1993. In May 1993 the Government Guarantee Fund (GGF) injected Fmk 700 million in preference capital into the bank. Skopbank went to the international capital markets in July and September 1993 to borrow a total of $150 million (by issuing a three-year bond), but in December it announced that it needed a further capital injection of Fmk 350 million in order to meet its capital requirements. This brought the total amount of GGF funds invested in this bank to Fmk 3.7 billion, and the GGF now owns 53 percent of Skopbank's equity and 63 percent of its voting shares. The Bank of Finland had provided Fmk 11.1 billion in assistance to Skopbank by the end of 1993.

In October 1993, the Government announced that the GGF had negotiated the takeover of the Savings Bank of Finland by KOP, Unitas, Postipankki, and the Okobank group.[9] Each of these four groups would acquire a quarter of the Savings Bank for a price of Fmk 1.4 billion; each will receive about Fmk 12 billion of assets. All of the Savings Bank's bad loans will be transferred to a separate company to be wholly owned by the GGF.

Following on favorable midyear results and the success of KOP's equity issues, the Norwegian banks have also raised additional equity, which has in some cases reduced the Government's equity share to 70 percent. Swedish commercial banks reported significantly improved results in the first half of 1993—particularly Nordbanken which, as a result of the divestiture of most of its nonperforming loans, recorded a SKr 12.6 billion turnaround in pretax profits to SKr 2.5 billion. Nordbanken's improved position provided the necessary support for the issue of a $30 million bond. Following the announcement of an increase in net profit to SKr 837 million from SKr 658 million during the first half of 1992, Svenska Handelsbanken, the largest commercial bank, announced a SKr 2.5 billion rights offering. Most significantly, the improved operating environment reduced net losses at Skandinaviska Enskilda Banken (SEB) to SKr 298 million from SKr 2.5 billion in the first half of 1993. As a result, in August 1993 SEB withdrew its application for government support and announced plans for a SKr 5.3 billion rights issue. SEB had also employed the "good bank/bad bank" model in 1993, by transferring 513 real estate properties, worth SKr 12.4 billion, to its real estate unit, Diligentia Fastigheter.

Likewise, the remaining two Swedish applicants for government assistance withdrew their requests after posting improved results for the first half of 1993. Foreningsbanken, a former rural cooperative institution, successfully launched a SKr 3.5 billion

initial public offering in December 1993, which was followed early in 1994 by a $100 million bond issue.[10] Swedbank followed suit with the announcement of a proposed SKr 8 billion restructuring plan in December 1993, which will include a SKr 2.1 billion stock issue.

The situation at Gota Bank took somewhat longer to be resolved. It was taken over by the Government in December 1992 after its parent company, Gota AB, declared bankruptcy. As a result of the government guarantee, Gota was able to issue $200 million in two equal tranches of five- and eight-year bonds. In the fall of 1993, the Government announced its intention to sell Gota Bank and began approaching other banks, domestic and foreign. Eventually all of the banks that expressed interest, except Nordbanken, declined to bid. Consequently, in December 1993, these two banks were merged. Prior to the merger, however, SKr 38 billion of Gota Bank's bad assets—all bad loans greater than SKr 5 million—were transferred to a new company, called Retriva, which was capitalized by the Government to the amount of SKr 3.8 billion and received loan guarantees of SKr 3.5 billion. As a result of this operation, Gota Bank's stock of nonperforming loans was reduced to 4 percent of total loans, from 36 percent. In addition, the BSA provided a capital injection of SKr 20 billion to Gota Bank in order to cover remaining loan losses.

Balance Sheet Difficulties in Japan

Steep declines in equity and real estate prices after 1990 were the key factors that precipitated banking difficulties in Japan. Since a significant proportion of bank loans were secured directly or indirectly by real estate collateral or extended to real estate companies and developers, the decline in land prices soon resulted in the accumulation of increasing stocks of nonperforming loans on the balance sheets of the major banks. These difficulties were compounded since 1991 by a general slowdown in the real economy, which led to further additions to the stock of bad loans.

As discussed in Part II of last year's *International Capital Markets* report, the banks' ability to strengthen their balance sheets depends to a considerable extent on external factors such as developments in the equity and real estate markets and in the real economy more generally. While equity prices have recovered from cyclical lows and a bottoming out of real estate prices may be in sight,

---

[9]The Savings Bank of Finland was itself formed in 1992 by the merger of 41 small savings banks.

[10]The BSA provided a SKr 2.5 billion capital-adequacy guarantee for the initial public offering. This guarantee can be utilized if the bank's capital falls below 9 percent of its risk-weighted assets. If fully utilized, this facility would result in a 54 percent BSA share in Foreningsbanken equity (86 percent of the votes).

banks must rely on improved revenue—in particular, an increase in interest earnings—in order to be able to increase their reserves against bad loans.

With economic growth slowing sharply from mid-1991 on, monetary and fiscal actions were taken to support activity. The official discount rate was reduced from 6 percent in mid-1991 to a historic low of 1.75 percent in September 1993, and fiscal expenditure was increased in a series of four supplementary budgets announced since August 1992, the latest of which was announced in February 1994.[11] Banks' interest rate margins, which had, if anything, narrowed slightly in the early part of 1993, widened appreciably in the fourth quarter. The spread between the average long-term loan rate and the interest rate paid on large (in excess of ¥ 10 million) one- to two-year term deposits fluctuated between a high of 211 basis points and a low of 185 basis points during the first eight months, but it jumped to 256 basis points in September and finished the calendar year at 286 basis points. A similar, although less dramatic, increase is observed in spreads between short-term lending and deposit rates, and in spreads over many other sources of funding.

While these wider spreads improved banks' operating revenue—particularly in the second half of the fiscal year—commercial property values continued to decline in 1993 and in the first quarter of 1994. Commercial real estate prices fell by 18.3 percent in Tokyo and by 19.1 percent in Osaka in 1993; further declines of 4 percent and 3.9 percent, respectively, were registered in the first quarter of 1994. Prices for commercial real estate in these cities have fallen by approximately 40 percent and 60 percent, respectively, from the peak level in 1990.

Developments in the equity and property markets are relevant for a number of reasons. As regards equity prices, banks are allowed to claim 45 percent of the unrealized gains on their equity portfolios as tier 2 capital. Thus, a decline in equity prices results in a direct decline in capital. This factor has been considerably alleviated by the permission banks received in July 1992 to include perpetual subordinated debt in tier 2 capital. Between March 1992 and March 1994, the major banks increased their subordinated debt by ¥ 2.9 trillion. The accounting for unrealized gains or losses on equity holdings, however, exposes banks to a potential problem. Since banks must report the value of their holdings at the lesser of the market value and the book value, a decline in the price of these shares must be recorded as a loss on their income statement. Land prices affect the banks' balance sheets by changing the value of their loans. A significant

proportion of banks' lending has been extended to real estate developers, to construction firms, or to housing loan companies; real estate serves as the collateral for such loans.

Equity prices fluctuated widely in 1993. The key Nikkei 225 index rose from ¥ 16,925 at the end of 1992 to a peak of ¥ 21,148 in mid-September 1993 before falling to a low of ¥ 16,079 at the end of November. Since early January 1994, the index has fluctuated within a relatively narrower band of ¥ 19,000 to ¥ 21,000.

The continued slowdown in economic activity, combined with declines in land prices, contributed to an increase in nonperforming loans in the fiscal year 1993/94. At the end of March 1994, the 21 major banks reported nonperforming loans of ¥ 13,573 billion, up from ¥ 12,775 billion at the end of March 1993 (Table 16).[12] Most of the problem assets are on the books of the city banks, whose reported nonperforming loans increased by 6.1 percent to ¥ 8,974 billion. The problems are most pronounced, however, at the trust banks, whose ¥ 2,712 billion in nonperforming loans represent almost 4 percent of their lending.

The banks' first line of defense against balance sheet weakness is an increase in loan-loss reserves. There are two kinds of reserves: (i) general reserves, additions to which are exempt from tax up to the legal maximum of 0.3 percent of the value of loans made; and (ii) specific reserves held against individual loans. Until recently, banks could only create specific reserves with the approval of the Ministry of Finance's Banking Bureau. This could be a time-consuming process because the bank would have to submit each loan for consideration individually to a Banking Bureau examiner. The tax liability of these provisions was determined by the Tax Bureau, which generally required proof of legal bankruptcy before exempting specific reserves from taxation. The February 1994 stimulus package eased these constraints somewhat by allowing banks more discretion in creating specific reserves: banks were freed of the need to present each loan for consideration and could make provisions against loans that they decided were nonperforming or doubtful.

Banks are permitted to write off losses equal to the difference between the book value and the mar-

---

[11]See International Monetary Fund (1994).

[12]The official definition of nonperforming loans includes loans to borrowers that have legally been declared bankrupt (¥ 2.3 trillion) and loans on which interest has not been paid for 180 days (¥ 11.3 trillion). These figures on nonperforming loans do not include restructured loans. The Japan Center for International Finance estimates the stock of restructured loans at ¥ 13–14 trillion. The increase in nonperforming loans between March and September 1993 is a net number: nonperforming loans that have been sold to the Cooperative Credit Purchasing Company or charged off are removed from the nonperforming category, as well as from the balance sheets of banks.

Table 16. Japan: Indicators of Banking Performance

(In billions of yen, except where indicated)

	Mar. 1992	Sept. 1992	Mar. 1993	Sept. 1993	Mar. 1994
All banks					
Nonperforming loans	7,900.00	12,300.00	12,774.60	13,756.00	13,573.00
Net interest income	5,213.10	3,032.30	5,908.70	2,687.10	5,580.60
Net operating income[1]	2,610.30	1,613.30	3,091.80	1,317.40	2,724.90
Provisions and charge-offs[2]	550.30	434.90	1,321.40	1,058.30	3,538.70
Net income	940.90	365.30	505.90	290.10	447.80
Specific reserves	1,044.20	1,361.20	1,866.00	2,263.00	3,022.40
Hidden reserves	16,754.90	13,871.40	17,429.70	23,728.50	20,325.60
Loans	397,464.50	393,928.20	390,761.40	391,122.50	. . .
Risk-weighted capital ratio					
(in percent)	8.27	8.78	9.32	9.82	9.73
City banks					
Nonperforming loans	. . .	8,118.00	8,454.90	9,273.00	8,973.90
Net interest income	4,145.80	2,372.80	4,657.80	2,159.70	4,439.60
Net operating income[1]	2,167.90	1,295.40	2,512.40	1,094.50	2,179.70
Provisions and charge-offs[2]	437.30	356.70	1,011.60	850.30	2,490.00
Net income	647.40	258.60	367.70	221.40	318.30
Specific reserves	835.90	1,099.20	1,459.00	1,793.00	2,102.10
Hidden reserves	10,575.50	8,625.40	10,845.40	14,863.10	13,024.90
Loans	274,757.60	274,089.70	269,616.00	272,072.10	. . .
Risk-weighted capital ratio					
(in percent)	8.19	8.69	9.62	9.75	9.69
Long-term credit banks					
Nonperforming loans	. . .	1,722.00	1,850.20	1,899.00	1,887.50
Net interest income	470.70	321.20	526.20	182.70	341.20
Net operating income[1]	270.90	223.60	336.40	96.40	175.60
Provisions and charge-offs[2]	49.00	39.90	197.30	122.30	546.90
Net income	161.50	53.20	70.40	35.00	68.10
Specific reserves	123.10	155.00	231.00	266.00	493.80
Hidden reserves	3,350.50	3,077.10	3,643.70	4,758.00	3,908.60
Loans	56,374.90	53,974.30	54,548.80	54,337.00	. . .
Risk-weighted capital ratio					
(in percent)	8.31	9.12	9.14	9.23	9.25
Trust banks					
Nonperforming loans	. . .	2,460.00	2,469.50	2,587.00	2,711.60
Net interest income	596.60	338.30	724.70	344.70	799.80
Net operating income[1]	171.50	94.30	243.00	126.50	369.60
Provisions and charge-offs[2]	64.00	38.30	112.50	85.70	501.80
Net income	132.00	53.50	67.80	33.70	61.40
Specific reserves	85.20	107.00	175.00	203.00	426.90
Hidden reserves	2,828.90	2,168.90	2,940.60	4,107.40	3,392.40
Loans	66,332.00	65,864.20	66,596.60	64,713.40	. . .
Risk-weighted capital ratio					
(in percent)	8.66	8.92	10.01	10.90	10.46
Memorandum item					
Nikkei 225 index	19,345.95	17,399.08	18,591.45	20,105.71	19,111.92

Sources: Bloomberg Financial Markets; IBCA Limited; Japan, Ministry of Finance; and IMF staff estimates.

[1]Adjusted to exclude investment bond profits and losses.

[2]Specific provisions and charge-offs against nondeveloping country loans plus losses on loans sold to the Cooperative Credit Purchasing Company (CCPC).

ket value of a loan when it is sold. In addition, when losses arise from loans against which sufficient provisions have not been made, they must be charged against current income; interest accrued but not paid in two years must also be charged off. However, while banks' foreign subsidiaries have begun to make use of the secondary market for loans elsewhere, there is no such market in Japan as of yet. In the absence of a market for loans, the major Japanese banks, together with many regional banks, insurance companies, and cooperative credit institutions, set up the Cooperative Credit Purchasing Company (CCPC) in early 1993. This essentially serves as a vehicle through which banks can realize the losses on their nonperforming loans and thereby make them eligible for tax deductibility. In the 1993/94 fiscal year, ¥ 3,838 billion in loans were sold to the CCPC; the discount on these loans

Table 17.   Business Results of the Cooperative Credit Purchasing Company (CCPC)

	Number of Transactions	Face Value (In billions of yen)	Price	Discount (In percent)
1993				
March	229	681.7	452.1	33.7
April	1	0.1	0.1	20.0
May	9	10.0	6.7	33.0
June	12	24.3	17.6	27.6
July	14	64.2	26.1	59.3
August	60	130.8	66.7	49.0
September	414	954.7	485.7	49.1
October	16	54.1	29.3	45.8
November	19	51.4	20.2	60.7
December	116	231.2	105.0	54.6
1994				
January	103	187.6	98.8	47.3
February	226	467.0	213.9	54.2
March	901	1,662.8	708.9	57.4
Total for 1993 and 1994	2,120	4,519.9	2,231.0	50.6
Memorandum item				
FY 1993	1,891	3,838.2	1,778.9	53.7

Sources: Bloomberg Financial Markets; IBCA Limited; Japan, Ministry of Finance; and IMF staff estimates.

averaged 54 percent (Table 17).[13] The 21 major banks claimed tax deductions of ¥ 1,775 billion. During the same period, banks made specific provisions of ¥ 1,378 billion and charged off ¥ 385 billion against nondeveloping-country loans.

Loans sold to the CCPC are evaluated by a pricing committee that determines an approximate market value for the collateral. The loans are then purchased by the CCPC at this price, with the financing provided by a loan from the selling bank. Interest and principal payments on these loans commence only after the collateral is sold. Hence the bank essentially exchanges a nonperforming loan for a performing loan to the CCPC and obtains a tax deduction for the difference. However, since the bank remains responsible for losses incurred by the CCPC if it is unable to sell the collateral (at its new estimated value), the bank is not as clear of the problem as it would be if it had sold the loan on a secondary market.

The Ministry of Finance has recently encouraged banks to make more aggressive use of the CCPC and has permitted banks to set up similar units to purchase restructured loans of nonbank affiliates— loans that often are not already included in the estimate of nonperforming loans. Reportedly, the first such entity has been proposed by a group of banks to purchase the restructured loans due to ten nonbank affiliates of Hyogo Bank.

As of March 31, 1994, the 21 major banks reported adjusted operating earnings, defined as net interest revenue plus noninterest revenue less noninterest expenses, of ¥ 2,725 billion, 12 percent less than for 1992/93.[14] Among the three groups of banks, the adjusted operating earnings of long-term credit banks suffered the largest decline, falling by 48 percent. Contrary to the experience of the other two groups, the earnings of the trust banks increased by 52 percent. Changes in net interest revenues were the driving force for changes in adjusted operating income: city banks' net interest revenues declined by ¥218 billion and long-term credit banks' net interest revenue declined by ¥ 185 billion. For the trust banks, in contrast, net interest revenues increased by some ¥ 75 billion.

Net operating income is an important element of banks' efforts to resolve the bad loans problem, because higher operating income allows for faster provisioning and write-offs. Assuming an average discount of 50 percent on the value of the nonperforming loans remaining at end-March 1994, the noncollateralized portion of these bad loans was approximately ¥ 6.8 trillion;[15] the combined specific reserves of the major banks at that time was ¥ 3 trillion. In 1993/94, banks' provisions and

---

[13]As the data in Table 17 show, most loan sales to the CCPC have been arranged immediately prior to the end-September and end-March reporting dates.

[14]This measure differs from the Japanese definition of operating earnings, which includes unrealized gains and losses on the investment bond portfolio. These are removed to approximate banks' cash flow.

[15]In 1993/94, loans were sold to the CCPC at an average discount of 51 percent.

charge-offs, including losses on CCPC loans, amounted to ¥ 3.5 trillion—130 percent of net operating income. With similar levels of provisioning, banks could increase reserves by the additional ¥ 3.8 trillion needed to fully cover the decline in portfolio value in just over a year.

However, the banks were only able to make such large provisions and write-offs by drawing on their unrealized gains on securities holdings—particularly equities. In 1993/94, the 21 major banks recorded ¥ 1.8 trillion in net profits on their equity holdings. As of March 31, 1994, the major banks had unrealized gains on equities of ¥ 19.6 trillion. While these gains can be realized by some institutions and used as a means to increase provisions, it would be difficult for all banks to do so since they hold a significant share of Japanese equities. At the end of September 1993, the 21 major banks' equity portfolios were valued at an estimated ¥ 36 trillion, or 10 percent of the market capitalization of the first two sections of the Tokyo Stock Exchange.[16]

---

[16]Based on data provided by IBCA Limited.

Annex IV

Developments in Private Market Financing for Developing Countries

Private financing to developing countries increased substantially in 1993; it was associated with a further improvement in the terms of borrowing and strong increases in equity prices in many local stock markets. Developing country borrowers issued almost $60 billion of bonds in 1993, by far their most widely used financing instrument. Much of this inflow represented net financing, because most bonds issued so far have bullet repayments that have not yet fallen due. A large share of these bond flows went to borrowers in about six to eight countries in Asia, Europe, and Latin America, but the range of countries accessing this market continued to expand in 1993. In contrast, international equity placements by developing country issuers rose only moderately from $9 billion in 1992 to $12 billion in 1993, with an important share of these issues made through American Depository Receipts (ADRs) or Global Depository Receipts (GDRs). This estimate of equity placements, however, misses direct purchases of equity in the local stock markets, which reportedly grew significantly in 1993. Banks continued to provide financing primarily through short-term trade credits, although their medium- and long-term lending to most developing countries picked up somewhat in 1993.

In the first quarter of 1994, the increase in U.S. interest rates, inter alia, helped spark a drop in demand for emerging markets assets (relative to their peaks in the fourth quarter of 1993), as financing to developing countries tapered off, together with strong declines in bond and equity prices. Developing country bond issuance had accelerated throughout 1993 to $24 billion in the fourth quarter and then fell off to $18 billion in the first quarter of 1994. A similar pattern occurred with international equity placements, which had reached over $5 billion in the fourth quarter of 1993 before declining to $4 billion in the first quarter of 1994.

The first part of this section reviews the recent experience with securitized capital flows (international bonds, short-term debt instruments, and equities) and with bank lending. The second part discusses two aspects of the development of the market in 1993. First, it explains the broadening of the investor base and the reasons behind the expansion. Second, it discusses the factors behind the assessment of risk.

Recent Experience

International Bonds

Issuance by developing country borrowers in international bond markets continued to show impressive growth, as bond placements more than doubled to $59 billion in 1993 following a doubling in the volume of bond issues in each year since 1990 (Table A10). During the course of the year, total bond issues accelerated from $10 billion in the first quarter to over $23 billion in the fourth quarter. The average size of bonds issued increased to $135 million in 1993, somewhat higher than the average of $110 million in 1992. In May, Cementos Mexicanos (Cemex), Mexico's largest cement producer, successfully placed a $1 billion issue, the largest Eurobond issued by a Latin American borrower to that date. In December, the Republic of Argentina launched the first global bond issue by an emerging markets issuer, a $1 billion bond payable in ten years. The share of developing countries in total bond issuance in international markets rose further to 12 percent in 1993, three times the share of 4 percent in 1991; and this share more than doubled from 7 percent in the first quarter of 1993 to 20 percent by the fourth quarter.

Bond issuance in 1993 was concentrated in three regions. Borrowers in the Western Hemisphere raised some $27 billion, with Mexico once again emerging as the leading borrower, raising over $10 billion. Besides the issue by Cemex, a wide range of Mexican corporations, such as Petroleos Mexicanos (Pemex) and several banks, placed sizable bond issues. Argentine issuers quadrupled their access to bond markets to $6 billion, which included several large issues by Telecomunicaciones. International bond offerings by Brazilian and Venezuelan entities also rose considerably, in spite of continued uncertainty about the course of economic policies and restrictions on the maturity of Brazilian bond issues. One of the Venezuelan issues was launched simultaneously in Colombia and outside Latin America, the first intra-regional bond issue in Latin America. Chile, Trinidad and Tobago, and Uruguay maintained their presence in these markets through a moderate amount of borrowing, and Colombia, Guatemala, and Peru tapped the market for the first time in many years.

Asian borrowers more than tripled their borrowing in international bond markets to $20 billion, reflecting in large part a sixfold increase in bonds issued by China and Hong Kong.[1] Borrowers in Korea and Thailand sharply increased their presence in international bond markets. Both the Philippines and Malaysia entered the market for the first time in many years, with the Philippines raising over $1 billion. India also returned to the market after being absent in 1992, with a sharp pickup in issuance in the fourth quarter of 1993.

Among European developing countries, Hungary stepped up its bond issues to the equivalent of $4.8 billion in 1993, in an effort to cover its present and future large external financing needs, while Turkey borrowed $3.9 billion on international bond markets. Other regions were relatively inactive in international bond markets in 1993, with the exception of the Middle East, where Israel floated $2 billion of bonds in 1993 as part of a loan-guarantee program granted by the United States.

All types of borrowers took part in the surge in bond financing in 1993. Private sector issuers more than doubled their bond issuance from $10 billion in 1992 to $27 billion in 1993, which accounted for 46 percent of total bond issues by developing countries. Almost three fourths of the private sector bond issues were placed by issuers in four countries or regions (Hong Kong and Mexico with about $6 billion each, followed by Brazil with $4.8 billion and Argentina with $3.8 billion). Sovereign borrowers roughly tripled their bond placements between 1992 and 1993, accounting for $16 billion, or 28 percent of bonds issued in 1993. Hungary and Turkey led sovereign bond issuers with $4.5 billion and $3.7 billion of bond placements, respectively, in 1993. Other public sector borrowers issued roughly the same amount of bonds in 1993 as the sovereign borrowers.

Terms on primary issues improved for many developing country borrowers during the year. The average yield spread against comparable U.S. Treasury securities at launch for all borrowers fell from 288 basis points in the first quarter of 1993 to 241 basis points by the fourth quarter of 1993. The average yield spread for sovereigns, however, actually increased slightly, reflecting the entrance of sovereign borrowing by the Philippines, the Slovak Republic, and Venezuela at spreads of over 300 basis points. For countries with a track record in the markets, sovereign yield spreads came down. In 1993, average yield spreads for other public sector

borrowers were below the spread on sovereign issues for the first time, reflecting the experience of Mexico, the Philippines, and Thailand. There was a strong variation in yield spreads across countries, with the lowest spreads for Asian borrowers, such as China, Korea, and Thailand (all below 100 basis points), while the private sector in Latin America typically paid a spread of 300 to 500 basis points. The average maturity of bond issues continued to lengthen in 1993 to about 6 1/2 years. Maturities were shortest in the private sector. Some sovereign borrowers pursued a strategy of lengthening the maturity structure of their country's debt; Hungary placed a 20-year bond issue, while a number of countries such as Argentina and Mexico placed 10-year bond issues.

Bond issues continued to be concentrated in three currency sectors, with the share of issues denominated in U.S. dollars, deutsche mark, or Japanese yen amounting to 95 percent of the total. The U.S. dollar sector continued to be the major funding source for developing country borrowers, even for non-U.S. investors. Most investors reportedly hedge their currency exposure and it is easier to hedge instruments denominated in U.S. dollars. German investors exhibit a strong home currency preference and tend to buy deutsche mark-denominated issues to avoid any exposure to exchange rate risk. Other reasons for the predominance of these three currencies would include their widespread use in international payments and the ease of settlement. While most borrowers—especially those in the Western Hemisphere—placed dollar-denominated bond issues, a number of countries—particularly in Europe—continued to try to diversify the currencies of denomination of their borrowings, as a means of broadening their investor base and in an effort to match the currency composition of their external assets and liabilities. Mexico has issued bonds in nine different currencies, and is followed by Hungary with bonds issued in eight currencies, including its first Matador bond and a forint medium-term note facility.[2]

Enhancement techniques continued to be employed by developing country issuers in 1993 to help reduce borrowing costs, and as in past years the pattern of enhancements differed among regions. Asian borrowers enhanced roughly $6 billion (35 percent) of their bond issues, relying principally on equity conversion options, while Western Hemisphere borrowers enhanced only $3 billion (12 percent) of their bond issues, mainly through put options or collateralization.

The bond market began to taper off somewhat in January and early February 1994, but experienced a

---

[1]For a description of China's external borrowing strategy, see Annex V of this report.

[2]A Matador bond is a bond issued in Spain by a nonresident.

Table 18. International Equity Issues by Developing Countries: Depository Receipts and Other Issues

(In millions of U.S. dollars)

	1990	1991	1992	1993
Developing countries	1,262	5,436	9,259	11,865
Africa	—	143	270	8
Depository receipts	—	—	—	—
Other	—	143	270	8
Asia	1,040	1,022	4,732	5,673
Depository receipts	1	200	1,056	937
Other	1,039	822	3,676	4,736
Europe	124	91	67	202
Depository receipts	—	—	10	105
Other	124	91	57	97
Middle East	—	60	127	257
Depository receipts	—	—	—	188
Other	—	60	127	69
Western Hemisphere	98	4,120	4,063	5,725
Depository receipts	98	2,166	1,781	5,246
Other	—	1,954	2,282	479

Sources: *Euroweek*; and *International Financing Review*.

more pronounced setback after U.S. interest rates were increased starting in early February. For the quarter as a whole, a decline in bond issuance compared with the last quarter of 1993 took place in all regions, and the fall-off was substantial for Hungary, Turkey, and several other major borrowers. Nonetheless, certain countries, such as China, Thailand, and Mexico, actually increased their bond issuance. Sovereign borrowers increased their level of bond issuance, while other public sector and private sector issuers registered sizable declines. The average maturity of the bonds became shorter in the first quarter, and a growing share of bonds relied on floating interest rates. Yield spreads at launch continued to improve, suggesting that lower quality borrowers lost access to the market, while the secondary market spreads rose for some countries but declined for others.

International Equity Placements

The market for international equity placements grew sevenfold between 1990 and 1992, reflecting in part the wave of privatization in several countries. In contrast to bonds, this expansion of the equity market moderated in 1993, as international equity placements reached $11.9 billion, up from $9.3 billion in 1992 (Table A11). In 1993, developing countries accounted for only 23 percent of all international equity placements, well below their share of 41 percent in 1992. Since 1990, companies from developing countries have raised over $28 billion through the international equity markets.

Latin American and Asian companies accounted for almost all of the international equity placements

in 1993. In Mexico, share prices and issuance activity were subdued in the first three quarters because of uncertainty about the passage of the North American Free Trade Agreement (NAFTA), but following the passage of the Agreement in the last quarter, Mexican corporations raised $1.7 billion in international equities, while local share prices rose rapidly (Chart 8). The shares sold by Mexican corporations in the fourth quarter were placed through ADR/GDR programs, with Grupo Televisa offering the largest GDR issue ever at $822 million (Table 18). For the year, Mexican firms issued $2.5 billion in international equities, down from the $3 billion issued in 1992. International equity issues from Argentina rose sharply in 1993 to $2.8 billion, reflecting a strong increase in share prices and the $2 billion privatization of Yacimientos Petroleros Fiscales in the second quarter. China and Hong Kong accounted for over half the equity issues from Asia.

For a number of developing countries, cross-border equity inflows have occurred through direct purchases on local exchanges. Although comprehensive statistics across countries are not available, recent estimates suggest that secondary market purchases in emerging markets by international investors amounted to some $14 billion in 1992, and many market participants believe that these flows increased substantially in 1993, with one source reporting an amount of $40 billion.[3] For India, direct purchases of equity amounted to an estimated $1.4 billion in 1993, following no purchases in 1992, while in Mexico these inflows are estimated to have held steady at about $6 billion in 1992 and 1993.

In the first quarter of 1994, international equity issues declined to $4 billion, but accounted for about one third of total international equity issues, up from roughly one fifth for 1993. Enterprises in both Asia and the Western Hemisphere issued less equity, except for India which experienced about a sevenfold increase in the volume of equity placements.

Bank Lending

Banks began to show a renewed interest in lending to developing countries in 1993, although bank activity remained subdued in comparison with the financing through bonds. To limit their risk exposure, banks restricted new lending to short-term credits (typically trade credits), project finance, and loans structured using a variety of risk-mitigating techniques, including asset securitization. Medium- and long-term bank loan commitments to capital

---

[3]Howell, Cozzini, and Greenwood (1994).

Chart 8. Share Price Indices for Selected Emerging Markets[1]
(In U.S. dollar terms, December 1988 = 100)

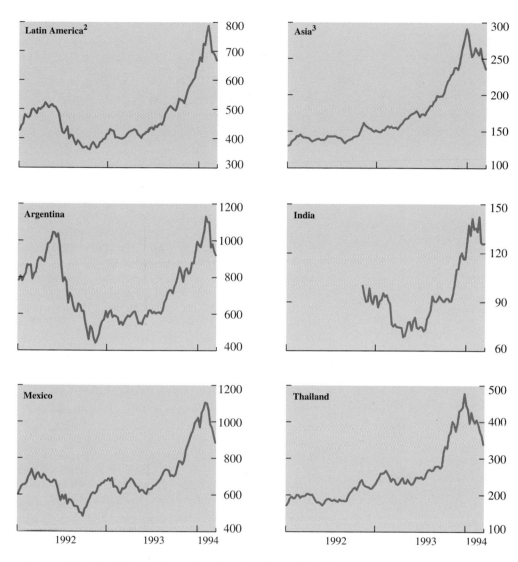

Source: International Finance Corporation, Emerging Markets Data Base.
[1]IFC weekly investable price indices.
[2]Argentina, Brazil, Chile, Colombia, Mexico, and Venezuela.
[3]India, Indonesia, Korea, Malaysia, Pakistan, the Philippines, Taiwan Province of China, and Thailand.

importing developing countries rose from $14.1 billion in 1992 to $18.5 billion in 1993 (Table 19).

Most notable was the increase in loan commitments to Latin America, which rose from $0.9 billion in 1992 to $2.4 billion in 1993. Each of the major restructuring countries (Argentina, Brazil, Mexico, and Venezuela) received loans ranging from $0.3 billion to $0.8 billion. Asian borrowers continued to account for three fourths of new syndicated bank credit commitments to capital importing countries, with China borrowing $3.8 billion, followed by Thailand ($3.3 billion), Korea ($2.1 bil-

lion), and Indonesia ($2.0 billion). In Europe, Turkey obtained close to $2 billion in bank loan commitments in 1993, while European countries in transition had little access to nonguaranteed medium- and long-term bank lending. Bank lending to the Middle East (including Kuwait and Saudi Arabia) fell to virtually nothing in 1993, down sharply from the historical high of $10 billion in 1991. Bank lending activity to Africa continued to be very low.

This pickup in bank lending to developing countries in 1993 was associated with a widening of the

Table 19. Bank Credit Commitments by Country or Region of Destination

(In billions of U.S. dollars)

	1990	1991	1992	1993
Developing countries[1]	21.0	27.0	17.0	18.7
Capital importing developing countries[1]	20.9	16.7	14.1	18.5
Africa	0.6	0.2	0.6	0.3
Algeria	—	0.1	—	—
Angola	—	—	0.3	—
Côte d'Ivoire	—	—	—	—
Ghana	0.1	0.1	0.1	—
Morocco	0.1	—	—	—
Nigeria	—	—	—	—
South Africa	—	—	—	—
Tunisia	—	—	0.1	0.1
Zimbabwe	—	0.1	—	0.1
Other	0.4	—	0.1	—
Asia	12.0	13.6	10.5	13.4
China	1.5	2.3	2.7	3.8
India	0.7	—	0.2	—
Indonesia	3.9	5.0	1.8	2.0
Korea	2.0	3.5	1.8	2.1
Malaysia	0.5	0.2	1.2	1.4
Pakistan	0.4	0.1	—	—
Papua New Guinea	0.1	0.3	—	—
Philippines	0.7	—	—	—
Taiwan Province of China	0.8	0.7	0.8	0.8
Thailand	1.3	1.6	2.0	3.3
Viet Nam	—	—	—	—
Other	0.1	—	—	—
Europe	4.9	1.9	2.1	2.3
Bulgaria	—	—	—	—
Czech Republic	—	—	—	0.2
Hungary	—	0.1	0.2	0.1
Slovak Republic	—	—	—	0.1
Turkey	1.8	1.6	1.8	1.9
Former U.S.S.R.	3.0	—	—	—
Other	0.1	0.2	0.1	—
Middle East	0.1	—	—	0.1
Egypt	—	—	—	—
Jordan	—	—	—	—
Other	0.1	—	—	0.1
Western Hemisphere	3.3	1.0	0.9	2.4
Argentina	—	—	—	0.4
Brazil	—	—	0.2	0.3
Chile	0.3	—	0.4	0.3
Colombia	—	0.2	—	0.1
Mexico	1.6	0.6	0.2	0.4
Uruguay	—	0.1	—	—
Venezuela	1.4	—	0.2	0.8
Other	—	0.1	—	0.1
Other developing countries	0.1	10.0	2.9	0.2
Kuwait	—	5.5	—	—
Saudi Arabia	0.1	4.5	2.9	0.2
Offshore banking centers	3.7	1.5	1.5	3.6
International organizations and unallocated	4.4	6.6	7.1	4.8
Total	124.5	116.0	117.9	138.3

Source: Organization for Economic Cooperation and Development, *Financial Statistics Monthly.*
[1]Excluding offshore banking centers.

average spread on voluntary loans to these countries to 106 basis points and a fall in the average maturity to 5.6 years in 1993, compared with 6.7 years in the previous year. The spreads differed widely according to the credit quality of the borrowing country, with spreads ranging from 57 basis points on loans to Malaysia to over 200 basis points on loans to India and Venezuela.

In contrast to the primary market for bank loans, the secondary market for bank claims on developing countries was very active. In October 1993, the Emerging Markets Traders Association issued the results of the first Trading Volume Survey. This report revealed that total trading volumes in the secondary market for developing country instruments exceeded $730 billion in 1992. Latin American instruments represented more than 80 percent of the volume, led by $209 billion for Brazil, $189 billion for Mexico, and $156 billion for Argentina. It is believed that the trading volume in 1993 was on the order of $1 trillion. By the end of 1993, securitized bank debt in developing countries had increased to some $90 billion, which includes about $25 billion of bonds issued in Argentina's 1993 debt restructuring.

Issues in Market Access

Broadening of the Investor Base

The rapid growth in private financing to developing countries in 1993 reflected a considerable broadening of the investor base. Prior to 1993, the investor base in this market displayed a regional specialization. Asian countries that maintained access to the international markets continued to attract a moderate level of investment from the mainstream institutional investors such as pension funds and insurance companies from industrial countries, especially the United States and the United Kingdom. In contrast, Latin American countries, which began to regain market access in 1989, received inflows primarily from flight capital investors—who in many cases were repatriating money to their home countries—and from wealthy individuals. Hedge funds and other highly leveraged speculators have generally remained on the sidelines of this market, but have entered for short periods when they have perceived a good profit opportunity.

Starting in late 1992, some U.S. pension funds, such as ARCO and GTE, began to purchase investments, including Brady bonds, in Latin America.[4] According to market participants, U.S. mutual funds significantly increased their participation in

---

[4]See *Pensions and Investments,* January 25, 1993.

all segments of this market in mid-1993 and were followed by another round of buying by pension funds and insurance companies. At the end of 1993, U.S. mutual funds held about 2 percent of their assets (roughly $30 billion) in emerging markets, principally in the form of equity.[5] The 200 largest pension funds in the United States increased the share of their portfolio placed in investments outside the country from 5.2 percent at the end of September 1992 to 7 percent at the end of September 1993, with slightly over one half of this increase due to new cash investments and with the remainder deriving from appreciation in the market value of the assets.[6] U.S. pension funds engaging in international investment tended to be defined benefit plans and included public as well as private pension plans. There is little evidence on the investments of U.S. insurance companies in emerging markets in 1993, but they probably allocated an even smaller share than pension funds to foreign assets. European institutional investors also increased their participation in this market, although more moderately, perhaps taking a cue from the heightened interest of the U.S. institutions. While the shares of the international investments allocated to emerging markets are difficult to obtain, a recent survey of institutional fund managers reports that these managers allocated 13 percent of their international portfolios in 1993 to emerging markets assets, up from 10 percent in 1992 and 2.5 percent in 1989.[7] The major institutions manage very sizable portfolios. The portfolios of U.S. mutual funds amount to $2 trillion.[8] U.S. pension funds and insurance companies manage almost $6 trillion, while the assets of these institutional investors in France, Germany, Japan, and the United Kingdom amounted to $5.7 trillion at the end of 1991.[9]

Investor preferences continue to vary widely across countries. U.S. investors continue to play the largest role and purchase debt and equity principally from Latin American and Asian issuers. U.K. investors are also active in this market and tend to buy assets in Asia and to a lesser extent in Latin America. German investors focus principally on Eastern Europe, although their interest in Latin American instruments is picking up, and they prefer deutsche mark-denominated bond issues to avoid

any exchange rate risk. Japanese investors have invested a small share of their assets in securities issued by the fast-growing economies of East and Southeast Asia and by other developing countries that maintained a good debt-servicing record during the 1980s. Investors outside these four countries have largely stayed on the sidelines of this market, although they have shown modest interest, mostly for opportunities in Asia.

Factors Behind the Expansion of the Investor Base

Starting in 1989, a number of developing countries proved they could sustain a program of sound macroeconomic policies and structural reforms (especially privatization), which helped open up investment opportunities with rates of return sufficiently high to attract international investors. In addition, several of the developing countries, including China and Mexico, began to improve financial reporting and the supervision of their financial markets, which helped boost investor confidence further. The reputation of the strong performing countries rubbed off on neighboring countries that embarked on a reform path later and made investors more willing to invest at an earlier stage in the reform process.

In 1993, high returns in emerging markets relative to those in industrial countries put pressure on some institutional investors, who face short-term performance goals, to enter these markets. The dollar return on equity investments in emerging markets reached 80 percent in 1993, ten times higher than the 8 percent return on U.S. equities and almost three times the gain in other industrial country stock markets (Table 20). In 1990–92, emerging market equity returns only matched those of the U.S. stock market after a strong relative performance in 1989. In addition, the equities in a number of emerging markets have price-earnings and price-book value ratios that are low in relation to the rest of the world (Table A12); and although a great deal of caution is needed in interpreting these indicators, these may lead investors to view emerging markets equities as undervalued. The average return for equities in all emerging markets, however, masks the strong variation in returns across countries as well as the volatility over time of returns in each country (Table 20). Similar to the returns on emerging market equity, the total return on Latin American bonds rose from about 10 percent in 1992 to 18 percent in 1993.[10] Total returns on bonds appear to show a much greater degree of stability than emerging market equity returns.

---

[5]Information provided by Morningstar and is based on its data base of about 3,500 U.S. open-end mutual funds. These data exclude closed-end funds. Information for before 1993 is not available.

[6]See *Pensions and Investments*, January 24, 1994, p. 17.

[7]Kleiman International Consultants (1993).

[8]Board of Governors of the Federal Reserve System (1993). The information on mutual funds includes open-end and closed-end funds and money market mutual funds.

[9]Chuhan (1994).

---

[10]J.P. Morgan, Latin American Eurobond Index.

Table 20. Total Return on Equity in Selected Emerging Markets

(In percent)

	1989	1990	1991	1992	1993
IFC composite	61.5	−2.2	39.5	3.3	79.2
Latin America	76.2	9.1	139.2	3.4	60.2
Of which:					
Argentina	204.4	−42.5	444.9	−25.7	76.7
Brazil	23.0	−69.5	285.1	1.0	94.2
Mexico	129.8	27.2	113.9	16.7	54.8
Venezuela	—	—	56.9	−50.7	50.7
Asia	54.1	−19.2	12.4	18.5	97.6
Of which:					
China	...	...	...	...	49.8
India	...	...	...	...	26.0
Malaysia	47.4	−9.4	10.3	24.1	110.0
Thailand	105.8	−24.4	20.6	38.5	114.0
Europe, Middle East, and Africa	75.8	13.9	−29.2	−32.7	122.4
Of which:					
Turkey	...	2.5	−45.8	−50.7	230.7
United States S&P 500	31.6	−3.1	30.4	7.6	7.5
Europe, Australia, and Far East	10.8	−23.2	12.5	−11.9	30.5

Source: International Finance Corporation.

The high rate of return compensates the investors for the fact that the returns on emerging markets equities have been considerably more volatile than those in industrial countries. Investors may also be attracted by diversification arguments since returns in emerging markets tend to be relatively uncorrelated with returns in developed countries.[11]

Institutional Issues

The investment decisions of insurance companies and pension funds in industrial countries are also affected by a variety of prudential limits on their ability to invest in foreign assets. Nonetheless, it is important to stress that these constraints do not appear to have been binding so far for most of these institutional investors. A recent World Bank study reviewed these restrictions in five major industrial countries and found the intensity of these restrictions varied across countries and differed for insurance companies as opposed to pension funds.[12] Of these five countries, Germany imposes the strictest limits on both insurance companies and pension funds, setting a maximum portfolio share of 5 percent for foreign investments and prohibiting net exposure in any foreign currency (Table A13). In the other four countries, pension funds are treated differently from the insurance companies. In the United States, private pension funds are free from mandatory ceilings on holdings of foreign assets, but are subject to a "prudent man" rule and review by their boards or shareholders.[13] Public pension funds in the United States are often subject to binding limits. In the United Kingdom, there are no limits, while in Japan there is a limit of 30 percent. Canada sets a ceiling that will reach 20 percent in 1994 on the foreign asset share of pension funds. Insurance companies in Canada, Japan, and the United Kingdom are free from any mandatory ceilings on their holdings of foreign assets, while the ceilings in the United States are set by state insurance regulators. Not surprisingly, insurance companies and pension funds in all five countries must meet certain minimum standards on the credit quality of their assets, which are often self-imposed, and in several countries these funds are subject to a prudent man rule.

The expansion of the investor base for emerging markets assets has been facilitated by the development of an infrastructure of the market. In recent years, many emerging market countries have improved the information that is available about their markets and have established investor safeguards, such as tougher laws against insider trading. Nonetheless, investments in these markets are affected by the host country's macroeconomic policies as well as its regulations, taxes and settlement, and custodial procedures. As a result, pension funds and insurance companies tend to rely on specialized fund managers to select investments in emerging markets. Almost four fifths of the U.S. pension funds decide on an allocation for international investments and let a specialized manager place these funds as they see fit among non-U.S. investments.[14]

One common way to invest in emerging markets is to purchase shares in a country fund, a mutual fund that invests in a variety of emerging markets or in just a single country. The first country fund—the Mexico Fund—was launched in 1981, and by the end of 1993 there were nearly 500 country funds listed in a number of major financial centers. There is a wide variety of country funds, ranging from global funds that may invest in any emerging market, to funds dedicated to a specific region, to funds that specialize in a single country. Country funds require relatively low minimum investment and offer more liquidity than directly investing in the

---

[11]International Finance Corporation (1994).
[12]Chuhan (1994).

[13]Under this type of rule, a regulator requires a pension fund or an insurance company to exercise prudence—which is not defined precisely—in their investment decisions.
[14]*Pensions and Investments*, January 24, 1994.

local market of the developing country, because the funds are traded in major financial markets. Also, a number of emerging market countries restrict portfolio capital inflows, and country funds may be the only vehicle for investing in such countries. Multi-country funds lower the cost of diversifying across emerging markets.

Many country funds are closed-end mutual funds in which a fixed number of shares are issued and shares may be sold only if another investor is willing to buy them, meaning that there are no net redemptions on the fund. In 1993, these funds invested $4 billion in emerging markets, bringing the combined portfolio of all emerging market closed-end funds to $33 billion at the end of 1993 (Table A14). The structure of a single-country closed-end fund protects the country from sudden swings in capital flows, because the shares invested in the country remain relatively stable. This also frees the fund from the risk of large net redemptions, allowing the manager to invest in less liquid assets. With a fixed number of shares, the market price of the share may trade at a discount or a premium from the net asset value of the fund, which is the total value of the assets divided by the number of shares. A discount or premium can persist for several reasons, including restrictions on the access of nonresidents to domestic capital markets of the issuing countries. At the end of 1993, closed-end equity funds on average had a discount of 11 percent.

Depository receipts are another instrument that facilitates investment in emerging markets. These instruments offer several advantages: they are denominated in and pay interest or dividends in U.S. dollars; settlement occurs in five days in the United States, which may be faster than in the issuer's home market; tax payments on the underlying asset may be simpler, particularly when the host country has a withholding requirement; and the investor avoids global custodian safekeeping charges. Companies from many countries, both developing and industrial, rely on this mechanism to raise capital, and the number of depository receipts currently trading exceeds 900.

There are three levels of depository receipt programs, which differ in the degree of disclosure required.[15] A level I program must obtain an exemption from the SEC's registration and periodic reporting requirements, which allows it to trade these instruments only on the OTC market. This type of program is useful to get investors accus-

tomed to trading in a particular stock, and most depository receipts use a level I program. A level II program is subject to a fairly complete registration and reporting requirement and is used mainly by issuers wishing to sell new shares through ADRs on NASDAQ or an exchange. A level III program requires full compliance with disclosure requirements of the SEC and is for foreign firms issuing new shares through a public offering.

Investors may also purchase a private placement of shares issued by a non-U.S. firm, and this private placement may take place through an ADR program. A private placement may qualify for an exemption from SEC reporting requirements if it meets a certain number of conditions, such as whether the potential investors have access to the kind of information that would be available in a registered public offering and whether they are sufficiently sophisticated. Rule 144a was adopted in 1990 to make securities privately placed under this exemption more liquid. Rule 144a permits holders of these securities to sell them freely to qualified institutional buyers (QIBs) under certain conditions without being subject to the two-year minimum holding period. Rule 144a does not apply to securities that are of the same class as "listed securities," that is, securities that are listed on NASDAQ or an exchange. Although not necessarily required by U.S. securities law, non-U.S. companies selling newly issued stock or debt securities under Rule 144a have typically prepared extensive placement memoranda or offering circulars, and the amount of disclosure contained in such material is not much less than that required for complete disclosure under the U.S. Securities Act.

Assessment and Pricing of Risk

The nature of the credit risk associated with developing country debt instruments makes risk assessment and pricing more complex than for bonds issued in industrial countries. The likelihood of repayment for a developing country sovereign bond issue is affected by the country's macroeconomic policies and in particular by the government's ability to service its debt obligations. The political situation also matters because of its impact on a country's ability to sustain sound fiscal and other economic policies. Other factors also count, such as the market for the product of the issuer, the financial structure of the issuer, and the domestic legal and regulatory environment of the issuer. These factors are of course relevant for assessing risk more generally. But the recent wide-ranging structural changes in a number of these countries diminish the value of historical information about an issuer. Also, transfer risk—the possibility of restrictions on a corporation's access to foreign

---

[15]There are also unsponsored depository receipts, but these are now obsolete. This discussion of depository receipts and private placements is based on Bank of New York (1993) and Quale (1993).

exchange—can be important for many developing country bonds. Because the bond market for developing countries has expanded so quickly, investors, especially those who entered the market in 1993, are still learning to understand the available information. Likewise, many corporate issuers are new to the market and are just becoming acquainted with the needs of their investor base.

The market measures the degree of risk of a particular bond in terms of the spread over the comparable U.S. Treasury obligations—that is, the difference between the yields to maturity on the bond and on the U.S. Treasury instrument with the same maturity.[16] Bond issues are sold initially at a particular spread, which may subsequently change over time through secondary market transactions. Because of the complexities associated with processing and evaluating the information, the market looks for certain benchmarks and arrives at a spread through a process of trial and error. Mexico, as the first debt-restructuring country to regain access to voluntary financing in recent years, has come to serve as the benchmark for measuring the risk of new sovereign debt issues from other developing countries in Latin America and in other regions, particularly for those with subinvestment grade ratings. In 1989, Mexico placed a bond at a spread of about 800 basis points over the comparable U.S. Treasury instrument. Mexico's economic performance improved steadily since 1989, and over time the market was willing to accept a larger stock of Mexican sovereign bonds at spreads that declined to around 200 basis points by late 1993.

Some analysts suggest that investors evaluate developing country bonds by reference to U.S. corporate bonds with comparable credit ratings. According to Moody's Investor Service, a U.S. Aaa corporate bond trades at a yield to maturity about 60 basis points above the yield on a long-term U.S. Treasury instrument, although this spread has at times reached 100 basis points.[17] A U.S. Baa corporate bond—the lowest investment grade category—pays a spread of about 75 basis points above the Aaa bond, or 135 basis points above long-term U.S. Treasury instruments. Like the spreads on developing country bonds, these spreads are determined by market forces. But because the U.S. corporate bond market is stable and established, bond investors have access to financial information about the borrower that meets the investors' standards, and the spreads can more accurately reflect the costs

associated with delinquent payments or outright defaults. Bond default rates for different classes of U.S. borrowers are known by the market. It has been estimated, for example, that AAA bonds experienced a default rate of 0.21 percent in the ten years after issuance, while the ten-year default rate for the lowest investment grade bonds was 2.1 percent. Default was much more common in subinvestment grade issues, with 10.7 percent of BB bonds and 30.9 percent of B bonds defaulting in the ten years after issuance.[18]

In January, the market was anticipating that Standard and Poor's would upgrade Mexico from the highest subinvestment grade rating, which for a U.S. corporate bond reportedly trades at a spread of about 200 basis points, to the lowest investment grade rating, which in the U.S. market would trade at a spread of about 130 basis points. As a result, the spread on Mexican sovereign issues fell to about 150 basis points, before the current market correction pushed the spread back up to about 200 basis points.

Argentina's debt trades at a spread about 50 to 100 basis points above Mexico's. Argentina is perceived as having made substantial progress in controlling inflation and implementing structural reforms, but is regarded as being at an earlier stage in the reform process and as having not yet resolved doubts about its external competitiveness. The market clearly regards both Brazil and Venezuela as much greater risks, and these countries' bonds trade at spreads of about 200 to 300 basis points above Mexico's. With regard to Eastern Europe, bonds of the Czech Republic currently obtain spreads below Mexico's, mainly because of the Czech Republic's investment grade rating, while Hungary's spread has risen above Mexico's because of the former's high and increasing external debt. China's $1 billion global bond issue was priced at a spread of about 80 basis points, in part because China received an investment grade rating and has relatively little external debt compared with Mexico and other countries.

Since 1989, Mexico has consistently paid the lowest spread of the major Latin American borrowers; the spread fell to below 200 basis points after NAFTA was approved in November 1993. The spread on Argentine bonds peaked at over 400 basis points in early 1993, but has hovered around 300 basis points since the completion of its bank debt restructuring in April 1993. The spread on Venezuelan bond issues has been the most volatile, rising from less than Argentina's spread in early 1992 to more than Brazil's spread of about 500 basis

---

[16]A U.S. dollar interest rate is presented here for illustrative purposes. For bonds denominated in other currencies, the appropriate comparison would be with a government instrument denominated in the same currency.

[17]*Moody's Bond Survey*, March 7, 1994, p. 6838.

[18]Altman (1989).

Chart 9. Yield Spreads at Launch for Selected Developing Countries[1]

(In basis points)

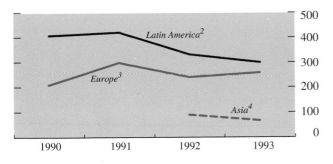

Sources: *International Financing Review* and *Financial Times*.

[1]Yield spread measured as the difference between the bond yield of U.S. dollar-denominated bonds and the corresponding U.S. Treasury security. Figures are weighted averages for sovereign and other public issuers.

[2]Argentina, Brazil, Mexico, and Venezuela.

[3]Czech Republic, Hungary, and Turkey.

[4]Korea, Malaysia, and Thailand.

points by mid-1993. Brazilian bonds have generally paid the highest spread in Latin America.

The bonds of many countries that avoided debt restructurings in the 1980s generally have paid lower spreads compared with the Latin American borrowers other than Mexico (Chart 9). Korea has consistently paid a spread of less than 100 basis points. Turkey's spread was 250 basis points at the end of 1993, but fluctuated considerably in early 1994, reaching 900 basis points. In the wake of the uncertainties surrounding the dissolution of Czechoslovakia, spreads on the bond of the Czech

Republic reached almost 500 basis points in late 1992, even though its external debt was relatively low, but its spreads have fallen sharply since then to about 150 basis points.

These spreads are linked to the secondary market prices for Brady bonds and other bank claims on developing countries. The market arbitrages away differences between the yields to maturities on new issue and Brady bonds, but the arbitrage possibilities are often complicated by the different characteristics of these two types of instruments. For example, Brady bonds are typically collateralized, while new issues usually carry no collateral and instead may feature different types of credit enhancements, such as put options. Brady bonds also have much longer maturities than the new issues. Some market participants use Mexico and other countries that have completed Brady operations as a benchmark for setting the price of claims on countries (such as Peru and Russia) still to complete bank debt restructurings.

Sovereign bond issues in each country serve as a benchmark for the bond issues by other borrowers in that country. Mexico pursued a deliberate strategy of issuing sovereign bonds at different points along the yield curve to facilitate the pricing of bonds issued by Mexican public and private enterprises.[19] In 1990, private bond issues paid spreads of 400 to 500 basis points above sovereigns, but by 1993, this margin had come down to 100 to 150 basis points.

---

[19]This strategy is explained in more detail in Loser and Kalter (1992) and Collyns and others (1993), Section V.

Annex V

Role of Capital Markets in Financing Chinese Enterprises

The development of securities markets in China has become one of the most visible aspects of that country's 15-year reform program. Drawn by the lure of double-digit growth rates in the most populous country in the world, foreign firms and investors rushed to establish a presence in China. Foreign direct investment commitments soared to $100 million in 1993, while portfolio investors responded eagerly to opportunities to invest in mainland Chinese firms. Equity placements on the Stock Exchange of Hong Kong (SEHK) amounted to $1.1 billion in 1993. International bond issuance increased to $2.9 billion, compared with $1.3 billion in 1992 and only $0.4 billion between 1989 and 1991. Demand for securities issued by Chinese enterprises was even stronger within China as individual Chinese, once given opportunities to invest in assets whose returns were market determined, proved eager to do so.

This annex examines the development of Chinese securities markets from their beginnings in the early 1980s. The Chinese approach to reform in the financial sector, as in other sectors, has been one of cautious experimentation, gradual relaxation of control, and decentralization of responsibility. Recently, however, it became necessary to retrench temporarily as the pace and direction of recent market activity exceeded the authorities' intentions.[1]

Development of Securities Markets in China

Although government bonds had been issued between 1952 and 1958, the systematic development of a *bond market* in China began in the early 1980s, when the Central Government recognized that an alternative to central bank financing would be needed to minimize the inflationary consequences of budget deficits. In 1981, the Government issued Y 4.9 billion in ten-year Treasury bonds (Table 21). These were allocated to state-owned enterprises, collectives, and local governments, which then passed them on to individuals through compulsory subscriptions.

In 1985, issuing privileges were extended to financial institutions as a means of supplementing the funds provided by the Ministry of Finance. These bonds were issued in shorter maturities—between one and five years—and with higher interest rates than those on Treasury bonds. Subscription to these bonds was usually voluntary, although local governments occasionally resorted to forced allocation methods similar to those employed to distribute Treasury bonds. From the mid-1980s, the range of bonds broadened, as different types of bonds were introduced—each issued by a different group of institutions and often targeted to different investors—to finance particular kinds of activities. In 1988, the first bonds issued directly by the Ministry of Finance and placed with financial institutions appeared.

The issuance of corporate bonds progressed much more slowly than that of government bonds and financial bonds. As a result of the financial reforms introduced in the early 1980s, it became more difficult for enterprises, particularly those outside the state sector, to obtain bank financing for investment or for working capital. Approval for enterprise bond issues was first made in 1982 on a very limited basis. Initially, the enterprise bond market was only loosely regulated, a situation that allowed enterprises to promise interest rates much higher than those paid on bank deposits. This led to a drain of resources away from the banks and caused the People's Bank of China (PBOC) to respond with regulations in 1986; these required that enterprise bonds be approved by the PBOC, subject to an overall quota and a 15 percent ceiling on their interest rates. Enterprise bonds had relatively short maturities of two or three years and were usually issued to the enterprise's employees—often by forced subscription—and were nontransferable.

Through the mid-1980s, as inflationary pressures built up, resistance to the forced allocation of Treasury bonds with negative real interest rates grew, particularly since some nongovernment issuers, especially enterprises, greatly increased the interest rates they paid on their bonds. Consequently, the Ministry of Finance was induced gradually to reduce the maturity of Treasury bonds, first to five years in 1985 and then to three years in 1988, and to

---

[1]See Bell and others (1993).

92

Table 21. Issues of Securities in China

(In billions of Chinese yuan)

	1981	1982	1983	1984	1985	1986	1987	1988	1989	1990	1991	Total
State bonds	4.866	4.383	4.158	4.253	6.061	6.251	11.787	18.888	18.725	23.416	28.000	130.788
Treasury bonds	4.866	4.383	4.158	4.253	6.061	6.251	6.287	9.216	5.612	9.328	19.900	80.315
Ministry of Finance notes	—	—	—	—	—	—	—	6.607	—	7.109	6.500	20.216
Construction bonds	—	—	—	—	—	—	—	3.065	—	—	—	3.065
Key construction bonds	—	—	—	—	—	—	5.500	—	—	—	—	5.500
Special bonds	—	—	—	—	—	—	—	—	4.370	3.239	1.600	9.209
"Inflation-proof" bonds	—	—	—	—	—	—	—	—	8.743	3.740	—	12.483
Financial institution bonds	—	—	—	—	0.500	3.000	9.000	15.500	8.319	7.055	16.420	59.794
State investment bonds	—	—	—	—	—	—	—	—	—	—	9.500	9.500
Financial bonds	—	—	—	—	0.500	3.000	6.000	6.500	6.066	6.440	6.691	35.197
Capital construction bonds	—	—	—	—	—	—	—	8.000	1.459	—	0.002	9.461
Key enterprise bonds	—	—	—	—	—	—	3.000	1.000	0.794	0.615	0.227	5.636
Enterprise bonds	—	—	—	—	—	10.000	3.000	7.541	7.526	12.637	24.996	65.700
Local enterprise bonds[1]	—	—	—	—	—	10.000	3.000	3.000	1.483	4.933	11.525	33.941
Short-term borrowing certificates	—	—	—	—	—	—	—	1.172	2.972	5.015	10.444	19.603
Interenterprise bonds	—	—	—	—	—	—	—	3.369	3.071	2.689	3.027	12.156
Certificates of deposit	—	—	—	—	—	—	—	5.926	14.180	50.353	42.685	113.144
Stocks[1]	—	—	—	—	—	—	1.000	2.500	0.662	0.428	2.952	7.542
Total	4.866	4.383	4.158	4.253	6.561	19.251	24.787	50.355	49.412	93.889	115.053	376.968

Sources: Data provided by the Chinese authorities; *Almanac of China's Finance and Banking* (Beijing: China Financial Publishing House, 1992); Chen (1991); and IMF staff estimates.

[1]Data for earliest entry include all previous issues.

increase the interest rates (Table A15).[2] Even in 1985 however, these rates still compared unfavorably to the rates paid on bank deposits.

As a result of the widening of bond issuing privileges, the amount of bonds issued each year rose substantially after 1985 (see Table 21). However, Treasury bonds became a smaller proportion of total issues as they were supplanted by bonds issued by financial institutions and enterprises, in particular certificates of deposit. That being said, enterprise bonds still amounted to only 15 percent of total securities issued up to the end of 1990 (or 11 percent of the outstanding stock at year-end).

Chinese *equity markets* also have their roots in the reforms initiated in 1979. As part of the Government's policy of financial decentralization, enterprises were given limited permission to issue shares. These securities had several unusual characteristics. For one thing, they frequently offered a guaranteed minimum annual rate of return. In principle, this return would consist of some fixed rate plus a share of the firm's profits. However, in practice, most enterprises simply promised the maximum allowable rate of return and in some cases were able to provide much greater returns. During

1985–86, returns of 20–40 percent a year (four to six times the annual rates of interest on bank deposits or government bonds) were common, and in 1988 some enterprise equities earned 50–100 percent. A second characteristic of shares in the earlier years was that they carried a maturity date, usually between one and five years, and their holders frequently had the option of early redemption. Finally, enterprise shares generally carried no ownership rights.[3] Consequently, these securities were more like bonds or preference shares with an embedded redemption option than straight equities. A further complicating factor was that in many cases shares, like bonds, gave investors special advantages such as priority in obtaining enterprise-provided housing or health care.

Central control over the equity market was first exerted in 1984 when the Central Government approved share issues on an experimental basis in five cities. In the same year, the municipal government in Shanghai—which was not one of the approved cities—permitted state-owned enterprises to issue shares. This made it easier for state-owned enterprises in these locations to issue equity, and as credit was tightened in late 1984 and in 1985, this became a more common means of raising capital.

[2]The ten-year bonds issued prior to 1985 actually had an effective maturity of seven and one half years, since the maturity date of a certificate was determined by lottery, with 20 percent of each issue maturing in each year after the fifth year following issue.

[3]Although in some cases, the purchase of a certain large number of shares gave the investor the right to nominate a member of the board of directors.

Table 22. Transactions in Debt Securities in China

(In billions of Chinese yuan)

	1987	1988	1989	1990	1991	Total
State bonds	—	2.421	2.129	11.594	37.017	53.161
Treasury bonds	—	2.383	2.094	10.489	33.955	48.921
Ministry of Finance notes	—	—	—	—	—	—
Construction bonds	—	—	0.018	0.005	—	0.023
Key construction bonds	—	0.038	0.017	0.010	0.029	0.094
Special state bonds	—	—	—	—	—	—
"Inflation-proof" bonds	—	—	—	1.090	3.033	4.123
Financial institution bonds	0.012	0.070	0.063	0.097	1.213	1.455
State investment bonds	—	—	0.009	0.026	0.216	0.251
Financial bonds	0.012	0.070	0.046	0.046	0.781	0.955
Capital construction bonds	—	—	0.006	0.025	0.216	0.247
Key enterprise bonds	—	—	0.002	—	—	0.002
Enterprise bonds	0.092	0.116	0.085	0.140	3.177	3.610
Local enterprise bonds	0.092	0.116	0.079	0.106	2.163	2.556
Short-term borrowing certificates	—	—	0.006	0.034	1.014	1.054
Certificates of deposit	—	0.013	0.012	0.042	0.102	0.169
Total	0.104	2.620	2.289	11.873	41.509	58.395

Source: *Almanac of China's Finance and Banking* (Beijing: China Financial Publishing House, 1992).

Most shares, even those issued publicly rather than placed privately, were purchased by state and collective enterprises. Hence, effective state ownership was maintained.

Secondary markets for debt and equity developed slowly. In the early 1980s, all securities were officially nontransferable. After 1985, Treasury bonds could be discounted at the PBOC or used as collateral for loans. However, since these bonds were unattractive as investment vehicles, a thriving illegal market soon developed in which individuals who had been forced to purchase bonds sought to sell them. Since bonds held by individuals were in bearer form, speculators could purchase them at steep discounts, hold them to maturity, and then redeem them for substantial profits. Similarly, early enterprise bonds were mostly nontransferable; however, some issues included a tranche that was made available to individuals on a voluntary basis, and these were transferable.

Officially sanctioned securities trading did not begin until August 1986, when a secondary market was established on an experimental basis in Shenyang. This was an OTC market in which two corporate bonds were available for trading at prices determined on a daily basis by the authorities. However, the market was quite illiquid because of the lack of supply. Since enterprise bonds, like equities, offered fringe benefits to investors, there was little incentive to sell them once they were acquired.

An official market in government debt securities was established on a trial basis in seven cities in April 1988. This experiment proved so successful that it was extended to more than 60 cities by June 1988 and the range of securities eligible for trading was expanded to include key construction bonds, enterprise and financial bonds, shares, commercial paper, and certificates of deposit. Turnover of Treasury bonds in 1988 was Y 2.4 billion (Table 22). The legitimization of trading led to the creation of a number of securities companies and a renewed drive to recognize securities markets throughout the country. However, the events of June 1989 resulted in a temporary freeze on securities market development. It was not until late in 1990 that the central authorities resumed their experimentation with securities, and it was only in March 1991 that securities trading was legalized throughout the country.

Although the authorities had allowed secondary markets for government securities to be established, they had not allowed a truly national market to develop. While individuals were free to trade eligible bonds in any one of these cities, they were not permitted to transfer bonds from one trading center to another until October 1990.[4] As a result of different market conditions around the country, large differences in prices for the same issues developed. A comparison of the market prices of the five-year Treasury bonds issued in June 1986 in the ten most active trading centers during 1990 reveals that the yields to maturity differed greatly between these trading centers. The difference between the highest and lowest yields ranged from a low of 221 basis points in April to a high of 716 in December.

Official secondary markets for equity also took form in 1986. In September 1986, the Shanghai branch of the Industrial and Commercial Bank of China (ICBC) opened a securities trading counter

---

[4]Bi (1993).

and offered to buy and sell enterprise shares at transaction prices set each day by the municipal government. However, there were practically no sellers. In 1987, when six equities with a total value of Y 60 million were available, turnover reached only Y 6 million.[5] By the end of 1988, there were 33 trading centers in Shanghai, trading seven enterprise shares and eight bonds. Turnover in that year was Y 535 million, although equity trading was only Y 11 million. Even in 1989, when total turnover reached Y 803 million, equity trading was still only a small share. In late 1990, the Central Government decided that it would extend the stock market experiment throughout the country, not by giving approval for a large number of exchanges to open, but by concentrating activity in a small number of centers and by providing investors around the country with access to that market. The first recognized stock market was in Shanghai, where the exchange opened officially on December 19, 1990 with seven equities, five state bonds, eight enterprise bonds, and nine financial bonds. The total value of equity issued by these seven enterprises amounted to Y 235.9 million, of which the state share was Y 156.5 million, institutions held Y 16.3 million, and individuals held Y 63.1 million. Only the last amount was available for trading on the exchange. Combined turnover in bonds and equity in Shanghai reached Y 2.7 billion in 1990.

The Shenzhen Securities Market began operations with the initial public equity offering in April 1987 of the Shenzhen Development Bank (SDB). Following official approval for securities trading in 1988, an OTC market for SDB shares emerged in Shenzhen. Turnover of both bonds and equity was only Y 4 million in 1988. By 1989, four more enterprises had issued shares and two more brokerage firms had opened up. Interest in securities waned as a result of an increase in deposit interest rates and a 20 percent tax on securities trading imposed by the Shenzhen government. However, later in that year, the SDB reported unusually strong profits and paid a dividend of Y 10 per share, which raised great public interest in equities. Turnover in equities in Shenzhen in 1989 was Y 23 million, and in 1990, with the addition of more issues, turnover jumped to Y 1.8 billion. The official OTC market could not handle the sudden increase in volume, and a large curb market emerged. In response to this, the municipal government opened a centralized trading center, which began trading in equities on December 1, 1990. The Shenzhen Stock Exchange did not receive official recognition until April 14, 1991 and opened officially on July 3, 1991 with five enterprises listed. These five enterprises had issued

Y 270 million of equity, of which only Y 91.7 million was held by individuals and therefore available for trading.

At the end of 1991, there were 9 stocks and 28 bonds listed on the Shanghai exchange, with a total capitalization of Y 2.9 billion. The Shenzhen exchange had 6 stocks listed, with a capitalized value of Y 7.4 billion. Despite liquidity problems and high volatility, the market continued to grow in terms of issues and capitalization through 1993. At the end of the year, there were 183 issues of both A and B shares listed on the two exchanges with a combined value of Y 347.4 billion ($39.9 billion).[6] New issues of shares reached Y 644 million in 1991, Y 7.15 billion in 1992, and Y 29.5 billion in 1993. Turnover in both classes of shares was Y 331.9 billion ($38.5 billion) in 1993, most of which was in A shares, despite a decline in turnover during the middle two quarters. During most of the year liquidity in the B share market was extremely low. At the end of February 1994, there were 234 companies listed—including 45 B shares—with a combined capitalization of Y 416.7 billion.

Steps toward the creation of a national securities trading network came with the introduction of the Securities Trading Automated Quotation System (STAQS).[7] The STAQS came on line on December 5, 1990, and provided a satellite computer link for 17 securities companies in six cities. STAQS provides on-screen pricing information and a centralized clearing and settlement system and is unique among securities markets in China in that it adopted the market-maker trading structure. At the end of 1991, the five circulating Treasury bonds—those issued between 1986 and 1990—were listed on STAQS. STAQS helped to narrow but did not eliminate the price differences between the regions. Also in 1990, Treasury bonds were listed on the Shanghai Securities Exchange (SSE).[8] In October 1993, turnover in the five-year 1992 bond on STAQS was Y 133 million, while trading in Wuhan, the most important regional trading center, amounted to Y 22.4 million, and turnover in SSE was Y 19.9 million.

Recently, a system similar to the STAQS has been established under the auspices of the PBOC and with the support of the specialized banks and the three national securities companies. The

---

[5]Data on trading activity in Shanghai and Shenzhen prior to 1991 are from Hu (1993), Chapter 3.

[6]Data from International Finance Corporation (1994). The distinction between A shares (which are reserved for mainland Chinese investors) and B shares (which are reserved for non-Chinese investors) is discussed below.

[7]In September 1990, the PBOC headquarters set up a Quotation Center for government securities, which provided on-line pricing information to securities dealers. However, it never provided a trading facility and has subsequently been overtaken by the STAQS.

[8]Renamed the Shanghai Stock Exchange in October 1993.

National Electronic Trading System (NETS) was officially opened in June 1993 to provide a nationwide electronic trading system for stocks and bonds. Trading is based on an order-driven, book-entry system in which orders are relayed through a network of more than 100 satellite-linked ground stations. At present no bonds are traded, only institutional shares, in which the market is relatively illiquid.

The development of a secondary bond market and particularly the creation of the STAQS system, which allowed for the issuance of bonds on a paperless, book-entry basis, facilitated an increase in government bond issues. In 1991, Treasury bond issuance doubled to Y 19.9 billion, compared with Y 9.3 billion in 1990. The 1991 Treasury bond issue is important because it represented the first attempt to distribute government debt to individuals through voluntary purchases. A syndicate of 70 financial institutions was appointed to market Y 2.5 billion of the planned Y 10 billion amount to be issued to households.[9] The bond issue was successful and the syndication method was repeated in 1992 when a total of Y 40 billion was issued.

The government bond market suffered a setback in 1993 as a result of the availability of more attractive returns in other markets—particularly the equity market. In March, the Ministry of Finance decided to issue, by voluntary subscription through a syndicate of 91 financial institutions, Y 30 billion in three- and five-year Treasury bonds, at interest rates of 10 percent and 12.52 percent, respectively. However, by the end of the subscription period in April, only about Y 4 billion of the issue had been taken up, and by the end of May only Y 8.3 billion had been sold. Investors were increasingly drawn to the equity markets (in which capital gains were much higher than bond yields), to financial and enterprise bonds issued by local governments and nonbank financial institutions, and to deposits, all of which paid much higher rates of interest. As a result, the Ministry of Finance raised the interest rates and offered holders of the five-year bond the option to cash in after only three years (Table A15). Still, demand did not increase sufficiently, and the Government was forced to return to forced subscriptions. Regional and local governments were assigned quotas of bond subscriptions and were told that new equity issues would not be approved until they met their quota. Employees of state enterprises and government offices were then forced to purchase bonds (Y 5 billion) as were employees in private enterprises (Y 3 billion); institutional

holders of maturing Treasury bonds were forced to roll them over into the new issue (Y 16 billion).

In 1993, the PBOC issued short-term financing bills for the first time. Another innovation in the domestic bond market in 1993 was the issue of bonds denominated in foreign currency. In June, the National Metallurgical Import and Export Company issued $40 million in one- and two-year bonds. In July, the China Investment Bank issued $50 million in one-year bonds. In the same month, the Ministry of Finance announced the adoption of a primary dealer system, to which 19 institutions—including only one bank—had been appointed. These dealers would be required to make a market in Treasury bonds.

For 1994, the Government has announced plans to sell about Y 100 billion in bonds with maturities between six months and ten years. Sales of long-term bonds—eight and ten years—are for the first time to be conducted through auctions. About Y 15 billion in short-term bonds—with maturities of less than one year—were sold through a syndicate of 35 financial institutions led by the ICBC by March 1994. Two-year bonds carry a 13 percent coupon, while the three-year bonds carry a rate of 14 percent—the three-year deposit rate plus 1 percent—which exceeds the forecast 10 percent inflation rate. Despite the fact that these yields are below the actual urban inflation rate, sales of Treasury bonds have been brisk. The target volume of two-year bond sales was actually met ahead of schedule.

Futures exchanges were first officially recognized in 1992 in Shenzhen. Since then, at least 30 recognized commodities futures exchanges have been established. Financial futures have also been introduced. In January 1993, the SSE listed its first futures contracts on government bonds, but the market was limited to the members of the exchange. In October participation was opened up to anyone, and turnover increased greatly to a daily average of Y 30 million.[10] However, bond futures are also traded on the Beijing Commodity Exchange, where turnover is reportedly much higher.

Recent Developments in External Financing

China's access to international bond and equity markets increased markedly in 1993, emulating the recent experience of many other developing countries. The supply of resources has shifted from commercial banks to the securities markets. Commercial banks' lending to developing countries has been constrained in some countries by capital weak-

[9]The interest rate was set at 1.5 percentage points above the deposit rate. Interestingly, the same year's Y 2 billion Ministry of Finance note issue was distributed through forced allocations.

[10]Bond futures were listed on the Shenzhen exchange in March 1994.

ness arising from losses on loans to other groups of borrowers, slow growth in deposits, and the capital constraints imposed by the implementation of the Basle capital adequacy guidelines.[11] As a consequence, banks have generally become more interested in loans that have lower capital requirements (such as short-term credits and officially guaranteed or structured lending) and in fee-generating, off-balance sheet business, such as underwriting the issuance of bonds. Moreover, some market participants noted that some banks had by the end of 1992 reached their internal limits on credit exposure to Chinese borrowers.

This combination of factors has been reflected in increased interest rates and shorter maturities on bank loans to China. Interest rate spreads appear to have increased by some 25–50 basis points during 1991–93 to around a yield of LIBOR plus 95 basis points. At the same time, average maturities in 1993 fell to 5 years, from 5.8 years in 1992 and over 10 years in 1991.

Bond Financing

China first issued a foreign bond in 1982 and was quite active up to 1989. In 1987 and 1988, various International Trust and Investment Corporations (ITICs) and banks raised $2.3 billion, with placements denominated in deutsche mark, yen, and dollars. The terms were in fact better than those achieved recently by Chinese issuers: interest rates were near LIBOR and maturities were rarely below seven years. Only one bond was issued in 1989, which raised $163 million. No bonds were sold in 1990, and in 1991 China resumed borrowing with two issues worth a combined $273 million. In 1992, activity picked up, with $1.3 billion in new bond issues (Table A16). At the end of 1992, international bond placements stood at about $6 billion and constituted approximately 10 percent of China's total external medium- and long-term debt, a ratio that has remained relatively constant over the recent past.[12] However, in 1993 China stepped up its external financing from the international bond markets, placing close to $3.0 billion.

Prior to 1993, China's borrowing from international bond markets was undertaken exclusively by the so-called ten windows, which consist of the

ITICs and certain financial institutions. The ten windows' monopoly of the issuance of bonds in the international markets has been led by the China International Trust and Investment Corporation (CITIC) (25 percent of total Chinese bond issuance in 1992–93) and the Bank of China (BOC) (17 percent).[13] The ten windows act as intermediaries, borrowing abroad with the advantage of an (implicit) government guarantee and then on-lending to domestic borrowers. Authorization for even these public sector institutions to borrow has been stringently regulated by the State Administration of Exchange Control (SAEC)—China's debt management supervisor.

In order to prevent lenders in the market becoming overexposed to the same borrowers—and therefore increasingly reluctant to lend—the ten windows have attempted to diversify their investor base since China's re-entry into the market in 1992. Although most borrowing has previously been concentrated in the Japanese domestic market—73 percent in 1992 and 43 percent in 1993—reflecting the familiarity of those investors with the Chinese market, the investor base has been diversified through re-entry into several major international bond markets.

The ten windows system has been recognized by the authorities as being limited, since the repetitive use of borrowers may eventually reach the limit of investor demand. Moreover, the balance sheets of the ten windows, in many cases, are in poorer condition than those of some of the enterprises seeking to access the international capital markets, and the ten windows' on-lending to domestic enterprises has reportedly been inefficient. In addition, as the number of bond issues multiplies, the case-by-case approval by the SAEC has also become cumbersome.

Meanwhile, nonstate enterprises have reportedly placed unauthorized issues privately with regional investors, especially in Hong Kong. The volumes are understandably hard to calculate, but the terms are reportedly much less favorable than those for the ten windows. For example, Hong Kong-based Guangdong Enterprises—which reportedly issued the first Chinese bond in the U.S. market not to carry a government guarantee—paid a spread of 300 basis points on its Rule 144a ADR in December 1993.

From 1993, the authorities planned to experiment with a more pragmatic approach, including the necessary first steps to giving enterprises direct access to the international bond markets. Following the lead of many other developing countries, especially

---

[11]For example, Japanese banks have reduced considerably their lending to developing countries. See Goldstein, Folkerts-Landau, and others (1992) for a discussion of the Basle accord and the treatment of exposures to developing countries.

[12]Foreign commercial banks and official (multilateral and bilateral) creditors have been the major source of external borrowing to date. At the end of June 1993, medium- and long-term debt stood at $16.7 billion to banks and $22.3 billion to official creditors, constituting about 25 percent and 34 percent, respectively, of the medium- and long-term debt at mid-1993.

[13]External debt is guaranteed by the ten windows and local governments, and not by the Central Government (except for what it borrows directly).

in Latin America, the Chinese authorities intend increasingly to allow direct access by the enterprises themselves—rather than through the ten intermediaries—and will use sovereign issues to establish benchmarks against which these enterprises' issues can be priced. In this regard, the Government entered the market directly in 1993 and early 1994 after a six-year absence and set three benchmark issues (Table A16).[14] Under the new approach, borrowing entities will be screened by an internal rating agency—ostensibly to provide potential lenders with better information—and then be provided a borrowing quota. To test the new approach, in 1993 CITIC was allowed to borrow up to a fixed limit without requiring case-by-case approval from the SAEC. To date, however, the SAEC has not opened up access to nonpublic enterprises, and at this initial stage access to the international markets continues to remain under the control of the authorities.

The Chinese authorities expect to place more emphasis on bond financing relative to bank financing, in view of the lower interest rates on bonds and the availability of longer maturities, which they believe to be more appropriate for their prospective infrastructure development.[15] The spread over government instruments of comparable maturity for most Chinese issues has been consistently tight, at about 100 basis points. Maturities have averaged 5.7 years and have exceeded the average maturity on uninsured bank credits of five years. Moreover, there is potential for lengthening maturities. For the group of developing country borrowers, average maturities in the bond market for (unenhanced) bonds—7.1 years—exceed those in the credit markets for uninsured credits—4.9 years; furthermore, the range is wider in the bond market.[16] The authorities place a special emphasis on the U.S. market, as they view it as the deepest market and most likely to produce the longest maturities, a fact already established by the recent elongation of maturities in the dollar market, to seven years in November 1992 (People's Construction Bank of China (PCBC)) and to ten years in July 1993 (CITIC).

Equity Financing

The stock markets were transformed in February 1992 with the issues of class B shares in Shanghai and Shenzhen.[17] These shares are reserved for foreign investors; they are denominated in U.S. dollars in Shanghai and in Hong Kong dollars in Shenzhen. In all other respects, they are identical to the class A shares reserved for mainland Chinese investors. The listing of B shares attracted the attention of international investors. The opportunity to invest in Chinese companies and thereby to benefit from the opening up of the Chinese economy proved to be highly attractive. By the end of 1992, 18 issues of B shares had been listed on the two exchanges, compared with 52 issues of A shares. In Shanghai, of the total capitalization (including bonds of Y 55.8 billion at the end of 1992), Y 3.1 billion was in A shares and Y 800 million in B shares. In Shenzhen, the corresponding figures were Y 48.3 billion, Y 2.6 billion, and Y 416 million, respectively. Enthusiasm for investment in Chinese equities was bolstered by the remarkable returns: an index of all Chinese equities—A and B shares combined—gained over 200 percent in the final quarter of 1992 alone, far outstripping returns in all other emerging markets.[18]

By early 1993 international investors apparently began to reconsider their headlong rush into B share investment. There were some reports that these investors were concerned about the adequacy of information disclosure and about the uses to which the funds that had been raised were being put. In addition, it was well known that the Chinese authorities were preparing to list nine enterprises on foreign stock markets where information disclosure requirements were more demanding. By the end of the first quarter of 1993, liquidity in B shares, never very high to begin with, declined, and with it average prices also fell (Chart 10).

The initial euphoria, occasioned by what was for many people the first opportunity to invest in equity since 1949, and the remarkable capital gains recorded in 1992 resulted in a surge of investment in late 1992 and early 1993. Of particular concern to the authorities was the fact that funds were being diverted from the banking sector—often by the banks themselves—into securities and real estate investment through bank-affiliated trust and investment companies and securities companies. The drainage of funds became so serious that shortages of working capital in the state-enterprise sector

---

[14]At this stage, it was also announced that CITIC would no longer borrow on behalf of the Government.

[15]The authorities have viewed official financing to be inflexible as its disbursement is conditional on various criteria—often linked to the use of the resources—despite its concessional terms.

[16]For export credit agency-insured or for cofinanced credits from international financial institutions, the average maturity for credits of 12 years is longer than for bonds, with the average for all loans—7.3 years—approximately equal to the average on unenhanced bonds.

[17]Only equity placements by companies based in China are considered as international equity placements, thus excluding international issues through special purpose vehicles (e.g., Bermuda-based subsidiaries) and secondary share listings. Notable examples of such exclusions are the New York Stock Exchange listings of Brilliance China Automobile (October 1992), China Tire (June 1993), and Ek Chor (July 1993). Other excluded secondary listings include those in Melbourne and Toronto.

[18]IFC Emerging Markets Data Base.

Chart 10. Selected Stock Exchange Indices in China and Hong Kong, 1993–February 1994
(January 2, 1993 = 100)

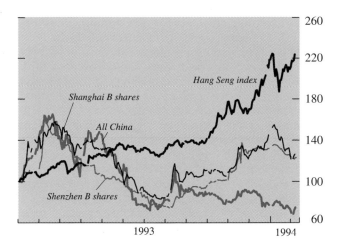

Source: Bloomberg Financial Markets.

became widespread, and funds were unavailable to pay farmers for their crops. The authorities responded in early July with a 16-point austerity program in which banks were ordered to cease their involvement with securities markets and securities companies and to call in loans made for unauthorized investments in real estate and securities.

After a modest increase in the first half of 1993, the overall trend in the A share markets was downward in the second half. This more than offset the increase in B share prices after the authorities stepped in to strengthen regulation in May.[19] As a result of these conflicting effects, at the end of 1993, the composite market index showed only a 7 percent gain over 1992, the worst performance among the emerging markets being followed by the IFC—a marked contrast to 1992. Prices of both A and B shares fell in the first quarter of 1994, resulting in a 20 percent decline in the market index.

Reflecting the problems affecting the B share market and the domestic credit market, many enterprises reverted to unauthorized listings ("backdoor listings") on the SEHK. Backdoor listings are takeovers by Chinese enterprises of publicly quoted Hong Kong companies. The primary incentives for such takeovers were that a Hong Kong listing enabled the enterprise to raise financing through new rights issues and that a Chinese enterprise could halve its effective tax rate by setting up a joint

venture with the overseas-registered entity that it controls.[20] Initially, most backdoor listings were undertaken by well-established and powerful mainland enterprises, such as China Resources, China Travel, China Overseas Land and Investment, and CITIC, which are referred to as "red chips." Market participants have estimated that Chinese companies injected HK$21 billion into Hong Kong during 1991–93 through 29 listings (with a current market capitalization of HK$100 billion or $13.2 billion). The largest are CITIC Pacific (HK$15.4 billion) and Guangdong Investment (HK$1.8 billion), a property developer.

The Hong Kong and Chinese authorities did not initially discourage these practices. However, many other enterprises that followed suit had more muddled accounts without clear title to mainland assets and poor standards of investor disclosure. In many cases, it was not clear if the resources raised from rights issues were eventually used for their intended purpose. There was also concern that enterprise assets were being transferred to the Hong Kong companies to protect the assets from a weakening of the yuan. Moreover, the extent of questionable takeovers— many of which were based on inflated real estate property in China—started to tarnish the reputation of the SEHK and led to unauthorized transfers of assets out of China.

On May 11, 1993, the Hong Kong authorities prohibited unlisted companies from taking control of listed firms in order to obtain an automatic listing. In August, newly listed firms were prohibited from making rights issues for 12 months after obtaining their listing and, in September, the minimum market capitalization for new issuers was increased from HK$50 million to HK$100 million, of which one half has to be in public hands.

The tightening up on backdoor listings in mid-1993 coincided with the listing on the SEHK of shares issued to foreign investors by mainland Chinese enterprises—H shares. On June 19, 1993, representatives of the Hong Kong and Chinese regulatory authorities and stock exchanges signed a Memorandum of Regulatory Cooperation, which paved the way for listings by nine selected Chinese companies after they met its standards for primary listings. The memorandum requires (i) the full, accurate, and immediate disclosure of information relevant to investors; (ii) action to be taken against insider trading; and (iii) the supervision of trading and settlement. Of key concern were a higher standard of disclosure requirements, which were to be cross-checked by international auditors for compli-

[19]An additional push to the B share market was given by the SEC assurance that U.S.-based investment funds could invest in China.

[20]Much of this capital is then recycled back to China in the form of direct investment. However, the extent of the financial linkages is hard to disentangle as Hong Kong maintains no balance of payments statistics.

ance with international accounting standards, and the possibility of recourse to arbitration in Hong Kong, based on Hong Kong legislation, both of which were considered to be the main misgivings of foreign investors concerning the B share market. The initial listings reportedly required hundreds of thousands of hours of work by international accounting firms to construct acceptable financial accounts and to separate the noneconomic activities (schools, hospitals, and so on). Obtaining adequate investor protection also required addendums to the listing firm's rules of incorporation in order to redress inadequacies in China's company laws.

Between July 1993 and May 1994, nine Chinese firms issued H shares in Hong Kong exchange, raising $1.5 billion (Table 23). Reflecting the gradual and experimental role of other reforms, the firms chosen for initial H share listings represented some of the highest-quality Chinese enterprises, mostly companies in heavy industry with good track records, comparatively good management, and high growth potentials.[21]

The Hong Kong and Chinese authorities recently announced the next group of enterprises (22 in total) for international listings, with 4 envisaged to have primary listings on the New York Stock Exchange (NYSE) and the other 18 on the SEHK. Though the first nine listings had an even geographic distribution, the subsequent H share listings appear to be more explicitly based on economic criteria, favoring especially infrastructure development—for example, the power generating sector. Once again, this second set of enterprises contains some of the highest quality firms in China. The attractions of the NYSE over the SEHK for Chinese companies are reportedly the much higher price/earnings ratios that Chinese companies have obtained on the former—which permits them to raise funds more cheaply—as well as intangibles such as the scarcity value and prestige of a NYSE listing. The highest quality enterprises are expected to list on the NYSE, specifically two power supply companies and two regional airlines.

Major constraints on the number of firms that can be listed include the legal framework—a national securities law has yet to be passed—and the speed of adoption of appropriate accounting and disclosure standards. The latter problem may be alleviated by China's new accounting standards, which are reportedly not much different from international standards. As the enterprises adopt these new standards, it will be easier for them to meet the listing requirements of the SEHK.

Though investor interest in Chinese equity has been heightened in the past two years, it has focused on indirect or diversified channels. Most investment in China is from retail investors (such as country funds), with institutional investors having shown the greatest enthusiasm for the NYSE listing of the Shanghai Petrochemical ADR. Country funds have three main channels for investing in China—H shares, B shares, and companies controlled by mainland Chinese corporations (backdoor listings and red chips) or companies closely related with Chinese interests. There are about 40 country funds that invest in China—all of which were established in the past two years—with a total of some $1.5–2.0 billion of assets under management. The B share listings have a market capitalization in the order of $5 billion, with average daily turnover varying from the high of $13 million to very low levels. Only about one fifth of fund managers invest more than 40 percent of their assets in B shares, whereas some three fifths invest over 40 percent of their assets in Hong Kong China plays. The preference for investing in China through companies listed in Hong Kong reportedly reflects the quality of the company managers, a familiar accounting system, and the perception that the local intermediaries have a comparative advantage in monitoring the quality of the investments.

Hong Kong's role as conduit for investing in China arises from the fact that most foreign direct investment in China and most external bank credits are advanced by Hong Kong enterprises—reportedly in search of a low cost manufacturing base—and banks based in Hong Kong. Foreign direct investment to China almost tripled in 1992 to $12.0 billion and for the first time exceeded loan financing; for 1993 it is estimated to have increased further to an estimated $26 billion in disbursements and over $100 billion in commitments. In 1992, foreign direct investment from Hong Kong amounted to $7.7 billion (64 percent of the total).[22]

The Chinese Approach to Securities Market Development

Despite appearances to the contrary since the beginning of 1993, the development of securities markets has been a relatively gradual one in China. In the early stages, the authorities reacted to developments in the markets rather than anticipating or leading them. For example, official approval of the issue of enterprise securities was given only after a large number of enterprises had done so on their own initiative; secondary markets for securities were recognized only after unofficial curb markets had been operating for some years; and securities

---

[21]All but one H share listing were issued through a fixed-price offering and were usually heavily oversubscribed.

[22]Of the remaining $4.3 billion, $0.7 billion came from Japan and $1.1 billion from Taiwan Province of China.

Table 23. Chinese H Shares

Issuer	Launch Date	Times Over-subscribed	No. of Shares Issued (In millions)	Value (In millions of Hong Kong dollars)	Value (In millions of U.S. dollars)	Price at Launch (In Hong Kong dollars)	Price at Close of First Day Trading (In Hong Kong dollars)	Price on Mar. 11, 1994 (In Hong Kong dollars)	Discount to A Share on Mar. 11, 1994 (In percent)	Market Capitalization on Mar. 11, 1994 (In millions of Hong Kong dollars)	Liquidity on Mar. 11, 1994[2] (In percent)	Volatility from Launch[3] (In percent)
Tsingtao Brewery Company Ltd.	July 1993	110.50	317.60	889.00	115.00	2.80	3.60	8.20	−27.00	2,619.90	0.40	3.64
Beiren Printing Machinery Holdings	July 1993	25.00	100.00	208.00	40.00	2.08	2.75	4.40	...	437.50	0.50	4.04
Guangzhou Shipyard International Company	July 1993	77.00	157.00	327.00	39.00	2.08	2.40	3.90	24.00	609.20	0.40	4.14
Shanghai Petrochemical Company[1]	July 1993	1.20	1,680.00	2,648.00	343.00	1.58	1.61	2.80	20.00	4,651.10	0.40	3.63
Maanshan Iron and Steel Company[1]	Oct. 1993	15.00	1,732.90	3,934.00	509.00	2.27	3.65	3.90	1.00	6,706.80	0.50	3.11
Kunming Machine Tool Plant	Dec. 1993	627.00	65.00	129.00	17.00	1.98	5.80	3.90	−10.00	250.30	0.40	4.13
Yizheng Joint Corporation of Chemical Fibre	Mar. 1994	10.00	1,000.00	2,380.00	307.00	2.38	2.42	...	...	2,380.00	...	...
Tianjin Bohai Chemical	May 1994	0.26	340.00	408.00	52.65	1.20	1.10	...	...	...	...	...
Dongfang Electrical Machinery	May 1994	15.00	170.00	481.10	61.70	2.83	3.17	...	...	...	...	...
Total				11,404.10	1,484.35					17,654.80	0.40	

Sources: *Euroweek*; *International Financing Review*; and IMF staff estimates.
[1]Including international tranches.
[2]Daily trading volume as percent of market capitalization.
[3]Standard deviation of daily price changes, at daily rate.

were traded on the Shanghai and Shenzhen exchanges long before they were officially opened in 1990 and 1991. Since 1990 the authorities have been more active in guiding market developments. New initiatives include official recognition of secondary markets for bonds and equity and efforts to create a national market. The Central Government has consistently attempted to maintain strict control over issuance by means of quotas for new share and bond issues by enterprises.

Banks' Involvement in Securities Markets

Overall, the securities markets remain relatively small as sources of funds. The data up to 1991 show that the substitution of securities issues for bank loans has been very modest. The ratio of securities issues by enterprises (enterprise bonds plus stock issues) to bank loans to enterprises rose from 0.4 percent in 1987 to 1.5 percent in 1991. The total stock of securities outstanding at the end of 1992—Y 330 billion—represented only 11 percent of all financial assets, although that proportion is increasing at a rate of 1 or 2 percentage points a year.

Until recently, banks were intimately involved in the securities markets. Many of the securities firms were bank subsidiaries or affiliates, and the markets were regulated by the central bank. In early 1993, however, when it became apparent that this mixing of banking and securities activities was resulting in the diversion of credit away from the productive sectors of the economy, the authorities introduced regulations providing for a complete separation of the industries. Banks had to close or sell their securities subsidiaries and call in "speculative" loans, and they were forbidden to have any further involvement with securities markets. As a result there is, for example, no margin lending, and securities firms and exchanges are not permitted to seek insurance from banks in the form of lines of credit. This of course has had an effect on liquidity in the secondary market. Individuals must put cash up front for securities they purchase and must retain minimum balances in accounts with securities firms. The firms themselves must keep relatively large balances in their accounts with the exchanges in order to finance their proprietary trading activities and to protect themselves against settlement failures.

The Approach to Equity Market Development

In China, the selection of issuing firms thus far has been determined on an administrative basis. Rather than simply having to meet the exchange's listing requirements and some national regulatory standards, Chinese firms that want to list must be transformed into joint-stock companies have their land and other assets valued by the State Assets Bureau and State Land Administration and have their financial statements audited and prepared according to international standards. They then must apply to the local government for approval to issue shares, and if that is successful, they apply to the China Securities Regulatory Commission (CSRC), which re-examines the application (in part to ensure that the exchange's listing requirements have been satisfied). One of the conditions of eligibility is that the company has earned positive profits for the three preceding years. Applications by enterprises owned by the Central Government for bond issues are examined by the PBOC and the State Planning Commission, whereas applications from private enterprises or enterprises owned by local governments are examined by the relevant local government.

The Central Government has a quota of A share listings for the country as a whole (this may be subdivided into quotas for different exchanges), which allows it to control market development. Compared with an estimated Y 10.9 billion in new issues in 1992, the quota in 1993 was Y 5 billion, and that for 1994 is Y 5.5 billion. Subject to this limit, approval will be given for one or two listings from each province or municipality on each exchange. The recent weakness in the markets has delayed scheduled issues, with the result that some issues that have been approved for 1994 may not be marketed until 1995. There is no quota for B shares, but the approval process is a little more complicated (at the very least enterprises have to prove a need for foreign exchange). There are also other mechanisms by which the center can control these issues—for example, in 1993 B share issues from provinces that had not taken up and distributed their allotment of Treasury bonds were prohibited.

The marketing of approved issues differs from practices followed elsewhere. A shares are underwritten by a securities firm—usually a domestic firm, but often with a foreign firm as an advisor—which sells share-order forms in which the holder applies to purchase a fixed number of shares. The price is generally not known at this stage. This modified book-building system allows the underwriter to gauge market demand for the issue and to better price the shares. In fact, public offers have generally been greatly oversubscribed, so the successful applications have been selected by lottery, and the underwriter bears minimal risk. Although the Government no longer sets the issue price—as the PBOC had done in the past—it apparently still has influence over the determination of the issue price. By contrast, B shares are generally marketed by private placement, most often in Hong Kong.

Because of their different investor base, A and B shares have very different liquidity characteristics.

For example, B shares generally are more thinly traded. As a result, prices of A and B shares for the same company (which differ only in their investor base and currency risk, but not in dividend or shareholder rights, and so on) frequently have very different prices. For example, on March 16, 1994, B shares in Shanghai traded at a 62 percent discount to the price of the same companies' A shares, while in Shenzhen the discount was 39 percent. For individual companies, the discounts reach as high as 84 percent, while only one company's B shares traded at a premium. It is not uncommon for developing countries to discriminate between foreign and domestic investors in their stock markets, but China may be alone in having the shares reserved for foreign investors trade at a discount.

In addition to strong "investor sentiment" pressures, one possible explanation for the B shares discount is that the required return for Chinese investors may be lower than for foreign investors because they have fewer alternative investment opportunities.[23] While the B share discounts for a selection of companies during March 1992–March 1993 did not respond to international interest rates and risk premiums, they do appear to be significantly correlated with the premiums on shares reserved for foreigners in Singapore and Thailand. As the discount on B shares falls, the premiums on foreign shares in Singapore and Thailand rise. This suggests that foreign investment in China may be motivated by similar factors as investment in these other two markets.

The segmentation of the equity market into A, B, and H shares is a distinguishing characteristic of securities market development in China. As mentioned earlier, although discrimination between domestic and foreign investors is not unusual—this occurs, for example, in Singapore and Thailand—the unique feature of the Chinese approach is that these classes of market differ in their information requirements. Thus, it was recognized early on that issuers of B shares would have to provide better information to the market than would issuers of A shares, and that H share issuers would need to disclose even more information. Thus, issuers of B shares have to prepare financial statements according to international accounting standards, which is not required of issuers of A shares. Moreover, issuers of H shares, have the added responsibility of meeting listing requirements on the SEHK, which has stricter information disclosure requirements than the two Chinese exchanges.

The informational asymmetries reflected the recognition that international investors would not be prepared to invest in companies in which they did

not have sufficient information (which was felt to be the case for the A shares). The local regulations in Shanghai and Shenzhen, for example, did not require issuers of A shares to use international accounting standards. The rules for B share issues were more demanding, and the regulators accepted foreign advice that accounts prepared according to Chinese standards would not then have been acceptable to foreign investors. The standards for H shares were set by the SEHK and are generally recognized to be the strictest.

The experience during 1993 has demonstrated that investors generally prefer markets with better disclosure. Foreign investors, with a choice of purchasing B or H shares, have gravitated toward the latter. Initially, when only B shares were available, the international investment community showed considerable interest in these shares, and turnover, while initially low, appeared to be improving. However, in the spring of 1993 when enterprises that had issued B shares began reporting their 1992 results, some of these firms chose not to prepare their reports according to international accounting standards, thus violating B share regulations. Moreover, it soon became apparent that some of them had misused the funds they had raised by speculating in real estate or securities markets, or simply by on-lending the foreign exchange. By the end of June, B share liquidity had all but disappeared. The emergence of Chinese companies listing on the SEHK, beginning in July, provided a superior alternative to B shares, and international investors quickly turned their attention to that market. With one exception, H share issues have been very well received in the primary market, and the secondary market for these shares has been very liquid since their listing.

A second element of the Chinese authorities' approach to stock market development is their decision to pick which firms will issue shares on the two regulated markets, subject to an overall quota and a concern for regional equity. The selection of H share issuers is not subject to a quota; however, the choice of companies is almost entirely made by the central authorities at the highest level. Rather than letting the market determine the issuers, subject to some minimum standards contained in securities and company law and in the exchange's listing requirements, the authorities are determined to follow a strategy of "picking winners." To a certain extent this approach was dictated by the absence of adequate disclosure, market regulation, and market-determined prices for competing assets. Since China did not have a market economy, a market-based approach to equity issues might not have been feasible. Perhaps more important in the authorities' opinion, there was a need to maintain control over the liberalization process. This is consistent with

_____
[23]Bailey (1994).

103

the general approach to reforms in China in which measures are implemented on a trial basis at first.

Suffice to say that given the large structural changes under way and the nature of the remaining distortions, it would not be easy for an outsider to identify the most profitable or best-managed firms. Local authorities may in fact be in the best position to do so. Government intervention of this sort may resolve a marked information asymmetry between domestic firms and foreign investors.

This strategy could run into trouble if non-economic factors, such as a desire to spread listings geographically, were to receive too much attention in the selection process. This could result in firms being allowed to issue shares, despite the fact more profitable firms in the same industry located elsewhere could not.

Corporate Governance

Another motivation for the development of corporate securities markets is to create a system of corporate governance that does not rely on bureaucrats. A first step in this process is to remove the enterprises from direct government control. Thus, the authorities have encouraged enterprises to transform themselves into joint-stock companies with majority (initially usually 100 percent) state ownership, but with independent management.[24] To date, more than 13,000 enterprises have taken on this status—9,500 in 1993 alone.

The second step is to allow enterprises to obtain their own financing. While the largest enterprises can still rely on fairly automatic bank credit, smaller ones would have to negotiate terms with the bank. Moreover, the intent has been that these loans should be repaid. In addition, subject to the approval of regulatory authorities, firms are allowed to issue debt and equity securities to the public. However, so far, equity issues have generally comprised less than 30 percent of the enterprises' enlarged capital.

Having released enterprises from direct bureaucratic control, the Government has recognized that some new source of discipline for managers must be found. It hopes to obtain this discipline from a reformed banking sector and from the securities markets. In assessing the scope for securities markets to exercise discipline, several factors need to be taken into account.[25]

Consider first the contribution of the banks. Banks can impose financial discipline on firms pri-

marily through the requirement to make regular payments on loans. If a firm does not obtain a regular cash flow from the investments financed by the borrowed funds, they may be unable to service the debt and be forced into bankruptcy. If bankruptcy is costly to managers, they will have an incentive to ensure timely service of their debts. Moreover, this obligation may mitigate any incentive managers may have to divert enterprise resources to their own personal uses.

Banks also have access to fairly detailed information on the financial condition of the firm—both as a condition for making or renewing a loan and from observing the firm's cash flow through its current account, which is often required to be maintained at the lending bank. Of course, banks will only enforce this discipline if they themselves face a cost to bad lending decisions. At this point, the only domestic financial institutions that have lent to the state-owned enterprises are themselves state owned. Since their cost of funds and lending interest rates are beyond their control, and since banks face no apparent penalty from accumulating bad loans, they have limited incentive to enforce their lending contracts. For example, although a bankruptcy act was passed in 1988, by the end of 1993 only 20 petitions for bankruptcy had been brought to court. Bank managers acknowledge that they would rather carry a bad loan on their accounts—effectively capitalizing unpaid interest—than force bankruptcy and closure of the firm.

Equity markets provide an alternative—and complementary—source of discipline through two possible avenues. In the first place, since shareholders own a claim to the firm's residual profits, they have an incentive to monitor the management of the firm and to ensure that the most profitable investments are undertaken in order to maximize the value of their shares. The second source of discipline derives from the marketability of the shares. At the very least, if shareholders become dissatisfied with the performance of the firm they can sell their shares. If this results in a significant decline in the market price of the equity, then the firm may find it more difficult to find new investors. If the price falls by a large enough amount, a rival manager may attempt a takeover, believing that he is more capable of managing the firm efficiently. Thus, managers for whom the loss of their position would be costly have an incentive to avoid this by managing the firm as efficiently as possible.

Equity markets in China face several constraints on their disciplining role. Investors need reliable information about the firms in which they are investing if they are to be able to closely monitor the firms' activities. Moreover, since private institutional investors have not yet emerged as significant shareholders, the shares the public holds are

---

[24]See Bell and others (1993) for a discussion of the history of enterprise reforms and especially the concept of ownership in China.

[25]The role of banks and securities markets in providing a market-based corporate governance mechanism is discussed in Blommestein and Spencer (1993).

widely dispersed; it is not clear therefore that any one individual has a large enough stake to compensate himself for the monitoring costs that would be incurred before effecting any change in management. Rather, it is possible that any indication of poor performance would result in a sale of shares. However, takeover regulations are drafted in a way that makes it difficult to rely on this mechanism for disciplining poor managers. Investors must make a public announcement when their stake reaches 5 percent of a firm's outstanding shares, and at every 2 percent increment thereafter. Moreover, the investor is barred from trading in that stock for two days after each announcement. Foreigners cannot mount a takeover through the secondary market because they are barred from purchasing any shares other than B and H shares, which generally amount to no more than 30 percent of the firm's capital.

Under present conditions, therefore, the main source of discipline is likely to come from the actual listing process itself. Both the authorities and Chinese and foreign securities houses report that preparing audited financial reports in line with international accounting standards and restructuring the operations of state-owned enterprises are highly instructive to management.

Supervision and Regulation of Domestic Capital Markets

The regulation of securities markets was rearranged in early 1993, which resulted in greater centralization and rationalization. Prior to April 1993, the PBOC took the initiative in developing and regulating securities markets through its securities regulatory office in Beijing. In this they were supported by the Ministry of Finance and the State Council for the Reform of the Economic System (SCRES). Because of the speed with which securities market activities emerged in centers all across the country, these responsibilities were soon decentralized. The local municipal governments and PBOC branches had the most important direct supervisory roles. The PBOC licensed securities firms and markets and approved new listings, while the local authorities were responsible for regulating the markets. In most cases, central government approval for a particular development—secondary market trading and issuance of a new kind of security—came long after the local authorities had approved them.

As a consequence of the decentralized regulatory structure, various markets formulated their own rules and regulations and created parallel systems for trading, clearing, and settlement. This duplication of effort made clear the need for a consistent, central regulatory structure. This was created in October 1992 when the State Council decided to centralize regulation. A two-tier structure was

established—the State Council Securities Policy Committee (SCSPC) and its executive arm, the CSRC—and became operational in April 1993. The SCSPC consists of representatives of 14 government ministries, including the Ministry of Finance and the SCRES, and is primarily responsible for drafting securities laws and regulations (or authorizing the CSRC to do so) and for formulating guidelines and rules governing securities market development. The CSRC is responsible primarily for implementing regulations and for supervising securities firms and markets. The exchanges continue to set their own listing requirements and operate as self-regulatory agencies.

The CSRC began operations in April 1993 by issuing the Interim Regulations on the Administration of the Issue and Trading of Shares, which replaced the provisional regulations promulgated by the various local authorities—particularly in Shanghai and Shenzhen—and formed the foundation for future national legislation, which is being drafted. These regulations prescribe issuing requirements—among others, the requirements that companies show at least three consecutive years of profits prior to issue and that intangible assets represent less than 20 percent of total assets—and acceptable practices in the primary and secondary markets. They specify the operating requirements for securities firms and explain how the firms will be supervised. They also include penalties for securities fraud and cover mergers and acquisitions.

The PBOC has retained its role of licensing securities firms, but the CSRC sets the conditions of eligibility and capital requirements and supervises the daily operations of these firms. Similarly, the Ministry of Finance licenses accounting firms and their professionals, but the CSRC sets the eligibility requirements and supervises their activity. The Ministry of Justice licenses lawyers, but the CSRC monitors their securities activities. The CSRC also monitors listed companies' compliance with reporting and other requirements.

Issues in External Financing

The Chinese authorities have chosen to list firms in Hong Kong rather than access international markets through issues of ADRs/GDRs—as is common in many other developing countries (see Annex IV). Both these vehicles, direct listing and ADRs/GDRs, raise an issue's liquidity and concomitantly its price through the broadening of the investor base, the reduction in settlement time and risk, the introduction of trade and settlement according to international standards and more established currencies, and the avoidance of foreign investment restrictions. However, ADRs/GDRs differ from direct placements in international markets in that they provide extra liquidity to the domestic market and not just the individual issue.[26] However, this route is made more difficult by the more rigorous accounting and disclosure standards required for a public listing of an ADR/GDR. Moreover, China has a close relationship with Hong Kong, which may increase the attraction of listing there rather than elsewhere.[27]

The pricing of Chinese equities highlights the market's concerns with the B share market. During 1993, the IFC's Asia investable index, the Hang Seng stock market index, and Standard Charter's B share index increased by 98 percent, 119 percent, and 35 percent, respectively. An index of red chip firms outperformed the Hang Seng index until the introduction of H shares in July 1993, with the former rising by 40 percent, compared with a 30 percent increase in the Hang Seng index. The Hang Seng and the B share indexes were substantially more volatile than the IFC index during 1993. Moreover, liquidity is relatively equal among all the China plays except for the B share market, where liquidity has been lower.

Broadening the analysis to include H shares is complicated by the relatively small period for which they have been issued, as well as by the upheavals in the Hong Kong market during this period. The first H share was issued in July 1993, while the largest H share started trading only in November 1993. The Hang Seng soared to record heights during the last quarter of the year and turned sharply downward in early January 1994. Neverthe-less, an H share index greatly outperformed the Hang Seng index over November 3–December 31, 1993, but fell slightly more than the Hang Seng over December 31, 1993–March 3, 1994.[28]

In the short run, China's access to the international securities markets, especially by entities carrying government guarantees in the bond markets, will be facilitated by the absence of debt-servicing difficulties in recent years and the opening of the economy under the reform program—along with the concomitant economic development. In recognition of these positive aspects, the major credit rating agencies having granted China an investment grade status. In setting this rating, Standard and Poor's cited China's demonstrated record and long-term prospects for strong economic growth, moderate external debt burdens, and cautious policy approach to managing economic development. Reconfirming the positive outlook, Moody's upgraded China from Baa1 to single A in September 1993.[29] These sovereign ratings exceed those of most other developing countries, other than a few of the other dynamic Asian economies. As the rating of a country's nonsovereign issues cannot exceed their respective sovereign rating, China's high rating should facilitate access by qualified enterprises to the markets when this is authorized. It is interesting to note that industrial country corporations with similar ratings can borrow at yields some 150 basis points over government paper of 20–25 years maturity, which—based on an extrapolation—is comparable to China's spreads on issues by the ten windows.

---

[26]Judging by the market's reaction to the prospects of level one ADRs for Shanghai B shares, this vehicle could prove to be useful in providing liquidity to the B share market; the Shanghai B share market was buoyed for several months at the beginning of 1993 by the prospects of ADR issues.

[27]Hong Kong is supposed to retain nominal financial independence for another 50 years following its transfer to China in 1997.

[28]The H share index is based on the Tsingtao, Shanghai Petrochemical Company, and Maanshan Iron and Steel issues weighted by their respective market capitalization.

[29]Moody's also upgraded three financial institutions (BOC, CITIC, and PCBC) to A3 in December 1993. Standard and Poor's rates China a BBB, though the rating was upgraded from stable to improving.

Annex VI
Glossary of Financial Terms

Auction

Discriminatory: Auction in which each successful bidder pays the price bid. Also known as a **multiple-price** auction.

Uniform-price: Auction in which all successful bidders pay the same price, usually the price of the lowest successful bid. Sometimes called a **Dutch** auction.

Sealed-bid: Auction in which all bids are submitted secretly, before some deadline, with no opportunity for revision.

Benchmark: Security used as the basis for interest rate calculations and for pricing other securities. Also denotes the most heavily traded and liquid security of a particular class.

Broker: Financial intermediary that solicits orders from buyers and sellers and then orchestrates trades, either by passing the identity of each party to the other or by making offsetting, simultaneous trades with each party. Brokers typically maintain computer screens with anonymous bid and offer quotes from dealers.

BTANs (Bons du Trésor à taux annuel): French fixed-rate, two- or five-year Treasury notes.

BTFs (Bons du Trésor à taux fixe): French fixed-rate, short-term discount Treasury bills.

Bunds (Bundesanleihen): German long-term Federal Government bonds.

Cash market: Market for sale of a security against immediate delivery, as opposed to the futures market.

Cherry-picking: The practice of a firm selectively enforcing only those contracts with positive net present value to itself in the event of the bankruptcy of its counterparty.

Coupon: Periodic interest payment on a bond. Some bonds have physical coupons that must be clipped and submitted to a bank. A **coupon rate** is the stated interest rate on the bond, equivalent to annual coupon payments as a percentage of the principal of the bond (par value).

Dealer: A financial intermediary that buys and sells securities or other instruments, by setting bid and offer quotes. Unlike brokers, dealers take positions in the instruments.

Depository receipt: A negotiable certificate that is issued by a U.S. bank and that is fully backed by shares that in turn, represent claims on the publicly traded debt or equity securities of a company. These receipts trade freely on an exchange or an OTC market. American Depository Receipts (ADRs) and Global Depository Receipts (GDRs) are identical from an operational point of view and the terms are used interchangeably, depending on the marketing strategy.

Dragon bonds: Bonds that are priced, launched, and syndicated in the Asia-Pacific region outside Japan and listed in at least two of the Hong Kong, Taiwan Province of China, or Singapore markets.

Duration: A weighted average of the terms of all cash flows from a debt instrument. The present values of these cash flows are used as the weights, with the yield to maturity used to compute the present values. Duration also represents the elasticity of the value of a bond with respect to changes in its yield to maturity. **Modified duration** is duration divided by a factor of one plus the interest rate.

EMTN (Euro medium-term note): Medium-term bonds issued on a tap basis on the Euromarkets.

Gilts (or gilt-edged securities): Irish or U.K. Government medium- and long-term debt securities.

Good bank/bad bank model: Method of restoring a bank with a large amount of bad loans by placing bad loans in a separate institution (the "bad bank") and adequately capitalizing the remaining bank (the "good bank").

GOVPX: Service in the United States that distributes real time price and quote information for all U.S. Treasury securities.

Margin: Amount of cash that must be provided when borrowing to purchase a security. For example, U.S. regulations limit margin to 50 percent for equity purchases, so that a customer may only borrow half the value of a stock purchased. Margin also refers to the amount by which value of a security in a repurchase agreement exceeds cash lent.

Market-maker: A dealer that posts ongoing quotes in a particular instrument.

Marking to market: Expressing assets or liabilities at current market values.

MATIF (Marché à Terme International de France): Financial futures exchange in Paris.

Netting by novation: A bilateral contract between two counterparties under which a new obligation to pay or receive a given currency is automatically amalgamated with all previous obligations in the same currency, thereby creating a single legally binding net position that replaces the larger number of gross obligations.

OATs (Obligations assimilables du Trésor): French fungible, long-term Treasury bonds.

On-the-run: Term used in the United States for the most recently issued Treasury security of a particular maturity class, which is also the most liquid and heavily traded (see **benchmark**). On-the-run status begins with when-issued trading.

Par: The principal of a bond.

Primary dealers: Group of dealers in the United States with a formal, ongoing trading relationship with the Federal Reserve Bank of New York and with certain obligations in the primary and secondary market for Treasury securities. Term also applies to similar entities in other countries.

Primary market: Market in which a security is first sold by issuer.

Price discovery: A general term for the process by which financial markets attain an equilibrium price, especially in the primary market. Usually refers to the incorporation of information into the price.

Pure discount: Zero-coupon (see below).

Repurchase agreement (repo): An agreement to sell a security and then repurchase it at a particular time and price.

Secondary market: Market in which a security is sold by one investor to another, as opposed to the primary market.

Settlement risk: Risk that one party or another in a securities trade will fail to deliver, especially when the other party has already delivered.

Short squeeze: Situation in which traders with short positions seeking to close their positions are required to pay an abnormally high price for the instrument because another trader has amassed a dominant long position in the instrument.

Strip: A pure-discount security created by the decomposition of a bond into separate securities for each coupon payment and for the final principal payment. The term strip comes from the U.S. Treasury acronym for "separate trading of registered interest and principal."

Syndicate: Group of intermediaries that purchase prearranged shares of a security in the primary market and sell the security to other investors.

Tap sales: Sales by a central bank of a new issue of government securities, usually on a gradual basis.

When-issued: The market for a security before it is sold on the primary market.

Winners' curse: Losses incurred by successful bidders at an auction, due to those bidders' having inaccurate, overoptimistic information on the value of the item auctioned.

Yield to maturity: Interest rate that makes a bond's present value equal to its market price. If the price of a bond is below par, the yield to maturity is greater than the bond's coupon rate, and the bond is said to trade at a discount.

Zero-coupon: A bond with no coupons, only a single principal payment at maturity.

Statistical Appendix

Table A1. United States: Estimated Ownership of Public Debt Securities by Private Investors[1]

(In percent of total privately held securities)[2]

	1980	1981	1982	1983	1984	1985	1986	1987	1988	1989	1990	1991	1992	1993
Total privately held	100.0	100.0	100.0	100.0	100.0	100.0	100.0	100.0	100.0	100.0	100.0	100.0	100.0	100.0
Domestic investors														
Commercial banks	18.2	16.0	15.5	17.6	15.0	13.4	12.3	11.2	9.9	8.2	7.5	9.1	10.4	10.4
Nonbank investors	60.8	64.3	66.9	66.2	68.0	70.8	71.2	71.5	70.6	70.5	72.5	71.7	70.3	69.2
Individuals														
Total	19.0	16.0	13.7	13.0	11.9	10.9	10.2	10.0	10.2	10.7	10.2	10.3	10.2	10.2
Savings bonds	11.8	9.8	8.1	7.0	6.1	5.6	5.8	5.8	5.9	5.8	5.5	5.4	5.5	5.6
Other securities	7.2	6.1	5.7	6.1	5.7	5.3	4.4	4.1	4.3	4.9	4.7	4.9	4.6	4.5
Insurance companies	3.9	4.2	5.2	4.5	5.3	5.7	6.3	6.2	6.4	6.2	6.2	7.1	7.0	7.1
Money market funds	0.6	3.1	5.0	2.2	2.1	1.8	1.8	0.8	0.6	0.7	2.0	3.1	2.8	2.6
Corporations[3]	3.1	2.6	2.9	3.9	4.1	4.2	4.3	4.9	4.6	4.6	4.8	5.9	6.8	7.0
State and local governments	14.3	13.9	13.7	15.0	15.5	21.4	21.6	24.2	25.4	24.2	21.4	20.3	18.8	18.5
Other investors[4]	19.9	24.6	26.3	27.6	29.1	26.8	27.0	25.4	23.3	24.0	27.9	25.0	24.7	23.8
Foreign and international	21.0	19.7	17.6	16.3	17.0	15.9	16.4	17.3	19.5	21.3	20.0	19.2	19.4	20.5

Sources: United States, Department of Treasury, *Treasury Bulletin* (March 1988, December 1993, and March 1994), Table OFS-2.

[1]As of end-December.

[2]Securities valued at par; some savings bonds are included at current redemption value.

[3]Exclusive of banks and insurance companies.

[4]Includes savings and loan associations, credit unions, nonprofit institutions, mutual savings banks, corporate pension trust funds, dealers and brokers, certain government deposit accounts, and government-sponsored enterprises.

Table A2. Financial Futures and Options: Exchanges, Contracts, and Volume of Contracts Traded

Exchange/Type	Face Value of Contract[1]	Volume of Contracts Traded					
		1988	1989	1990	1991	1992	1993
		(In thousands of contracts)					
United States							
Chicago Board of Trade (CBOT)							
Interest rate							
Futures							
Thirty-day federal funds	$5,000,000	19	68	81	116	234	182
U.S. Treasury notes[2]	$100,000[3]	5,708	7,891	8,698	10,013	18,105	25,257
U.S. Treasury bonds (15-year)	$100,000	70,308	70,303	75,499	67,887	70,005	79,428
Municipal bond index	$1,000 x index	1,274	1,068	697	549	776	1,121
Mortgage-backed securities[4]	$100,000	n.t.	25	17	6	—	—
Interest rate swap (three- and five-year)	$25,000,000	n.t.	n.t.	n.t.	7	2	—
Options							
Options on U.S. Treasury note futures[5]	$100,000	1,012	1,168	1,024	1,020	3,236	6,829
Options on U.S. Treasury bond futures	$100,000	19,509	20,784	27,315	21,926	20,259	23,435
Options on municipal bond index futures	$1,000 x index	172	89	86	53	38	69
Options on mortgage-backed securities futures[4]	$100,000	n.t.	14	19	10	—	—
Options on interest rate swap futures	$25,000,000	n.t.	n.t.	n.t.	6	—	—
Stock index							
Futures							
Major market index (MMI)	$500 x index	1,176	1,087	951	703	361	155
Wilshire Small Cap index	$500 x index	n.t.	n.t.	n.t.	n.t.	n.t.	2
Options							
Options on MMI futures	$500 x index	n.t.	n.t.	n.t.	3	2	1
Wilshire Small Cap index options	$500 x index	n.t.	n.t.	n.t.	n.t.	n.t.	—
Chicago Board Options Exchange (CBOE)							
Interest rate							
Options							
U.S. Treasury bonds and notes	$100,000	140	144	7	—	n.t.	n.t.
Stock index							
Options							
Standard & Poor's (S&P) 100 options	$100 x index	57,433	58,371	68,847	63,936	62,427	64,032
S&P 500 options	$100 x index	4,817	6,274	12,089	11,925	13,420	16,454
Russell 2000 index options	$100 x index	n.t.	n.t.	n.t.	n.t.	40	495
Financial Times stock index (FT-SE) options	$100 x 1/10 of index	n.t.	n.t.	n.t.	n.t.	16	22
Mid-America Commodity Exchange (MIDAM)							
Interest rate							
Futures							
Eurodollar (three-month)	$500,000	n.t.	n.t.	n.t.	n.t.	3	7
U.S. Treasury bills (90-day)	$500,000	22	9	4	1	2	1
U.S. Treasury notes (five- and ten-year)	$50,000	n.t.	n.t.	n.t.	n.t.	n.t.	12
U.S. Treasury bonds (15-year)	$50,000	1,414	1,307	1,461	1,397	1,342	1,126
Options							
Options on U.S. Treasury bond futures	$50,000	n.t.	n.t.	n.t.	2	4	2
Currency							
Futures							
Japanese yen	¥ 6,250,000	44	59	54	41	39	63
Deutsche mark	DM 62,500	50	54	83	94	106	124
Pound sterling	£12,500	28	24	26	30	44	67
Canadian dollar	Can$50,000	9	7	9	4	5	9
Swiss franc	Sw F 62,500	77	61	76	74	63	74
Chicago Mercantile Exchange (CME)							
Interest rate							
Futures							
London interbank offered rate— LIBOR (one-month)	$3,000,000	n.t.	n.t.	84	450	919	1,128
Eurodollar (three-month)[6]	$1,000,000	21,705	40,818	34,696	37,244	60,531	64,411
Euro-deutsche mark (three-month)	DM 1,000,000	n.t.	n.t.	n.t.	n.t.	n.t.	26
U.S. Treasury bills (90-day)	$1,000,000	1,374	1,502	1,870	2,012	1,337	1,017

Table A2 (*continued*)

Exchange/Type	Face Value of Contract[1]	Volume of Contracts Traded					
		1988	1989	1990	1991	1992	1993
		(In thousands of contracts)					
United States (*continued*)							
Options							
Options on LIBOR futures	$3,000,000	n.t.	n.t.	n.t.	75	99	91
Options on Eurodollar futures	$1,000,000	2,600	6,002	6,860	7,875	13,763	17,009
Options on Euro-deutsche mark futures	DM 1,000,000	n.t.	n.t.	n.t.	n.t.	n.t.	9
Options on U.S. Treasury bill futures	$1,000,000	6	17	32	49	30	14
Currency							
Futures							
Japanese yen[6]	¥ 12,500,000	6,433	7,824	7,437	6,017	4,520	6,023
Deutsche mark[6]	DM 125,000	5,662	8,186	9,169	10,929	11,593	12,866
Deutsche mark rolling spot	$250,000	n.t.	n.t.	n.t.	n.t.	n.t.	29
French franc	F 500,000	n.t.	n.t.	n.t.	n.t.	n.t.	19
Pound sterling[6]	£62,500	2,616	2,518	3,410	3,746	3,053	3,701
Pound sterling rolling spot	£250,000	n.t.	n.t.	n.t.	n.t.	n.t.	2
Canadian dollar	Can$100,000	1,409	1,264	1,409	1,139	1,172	1,411
Australian dollar	$A 100,000	76	114	105	76	90	199
Swiss franc	Sw F 125,000	5,283	6,094	6,525	5,835	5,135	5,605
Cross-rate deutsche mark/	DM 125,000 x DM/¥						
Japanese yen	cross rate	n.t.	n.t.	n.t.	9	11	—
Options							
Options on Japanese yen futures	¥ 12,500,000	2,945	3,127	3,116	2,397	1,518	2,262
Options on deutsche mark futures	DM 125,000	2,734	3,795	3,430	5,643	6,354	5,916
Options on deutsche mark							
rolling spot futures	$250,000	n.t.	n.t.	n.t.	n.t.	n.t.	—
Options on French franc futures	F 500,000	n.t.	n.t.	n.t.	n.t.	n.t.	6
Options on pound sterling futures	£62,500	543	406	501	650	597	528
Options on pound sterling							
rolling spot futures	£250,000	n.t.	n.t.	n.t.	n.t.	n.t.	—
Options on Canadian dollar futures	Can$100,000	314	274	284	337	307	177
Options on Australian dollar futures	$A 100,000	7	23	27	38	13	3
Options on Swiss franc futures	Sw F 125,000	1,070	1,489	1,130	998	1,027	628
Options on cross-rate deutsche mark/	DM 125,000 x DM/¥						
Japanese yen futures	cross rate	n.t.	n.t.	n.t.	3	29	—
Stock index							
Futures							
S&P 500 index	$500 x index	11,354	10,560	12,139	12,340	12,414	13,204
Nikkei stock index average	$5 x index	n.t.	n.t.	52	247	384	357
S&P MidCap 400 index	$500 x index	n.t.	n.t.	n.t.	n.t.	103	219
Goldman Sachs commodity index	$250 x index	n.t.	n.t.	n.t.	n.t.	36	122
Major market index (MMI)	$500 x index	n.t.	n.t.	n.t.	n.t.	n.t.	49
Russell 2000 stock price index	$500 x index	n.t.	n.t.	n.t.	n.t.	n.t.	19
Options							
Options on S&P 500 index futures	$500 x index	735	1,162	1,638	1,813	2,210	2,916
Options on Nikkei stock							
index average futures	$5 x index	n.t.	n.t.	9	12	14	10
Options on S&P MidCap 400							
index futures	$500 x index	n.t.	n.t.	n.t.	n.t.	3	5
Options on Goldman Sachs							
commodity index futures	$250 x index	n.t.	n.t.	n.t.	n.t.	8	38
MMI options	$500 x index	n.t.	n.t.	n.t.	n.t.	n.t.	—
Options on Russell 2000 stock							
price index futures	$500 x index	n.t.	n.t.	n.t.	n.t.	n.t.	1
Kansas City Board of Trade							
Stock index							
Futures							
Value Line index	$500 x index	80	41	36	58	46	46
Mini Value Line	$100 x index	14	8	14	27	34	41
Options							
Options on Mini Value Line futures	$100 x index	n.t.	n.t.	n.t.	n.t.	1	2

Table A2 (continued)

Exchange/Type	Face Value of Contract[1]	Volume of Contracts Traded					
		1988	1989	1990	1991	1992	1993
		(In thousands of contracts)					
United States *(continued)*							
New York Cotton Exchange (FINEX)							
Interest rate							
Futures							
U.S. Treasury notes[7]	$250,000[8]	790	599	292	81	81	51
Currency							
Futures							
U.S. dollar index	$1,000 x index	447	743	565	716	678	599
European currency unit (ECU)	ECU 100,000	24	16	12	2	1	—
Options							
U.S. dollar index	$1,000 x index	11	5	100	1,418	470	68
Options on ECU futures	ECU 100,000	n.t.	n.t.	n.t.	n.t.	5	—
New York Futures Exchange (NYFE)[9]							
Stock index							
Futures							
New York Stock Exchange (NYSE) composite stock index	$500 x index	1,669	1,580	1,575	1,486	1,315	849
Commodity Research Bureau (CRB) index	$500 x index	206	125	70	61	56	92
Options							
Options on NYSE composite stock index futures	$500 x index	23	39	26	35	43	30
Options on CRB index futures	$500 x index	1	4	4	4	4	7
New York Stock Exchange (NYSE)							
Stock index							
Options							
NYSE index options[10]	$100 x index	781	579	262	153	131	41
American Stock Exchange (AMEX)							
Stock index							
Options							
AMEX index options[11]	$100 x index	7,527	8,265	6,690	5,976	6,247	4,495
Commodity Exchange, Inc. (COMEX)							
Stock index							
Futures							
Eurotop 100 index	$100 x index	n.t.	n.t.	n.t.	n.t.	26	56
Options							
Options on Eurotop 100 index futures	$100 x index	n.t.	n.t.	n.t.	n.t.	n.t.	1
Pacific Stock Exchange (PSE)							
Stock index							
Options							
Financial News composite index options	$100 x index	280	226	130	72	70	6
Wilshire Small Cap index options	100 x value of index	n.t.	n.t.	n.t.	n.t.	n.t.	153
Philadelphia Stock Exchange (PHLX)							
Currency							
Futures							
Foreign currencies[12]		. . .	. . .	1	1	83	25
Options[13]							
Japanese yen	¥ 6,250,000	2,922	3,328	2,990	1,783	1,305	1,302
Deutsche mark	DM 62,500	3,407	5,277	4,892	7,472	7,966	6,218
French franc	F 250,000	256	60	40	146	1,261	3,979
Pound sterling	£31,250	1,303	482	646	587	789	529
Canadian dollar	Can$50,000	337	362	475	204	189	221
Australian dollar	$A 50,000	531	417	309	186	143	160
Swiss franc	Sw F 62,500	1,237	1,114	773	460	434	450
ECU	ECU 62,500	1	3	10	6	4	8
Pound sterling/deutsche mark	£500,000	n.t.	n.t.	n.t.	n.t.	18	153
Deutsche mark/Japanese yen	DM 1,000,000	n.t.	n.t.	n.t.	1	49	82
Stock index							
Options							
PHLX index options[14]	$100 x index	3,256	153	95	225	311	723

Table A2 (*continued*)

Exchange/Type	Face Value of Contract[1]	Volume of Contracts Traded					
		1988	1989	1990	1991	1992	1993
		(In thousands of contracts)					
Japan							
Osaka Securities Exchange							
Stock index							
Futures							
Nikkei 225	¥ 1,000 x index	1,892	5,443	13,589	21,643	11,927	8,461
Options							
Nikkei 225 options	¥ 1,000 x index	n.t.	6,610	9,188	11,836	9,257	6,090
Tokyo International Financial Futures Exchange (TIFFE)							
Interest rate							
Futures							
Eurodollar (three-month)	$1,000,000	n.t.	103	8	3	—	. . .
Euro-yen (three-month and one-year)	¥ 100,000,000	n.t.	4,495	14,414	14,666	14,969	23,391
Options							
Options on three-month Euro-yen futures	¥ 100,000,000	n.t.	n.t.	n.t.	332	486	687
Currency							
Futures							
U.S. dollar/Japanese yen	$50,000	n.t.	n.t.	n.t.	149	86	48
Tokyo Stock Exchange							
Interest rate							
Futures							
U.S. Treasury bonds	$100,000	n.t.	141	518	125	118	113
Japanese Government bonds (JGB)							
(10- and 20-year)	¥ 100,000,000	18,759	18,971	16,319	12,829	11,872	15,165
Options							
Options on ten-year JGB futures	¥ 100,000,000	n.t.	n.t.	2,288	1,850	1,141	1,507
Stock index							
Futures							
Tokyo Stock Price Index (TOPIX)	¥ 10,000 x index	1,887	3,728	3,091	1,677	1,359	2,157
Options							
TOPIX options	¥ 10,000 x index	n.t.	4,806	463	120	49	38
Germany							
Deutsche Terminbörse (DTB)							
Interest rate							
Futures							
Medium-term notional bond (Bobl)	DM 250,000	n.t.	n.t.	n.t.	236	1,668	4,534
Notional German Government bond (Bund)	DM 250,000	n.t.	n.t.	60	2,283	5,328	7,625
Options							
Options on Bobl futures	DM 250,000	n.t.	n.t.	n.t.	n.t.	n.t.	54
Options on Bund futures	DM 250,000	n.t.	n.t.	n.t.	164	498	252
Stock index and equity							
Futures							
German Stock Index (DAX)	DM 100 per DAX index point	n.t.	n.t.	51	1,251	3,271	3,977
Options							
Options on DAX futures	One DAX futures contract	n.t.	n.t.	n.t.	n.t.	136	63
DAX options	DM 10 per DAX index point	n.t.	n.t.	n.t.	2,046	13,945	21,420
DTB stock options	50 shares of underlying stocks	n.t.	n.t.	6,688	9,390	9,996	12,253
France							
Marché à Terme International de France (MATIF)							
Interest rate							
Futures							
Paris interbank offered rate—PIBOR (three-month)	F 5,000,000	452	2,296	1,901	3,000	6,437	11,864
Medium-term French Treasury bond	F 500,000	n.t.	n.t.	n.t.	n.t.	n.t.	99
ECU bond	ECU 100,000	n.t.	n.t.	56	546	1,354	873
Long-term French Treasury bond	F 500,000	n.t.	n.t.	n.t.	n.t.	n.t.	29
Notional bonds[15]	F 500,000	12,357	15,005	15,996	21,088	31,063	36,805
Options							
Options on three-month PIBOR futures	F 5,000,000	n.t.	n.t.	710	1,374	2,660	4,830
Options on ECU bond futures	ECU 100,000	n.t.	n.t.	n.t.	21	83	8
Options on notional bond futures	F 500,000	3,431	7,150	7,410	8,412	10,047	11,573

Table A2 (*continued*)

Exchange/Type	Face Value of Contract[1]	Volume of Contracts Traded					
		1988	1989	1990	1991	1992	1993
		(In thousands of contracts)					
France (*continued*)							
Stock index							
Futures							
CAC 40 stock index	F 200 x index	65	581	1,641	2,311	3,601	5,909
Marché des Options Negociables de Paris (MONEP)							
Stock index							
Options							
CAC 40 stock index options (short-term)	F 200 x index	50	816	2,470	3,718	3,171	2,452
CAC 40 stock index options (long-term)	F 50 x index	n.t.	n.t.	n.t.	87	547	1,761
Italy							
Mercato Italiano Futures							
Interest rate							
Futures							
BTP (five-year)[16]	Lit 250,000,000	n.t.	n.t.	n.t.	n.t.	49	1,637
BTP (ten-year)[16]	Lit 250,000,000	n.t.	n.t.	n.t.	n.t.	521	2,777
United Kingdom							
London International Financial Futures Exchange (LIFFE)							
Interest rate							
Futures							
Eurodollar (three-month)	$1,000,000	1,648	2,061	1,249	994	709	245
Euro-deutsche mark (three-month)	DM 1,000,000	n.t.	952	2,660	4,784	12,173	21,319
Euro-lira (three-month)	Lit 1,000,000,000	n.t.	n.t.	n.t.	n.t.	376	1,479
Short sterling (three-month)	£500,000	3,538	7,114	8,355	8,064	11,296	12,136
Euro-Swiss (three-month)	Sw F 1,000,000	n.t.	n.t.	n.t.	548	1,970	1,846
ECU (three-month)	ECU 1,000,000	n.t.	16	64	115	317	721
Medium-term German Government bond (Bobl)	DM 250,000	n.t.	n.t.	n.t.	n.t.	n.t.	1,050
U.S. Treasury bonds	$100,000	2,042	967	756	463	272	5
Japanese Government bond (JGB)[17]	¥ 100,000,000	122	117	46	106	221	421
German Government bond (Bund)	DM 250,000	315	5,330	9,582	10,112	13,605	20,440
Italian Government bond (BTP)[16]	Lit 200,000,000	n.t.	n.t.	n.t.	483	3,773	6,344
Long gilt (government bond)[18]	£50,000	5,641	4,063	5,643	5,639	8,805	11,809
ECU bond	ECU 200,000	n.t.	n.t.	n.t.	54	7	n.t.
Options							
Options on Eurodollar futures	$1,000,000	76	82	65	31	73	20
Options on Euro-deutsche mark futures	DM 1,000,000	n.t.	n.t.	248	514	1,964	2,906
Options on short sterling futures	£500,000	445	824	1,377	1,594	2,648	2,667
Options on Euro-Swiss futures	Sw F 1,000,000	n.t.	n.t.	n.t.	n.t.	17	32
Options on U.S. Treasury bond futures	$100,000	84	76	87	40	68	3
Options on Bund futures	DM 250,000	n.t.	469	1,804	2,453	2,750	4,416
Options on BTP futures[16]	Lit 200,000,000	n.t.	n.t.	n.t.	16	395	602
Options on long gilt futures	£50,000	1,141	727	790	844	1,813	2,059
Stock index							
Futures							
Financial Times stock index (FT-SE 100)	£25 x index	465	1,028	1,444	1,727	2,619	3,120
Options							
FT-SE 100 options	£10 x index	n.t.	n.t.	n.t.	n.t.	3,063	3,439
Canada							
Montreal Exchange							
Interest rate							
Futures							
Canadian Bankers' Acceptances[19]	Can$1,000,000	10	28	88	194	443	749
Canadian Government bonds (ten-year)	Can$100,000	n.t.	87	454	421	516	895
Options							
Canadian Government bond options	Can$25,000	335	323	139	47	51	61
Options on Canadian Government bond futures	Can$100,000	n.t.	n.t.	n.t.	15	5	9
Toronto Stock Exchange							
Equity							
Options							
Canadian equity options	100 shares	2,339	2,435	1,411	1,015	889	...

Table A2 (*continued*)

Exchange/Type	Face Value of Contract[1]	Volume of Contracts Traded					
		1988	1989	1990	1991	1992	1993
		(In thousands of contracts)					
Canada (*continued*)							
Toronto Futures Exchange							
Stock index							
Futures							
Toronto Stock Exchange (TSE) 35 index	Can$500 x index	27	35	53	61	59	69
Options							
TSE 35 index options	Can$100 x index	429	487	698	465	302	221
Spain							
Mercado de Opciones y Futuros Financieros, Meff Renta Fija							
Interest rate							
Futures							
Madrid interbank offered rate—MIBOR[20]	Ptas 10,000,000	n.t.	n.t.	17	456	747	2,363
Notional bond (three-, five-, and ten-year)	Ptas 10,000,000	n.t.	n.t.	171	535	1,015	4,553
Options							
Options on MIBOR futures	Ptas 10,000,000	n.t.	n.t.	n.t.	n.t.	8	140
Notional bond (three- and ten-year)	Ptas 10,000,000	n.t.	n.t.	n.t.	n.t.	382	1,088
Currency							
Futures							
Spanish peseta/U.S. dollar	$100,000	n.t.	n.t.	n.t.	4	12	—
Spanish peseta/deutsche mark	DM 125,000	n.t.	n.t.	n.t.	11	55	3
Netherlands							
European Options Exchange (EOE)							
Interest rate							
Options							
Dutch Government bond options	f. 10,000	537	486	260	232	270	436
Options on Dutch Government bond futures	f. 250,000	n.t.	n.t.	1	8	1	1
Currency							
Options							
U.S. dollar/guilder and pound sterling/guilder options	$10,000 £10,000	473	469	200	373	538	673
Stock index and equity							
Options							
EOE stock index and MMI U.S. stock index options[21]	f. 100 x index and $100 x index	793	1,995	2,003	2,384	2,471	2,701
Dutch Top 5 index options	100 x value of index	n.t.	n.t.	174	330	493	412
Eurotop 100 index options	50 x value of index	n.t.	n.t.	n.t.	10	10	3
Dutch stock options	100 shares	6,403	9,998	7,525	7,013	6,809	8,036
Financial Futures Market							
Interest rate							
Futures							
Notional guilder bond	f. 250,000	n.t.	62	54	29	25	70
Currency							
Futures							
U.S. dollar/guilder	$25,000	n.t.	n.t.	n.t.	2	11	22
Stock index							
Futures							
EOE stock index	f. 200 x index	34	238	437	485	492	812
Dutch Top 5 index	f. 200 x index	n.t.	n.t.	43	47	52	58
Eurotop 100 index	ECU 50 x index	n.t.	n.t.	n.t.	1	2	1
Australia							
Sydney Futures Exchange							
Interest rate							
Futures							
Bank bills (90-day)	$A 500,000	2,989	5,911	5,081	4,652	5,698	6,415
Treasury bonds (three-year)	$A 100,000	500	967	1,608	2,112	5,435	6,940
Commonwealth Treasury bonds (ten-year)	$A 100,000	2,712	3,222	3,174	3,602	4,253	4,782
Options							
Options on bank bill futures	$A 500,000	192	515	606	719	610	663
Options on Treasury bond futures	$A 100,000	18	25	75	107	317	515
Options on Commonwealth Treasury bond futures	$A 100,000	722	709	512	670	746	715

Table A2 (*continued*)

Exchange/Type	Face Value of Contract[1]	Volume of Contracts Traded					
		1988	1989	1990	1991	1992	1993
		(In thousands of contracts)					
Australia (*continued*)							
Stock index							
Futures							
All-ordinaries share price index	$A 25 x index	285	326	314	388	342	981
Options							
Options on All-ordinaries share price index futures	$A 25 x index	82	140	186	248	154	467
Switzerland							
Swiss Options and Financial Futures Exchange (SOFFEX)							
Interest rate							
Futures							
Euro-Swiss franc (three-month)	Sw F 1,000,000	n.t.	n.t.	n.t.	122	184	—
Swiss franc (five-year)	Sw F 100,000	n.t.	n.t.	n.t.	59	200	29
Swiss Government bond	Sw F 100,000	n.t.	n.t.	n.t.	n.t.	234	271
Stock index							
Futures							
Swiss market index	Sw F 50 x index	n.t.	n.t.	31	591	847	914
Options							
Swiss market index options	Sw F 5 x index	71	2,115	4,683	6,175	7,794	5,595
Belgium							
Belgian Futures and Options Exchange (BELFOX)							
Interest rate							
Futures							
Brussels interbank offered rate— BIBOR (three-month)	BF 25,000,000	n.t.	n.t.	n.t.	n.t.	52	191
Belgian Government bonds	BF 2,500,000	n.t.	n.t.	n.t.	13	264	585
Stock index and equity							
Futures							
Bel 20 index	BF 1,000 x index	n.t.	n.t.	n.t.	n.t.	n.t.	12
Options							
Bel 20 index options	BF 100 x index	n.t.	n.t.	n.t.	n.t.	n.t.	346
Stock options	20 shares of underlying stocks	n.t.	n.t.	n.t.	n.t.	104	275
Sweden							
Stockholm Options Market							
Interest rate							
Futures							
Interest rate	SKr 1,000,000	n.t.	n.t.	n.t.	4,134	7,420	11,343
Swedish Treasury bills	SKr 1,000,000	n.t.	n.t.	206	1,980	3,930	3,990
Swedish Government bonds (two-, five-, and ten-year)	SKr 1,000,000	n.t.	n.t.	116	1,720	2,483	3,814
Options							
Interest rate options	SKr 1,000,000	204	2	19	94	20	—
Stock index and equity							
Futures							
Stock futures	SKr 100 x index	6	—	3	5	21	119
OMX index	SKr 100 x index	312	—	4	117	450	628
GEMx index	DM 10 x index	n.t.	n.t.	n.t.	11	6	—
Options							
Stock options	SKr 100 x index	2,100	3,195	2,849	4,074	3,543	7,068
OMX index options	SKr 100 x index	4,467	5,016	5,169	4,826	5,605	4,074
GEMx index options	DM 10 x index	n.t.	n.t.	n.t.	181	7	—
Austria							
Austrian Futures and Options Exchange							
Interest rate							
Futures							
Austrian Government bonds	S 1,000,000	n.t.	n.t.	n.t.	n.t.	n.t.	43
Stock index							
Futures							
Austrian Traded index (ATX)	S 100 x index	n.t.	n.t.	n.t.	n.t.	67	174
Options							
ATX options	S 100 x index	n.t.	n.t.	n.t.	n.t.	176	673

Table A2 (*continued*)

Exchange/Type	Face Value of Contract[1]	Volume of Contracts Traded					
		1988	1989	1990	1991	1992	1993
		(In thousands of contracts)					
Denmark							
Guarantee Fund for Danish Options and Futures (FUTOP)							
Interest rate							
Futures							
Danish Government bonds	DKr 1,000,000	n.t.	11	22	283	548	578
Mortgage credit bonds	DKr 1,000,000	. . .	. . .	329	100	34	30
Copenhagen interbank offered rate—							
CIBOR (three-month)	DKr 5,000,000	n.t.	n.t.	n.t.	n.t.	n.t.	35
Options							
Options on Danish Government bond futures	DKr 1,000,000	n.t.	n.t.	n.t.	53	153	86
Options on mortgage credit bonds	DKr 1,000,000	. . .	. . .	87	35	—	n.t.
Stock index and equity							
Futures							
KFX stock index	DKr 1,000 x index	n.t.	7	243	336	407	339
Options							
Options on KFX stock index futures	DKr 1,000 x index	n.t.	n.t.	55	135	194	87
Options on Danish equities	100 underlying shares	n.t.	n.t.	3	143	187	163
Norway							
Oslo Stock Exchange							
Interest rate							
Futures							
Norwegian Government bonds (ten-year)	NKr 1,000,000	n.t.	n.t.	n.t.	n.t.	n.t.	28
Stock index							
Futures							
OBX index	NKr 100 x index	n.t.	n.t.	n.t.	n.t.	9	17
Options							
Options on the OBX index	NKr 100 x index	n.t.	n.t.	39	224	445	386
Finland							
Finnish Options Market Exchange and Clearing House							
Stock index							
Futures							
FOX index	Fmk 100 x index	32	70	43	35	37	54
Options							
FOX index options	Fmk 100 x index	362	931	747	636	398	378
Ireland							
Irish Futures and Options Exchange							
Interest rate							
Futures							
Dublin interbank offered rate—							
DIBOR (three-month)	£Ir 500,000	n.t.	15	37	27	28	19
Short gilt	£Ir 100,000	n.t.	n.t.	1	3	2	—
Long gilt	£Ir 50,000	n.t.	4	8	10	4	10
New Zealand							
New Zealand Futures and Options Exchange							
Interest rate							
Futures							
Bank bills (90-day)	$NZ 500,000	64	118	281	408	392	463
Government stock (three-, five-, and ten-year)	$NZ 100,000	295	349	308	267	208	146
Options							
Options on bank bill futures	$NZ 500,000	n.t.	2	3	30	39	8
Options on Government stock futures	$NZ 100,000	1	27	9	22	29	3
Stock index							
Futures							
Forty index	$NZ 20 x index	n.t.	n.t.	n.t.	3	5	4
Options							
Forty index options	$NZ 20 x index	n.t.	n.t.	n.t.	—	1	1

Table A2 (*continued*)

Exchange/Type	Face Value of Contract[1]	Volume of Contracts Traded					
		1988	1989	1990	1991	1992	1993
		(In thousands of contracts)					
Hong Kong							
Hong Kong Futures Exchange (HKFX)							
Interest rate							
Futures							
Hong Kong interbank offered rate—							
HIBOR (three-month)	HK$1,000,000	n.t.	n.t.	55	1	—	—
Stock index							
Futures							
Hang Seng index	HK$50 x index	140	236	236	499	1,089	2,416
Options							
Hang Seng index options	HK$50 x index	n.t.	n.t.	n.t.	n.t.	n.t.	282
Singapore							
Singapore International Monetary Exchange (SIMEX)							
Interest rate							
Futures							
Eurodollar (three-month)	$1,000,000	1,881	3,862	3,469	3,433	5,618	5,536
Euro-yen (three-month)	¥ 100,000,000	n.t.	169	816	1,492	2,473	3,533
Euro-deutsche mark (three-month)	DM 1,000,000	n.t.	n.t.	57	33	5	23
Options							
Options on Eurodollar futures	$1,000,000	11	10	13	5	12	7
Options on Euro-yen futures	¥ 100,000,000	n.t.	n.t.	62	81	81	57
Currency							
Futures							
Japanese yen	¥ 12,500,000	221	287	116	47	20	21
Deutsche mark	DM 125,000	98	84	64	60	45	16
Pound sterling	£62,500	3	3	3	4	4	4
Options							
Options on Japanese yen futures	¥ 12,500,000	61	2	—	—	—	—
Stock index							
Futures							
Nikkei stock average	¥ 500 x index	587	859	881	722	3,349	5,162
Options							
Options on Nikkei stock average futures	¥ 500 x index	n.t.	n.t.	n.t.	n.t.	269	898

Sources: American Stock Exchange; Battley(1993); Belgian Futures and Options Exchange; Chicago Board of Trade; Chicago Board Options Exchange; Chicago Mercantile Exchange; Deutsche Terminbörse; European Options Exchange; Financial Futures Market; Finnish Options Market Exchange and Clearing House; Futures Industry Association; Futures Industry Institute, *Fact Book 1993*; Guarantee Fund for Danish Options and Futures; Hong Kong Futures Exchange; London International Financial Futures Exchange; Marché à Terme International de France; Mid-America Commodity Exchange; Montreal Exchange; New York Cotton Exchange; New York Stock Exchange; Pacific Stock Exchange; Philadelphia Stock Exchange; Singapore International Monetary Exchange; Stockholm Options Market; and Toronto Futures Exchange.

Note: n.t. = not traded; — = either zero or less than 500 contracts; $A = Australian dollar; S = Austrian schilling; BF = Belgian franc; Can$ = Canadian dollar; DKr = Danish krone; DM = deutsche mark; ECU = European currency unit; Fmk = Finnish markka; F = French franc; HK$ = Hong Kong dollar; £Ir = Irish pound; Lit = Italian lira; ¥ = Japanese yen; f. = Netherlands guilder; $NZ = New Zealand dollar; NKr = Norwegian krone; £ = pound sterling; Ptas = Spanish pesetas; SKr = Swedish krona; Sw F = Swiss franc; and $ = U.S. dollar; Options volume is puts and calls combined.

[1]Blanks in this column indicate that information is not available.

[2]Data on 6½–10-year and 5-year notes for 1988 and 1989; from 1990 onward it also includes 2-year notes.

[3]Face value of contract is $100,000 for 6½–10-year and 5-year notes, and $200,000 for 2-year notes.

[4]There are five types: mortgage-backed 7.5 percent, 8.0 percent, 8.5 percent, 9.0 percent, and 9.5 percent. The value presented for each year is the total volume of contracts traded for those types existed in the respective year.

[5]Data on 10-year notes for 1988–89; 10- and 5-year notes for 1990–91; and 10-, 5-, and 2-year notes from 1992 onward. Face value of contract is $100,000 for 5- and 10-year notes; and $200,000 for 2-year notes.

[6]CME deutsche mark, Eurodollar, Japanese yen, and pound sterling contracts are listed on a mutual offset link with the Singapore International Monetary Exchange.

[7]Five-year notes for 1988; and 2- and 5-year notes from 1989 onward.

[8]Commodity size is $250,000 for 5-year notes and $500,000 for 2-year notes.

[9]NYFE is a subsidiary of the New York Stock Exchange.

[10]Includes NYSE composite index and NYSE beta index (discontinued trading in 1988).

Table A2 (*concluded*)

[11]Includes AMEX major market index, AMEX institutional index, AMEX computer technology index, AMEX oil index, Japan index (trading began September 1990), major market index LEAPS (major market index divided by 10; trading began November 1990), international market index (options on an index of American depository receipts; delisted June 21, 1991), AMEX major market index capped options (delisted June 22, 1992), AMEX institutional index capped options (a.m. settled index capped options were delisted September 21, 1992), S&P MidCap index options (trading began February 13, 1992), Eurotop index options (trading began October 26, 1992), Pharmaceutical index options (trading began June 26, 1992), Biotechnology index options (trading began October 9, 1992), Morgan Stanley cyclical and consumer index options (trading began September 21, 1993), and North American telecommunications index options (trading began November 23, 1993).

[12]Covers Australian dollar, Canadian dollar, deutsche mark, ECU, French franc, Japanese yen, pound sterling, and Swiss franc.

[13]Include American and European options.

[14]PHLX value line index, PHLX national OTC index, and bank index (since 1992).

[15]A contract identical to the MATIF treasury bond future is also traded on an over-the-counter basis outside exchange hours and is cleared by the clearinghouse.

[16]BTP stands for Buoni del Tesoro Poliennali.

[17]Trading began on July 13, 1987 for the old JGB. A new JGB was launched on April 3, 1991, with modified specifications.

[18]The 1988 data also contain 54,108 contracts traded on medium gilts (£50,000).

[19]Include one- and three-month futures. Face value of contract for the one-month futures is Can$3 million and for the three-month futures is Can$1 million.

[20]Includes 90-day MIBOR. Beginning from 1993, it also has data for 360-day MIBOR.

[21]The MMI option is also listed on the American Stock Exchange.

Table A3. Markets for Selected Derivative Financial Instruments: Notional Principal Amounts Outstanding

(In billions of U.S. dollars, end-year data)

	1986	1987	1988	1989	1990	1991	1992	1993
Interest rate futures	370.0	487.7	895.4	1,200.7	1,454.2	2,157.1	2,902.2	4,960.4
Futures on short-term interest rate instruments	274.3	338.9	721.7	1,002.6	1,271.1	1,906.3	2,652.8	4,627.0
Of which:								
Three-month Eurodollar[1]	229.5	307.8	588.8	671.9	662.6	1,100.5	1,389.5	2,178.6
Three-month Euro-yen[2]	—	—	—	109.5	243.5	254.5	431.8	1,080.1
Three-month Euro-deutsche mark[3]	—	—	—	14.4	47.2	109.6	229.2	421.2
Futures on long-term interest rate instruments	95.7	148.8	173.7	198.1	183.1	250.8	249.4	333.4
Of which:								
U.S. Treasury bond[4]	23.0	26.5	39.9	33.2	23.0	29.8	31.3	32.6
Notional French Government bond[5]	2.1	7.6	7.0	6.1	7.0	11.4	21.0	12.6
Ten-year Japanese Government bond[6]	63.5	104.8	105.6	129.1	112.7	122.0	105.9	136.0
German Government bond[7]	—	—	1.4	4.2	13.7	20.2	27.8	33.3
Interest rate options[8]	146.5	122.6	279.2	387.9	599.5	1,072.6	1,385.4	2,362.4
Currency futures	10.0	14.1	11.6	15.6	16.3	17.8	24.5	29.8
Currency options[8]	39.2	59.5	48.0	50.1	56.1	61.2	80.1	81.1
Stock market index futures	15.0	18.1	27.8	41.8	69.7	77.3	80.7	119.2
Options on stock market indices[8]	38.1	27.8	44.0	72.2	96.0	137.4	167.6	286.4
Total	618.8	729.9	1,306.0	1,768.3	2,291.7	3,523.4	4,640.5	7,839.3
Of which:								
In the United States	517.7	577.3	949.8	1,151.9	1,261.9	2,130.2	2,684.4	4,328.9
In Europe	13.1	13.3	177.7	250.8	461.2	710.2	1,110.1	1,819.9
In Japan	63.5	107.7	106.6	260.9	424.2	441.4	576.2	1,193.6

Sources: Bank for International Settlements.

[1]Traded on the Chicago Mercantile Exchange-International Monetary Market (CME-IMM), Singapore International Monetary Exchange (SIMEX), London International Financial Futures Exchange (LIFFE), Tokyo International Financial Futures Exchange (TIFFE), and Sydney Futures Exchange (SFE).

[2]Traded on the TIFFE and SIMEX.

[3]Traded on the Marché à Terme International de France (MATIF) and LIFFE.

[4]Traded on the Chicago Board of Trade (CBOT), LIFFE, Mid-America Commodity Exchange (MIDAM), New York Futures Exchange (NYFE), and Tokyo Stock Exchange (TSE).

[5]Traded on the MATIF.

[6]Traded on the TSE, LIFFE, and CBOT.

[7]Traded on the LIFFE and the Deutsche Terminbörse (DTB).

[8]Calls plus puts.

Table A4. Annual Turnover in Derivative Financial Instruments Traded on Organized Exchanges Worldwide

(In millions of contracts traded)

	1986	1987	1988	1989	1990	1991	1992	1993
Interest rate futures	91.0	145.7	156.3	201.0	219.1	230.9	330.1	427.0
Futures on short-term interest rate instruments	16.4	29.4	33.7	70.2	76.0	84.8	130.8	166.8
Of which:								
Three-month Eurodollar[1]	12.4	23.7	25.2	46.8	39.4	41.7	66.9	70.2
Three-month Euro-yen[2]	—	—	—	4.7	15.2	16.2	17.4	26.9
Three-month Euro-deutsche mark[3]	—	—	—	1.6	3.1	4.8	12.2	21.3
Futures on long-term interest rate instruments	74.6	116.3	122.6	130.8	143.1	146.1	199.3	260.2
Of which:								
U.S. Treasury bond[4]	54.6	69.4	73.8	72.8	78.2	69.9	71.7	80.7
Notional French Government bond[5]	1.1	11.9	12.4	15.0	16.0	21.1	31.1	36.8
Ten-year Japanese Government bond[6]	9.4	18.4	18.8	19.1	16.4	12.9	12.1	15.6
German Government bond[7]	—	—	0.3	5.3	9.6	12.4	18.9	28.1
Interest rate options[8]	22.3	29.3	30.5	39.5	52.0	50.8	64.8	82.9
Currency futures	19.7	20.8	22.1	27.5	29.1	29.2	30.7	38.0
Currency options[8]	13.0	18.3	18.2	20.7	18.9	22.9	23.4	23.8
Stock market index futures	28.4	36.1	29.6	30.1	39.4	54.6	52.0	60.7
Options on stock market indices[8]	140.4	139.1	79.1	101.7	119.1	121.4	133.9	141.8
Total	314.8	389.2	335.8	420.4	477.7	509.8	634.9	774.2
Of which:								
In the United States	288.2	317.2	251.0	286.2	310.3	300.7	339.4	379.0
In Europe	10.3	35.9	40.7	64.4	83.0	110.5	185.0	255.9
In Japan	9.4	18.5	23.1	45.7	60.6	66.2	51.7	57.8

Sources: Bank for International Settlements.

[1]Traded on the Chicago Mercantile Exchange-International Monetary Market (CME-IMM), Singapore International Monetary Exchange (SIMEX), London International Financial Futures Exchange (LIFFE), Tokyo International Financial Futures Exchange (TIFFE), and Sydney Futures Exchange (SFE).

[2]Traded on the TIFFE and SIMEX.

[3]Traded on the Marché à Terme International de France (MATIF) and LIFFE.

[4]Traded on the Chicago Board of Trade (CBOT), LIFFE, Mid-America Commodity Exchange (MIDAM), New York Futures Exchange (NYFE), and Tokyo Stock Exchange (TSE).

[5]Traded on the MATIF.

[6]Traded on the TSE, LIFFE, and CBOT.

[7]Traded on the LIFFE and the Deutsche Terminbörse (DTB).

[8]Calls plus puts.

Table A5. Notional Principal Value of Outstanding Interest Rate and Currency Swaps[1]

(In billions of U.S. dollars)

	1987	1988	1989	1990	1991	1992
Interest rate swaps						
All counterparties	682.9	1,010.2	1,502.6	2,311.5	3,065.1	3,850.8
Interbank (ISDA member)	206.6	341.3	547.1	909.5	1,342.3	1,880.8
Other (end-user and brokered)	476.2	668.9	955.5	1,402.0	1,722.8	1,970.1
Of which:						
End-user	476.2	668.9	955.5	1,402.0	1,722.8	1,970.1
Financial institutions	300.0	421.3	579.2	817.1	985.7	1,061.1
Governments[2]	47.6	63.2	76.2	136.9	165.5	242.8
Corporations[3]	128.6	168.9	295.2	447.9	571.7	666.2
Unallocated	. . .	15.5	4.9	—	—	. . .
Brokered	—	—	—	—	—	—
Currency swaps						
All counterparties	365.6	639.1	898.2	1,155.1	1,614.3	1,720.8
(Adjusted for reporting of both sides)	(182.8)	(319.6)	(449.1)	(577.5)	(807.2)	(860.4)
Interbank (ISDA member)	71.0	165.2	230.1	310.1	449.8	477.7
Other (end-user and brokered)	294.6	473.9	668.1	844.9	1,164.6	1,243.1
Of which:						
End-user[4]	147.3	237.0	334.1	422.5	582.3	621.5
Financial institutions	61.9	102.7	141.7	148.2	246.7	228.7
Governments[2]	33.9	54.0	65.6	83.2	96.9	110.6
Corporations[3]	51.6	76.5	116.5	191.1	238.7	282.2
Unallocated	. . .	3.8	10.3	—	—	—
Brokered	—	—	—	—	—	—
Total (interest rate and currency swaps for all counterparties)	1,048.5	1,649.3	2,400.8	3,466.6	4,679.4	5,571.6

Sources: Bank for International Settlements, *International Banking and Financial Market Developments*, various issues; and International Swaps and Derivatives Association (ISDA).

[1]End-December.
[2]Including international institutions.
[3]Including others.
[4]Adjusted for double-counting as each currency swap involves two currencies.

Table A6. New Interest Rate Swaps and Currency Swaps[1]
(In billions of U.S. dollars)

	1987		1988		1989		1990		1991		1992	
	First half	Second half	First half	Second half	First half	Second half	First half	Second half	First half	Second half	First half	Second half
Interest rate swaps												
All counterparties	181.5	206.3	250.5	317.6	389.2	444.4	561.5	702.8	762.1	859.7	1,318.3	1,504.3
Interbank (ISDA member)	58.9	67.0	86.6	106.5	140.4	177.6	223.2	261.3	335.4	426.4	617.7	718.7
Other (end-user and brokered)	122.6	139.3	163.9	211.1	248.7	266.8	338.2	441.5	426.8	433.3	700.6	785.6
Of which:												
End-user	121.0	136.0	162.3	209.1	242.8	260.6	334.5	370.8	419.2	425.5	681.0	755.7
Financial institutions	82.3	86.4	102.8	135.3	152.9	165.0	200.2	219.9	229.3	263.1	404.6	449.3
Governments[2]	10.9	10.8	15.7	17.2	23.0	16.6	33.7	41.0	43.4	35.5	64.9	84.0
Corporations[3]	27.8	34.8	43.9	54.3	60.5	79.0	100.6	110.0	146.4	126.9	211.5	222.4
Unallocated	. . .	4.1	—	2.3	6.5	—	—	—	—	—	—	—
Brokered	1.6	3.3	1.6	1.9	5.9	6.2	3.7	70.7	7.6	7.7	19.6	29.9
Currency swaps												
All counterparties	87.1	85.7	122.3	126.2	166.7	189.6	189.3	236.2	322.6	334.1	312.1	291.6
(Adjusted for reporting of both sides)	(43.5)	(42.8)	(61.1)	(63.1)	(83.4)	(94.8)	(94.6)	(118.1)	(161.3)	(167.1)	(156.1)	(145.8)
Interbank (ISDA member)	17.5	18.3	25.4	33.3	50.8	50.5	53.0	69.6	105.9	102.0	68.3	64.2
Other (end-user and brokered)	69.5	67.4	96.9	92.9	115.9	139.1	136.3	166.6	216.7	232.1	243.9	227.4
Of which:												
End-user[4]	34.3	33.5	47.5	46.4	57.5	69.6	67.7	83.0	103.1	116.0	121.6	113.1
Financial institutions	18.9	13.0	23.3	20.2	22.4	29.8	22.8	28.6	41.1	57.4	40.9	38.0
Governments[2]	7.6	6.3	10.6	8.7	13.2	9.8	12.5	10.9	13.7	17.1	23.6	18.5
Corporations[3]	7.9	13.6	12.9	16.2	18.5	27.7	32.4	43.5	48.2	41.5	57.1	56.6
Unallocated	. . .	0.6	0.7	1.3	3.5	2.2	—	—	—	—	—	—
Brokered	0.9	0.3	1.9	0.2	1.0	—	0.9	0.7	10.7	0.1	0.7	1.2

Sources: Bank for International Settlements, *International Banking and Financial Market Developments*, various issues; and International Swaps and Derivatives Association (ISDA).

[1]During the respective half of the year.
[2]Including international institutions.
[3]Including others.
[4]Adjusted for double-counting as each currency swap involves two currencies.

Table A7. Currency Composition of Notional Principal Value of Outstanding Interest Rate and Currency Swaps
(In billions of U.S. dollars)

	1987	1988	1989	1990	1991	1992
Interest rate swaps						
All counterparties	682.9	1,010.2	1,502.6	2,311.5	3,065.1	3,850.8
U.S. dollar	541.5	728.2	993.7	1,272.7	1,506.0	1,760.2
Japanese yen	40.5	78.5	128.0	231.9	478.9	706.0
Deutsche mark	31.6	56.5	84.6	193.4	263.4	344.4
Pound sterling	29.7	52.3	100.4	242.1	253.5	294.8
Other	39.5	94.8	195.8	371.5	563.3	745.3
Interbank (ISDA member)	206.6	341.3	547.1	909.5	1,342.3	1,880.8
U.S. dollar	161.6	243.9	371.1	492.8	675.0	853.9
Japanese yen	19.5	43.0	61.1	126.1	264.9	441.3
Deutsche mark	7.9	17.2	32.6	78.4	111.2	175.6
Pound sterling	10.4	17.6	40.0	100.1	106.3	137.2
Other	7.1	19.6	42.2	112.1	184.9	272.7
End-user	476.2	668.9	955.5	1,402.0	1,722.8	1,970.1
U.S. dollar	379.9	484.3	622.6	779.9	831.0	906.3
Japanese yen	21.0	35.5	66.9	105.8	214.0	264.7
Deutsche mark	23.7	39.3	52.0	115.0	152.2	168.8
Pound sterling	19.3	34.7	60.4	142.0	147.3	157.6
Other	32.4	75.2	153.6	259.4	378.3	472.7
Currency swaps[1]						
All counterparties	182.8	319.6	449.1	577.5	807.2	860.4
U.S. dollar	81.3	134.7	177.1	214.2	292.1	309.0
Japanese yen	29.9	65.5	100.6	122.4	180.1	154.3
Deutsche mark	10.7	17.0	26.9	36.2	47.6	53.3
Pound sterling	5.3	8.9	16.7	24.5	37.4	40.1
Other	55.7	93.5	127.8	180.3	250.0	303.6
Interbank (ISDA member)	35.5	82.6	115.1	155.1	224.9	238.9
U.S. dollar	16.7	34.1	48.2	59.7	86.8	90.9
Japanese yen	7.2	18.6	28.3	37.4	60.9	53.9
Deutsche mark	1.6	3.0	5.4	7.6	9.4	12.6
Pound sterling	1.1	1.6	4.3	6.2	8.4	10.4
Other	9.0	25.4	28.8	44.1	59.5	71.1
End-user	147.3	237.0	334.1	422.5	582.3	621.5
U.S. dollar	64.6	100.7	128.9	154.5	205.3	218.1
Japanese yen	22.7	47.0	72.2	85.0	119.2	100.4
Deutsche mark	9.1	14.0	21.5	28.5	38.2	40.7
Pound sterling	4.2	7.3	12.4	18.3	29.0	29.7
Other	46.7	68.1	99.0	136.2	190.6	232.6

Sources: Bank for International Settlements, *International Banking and Financial Market Developments*, various issues; and International Swaps and Derivatives Association (ISDA).

[1] Adjusted for double-counting as each currency swap involves two currencies.

Table A8. Changes in Claims on Nonbanks and Liabilities to Nonbanks[1]

(In billions of U.S. dollars)

	1986	1987	1988	1989	1990	1991	1992	1993
Changes in claims on[2]	89	139	74	186	265	96	140	191
Industrial countries	38	79	81	120	204	95	126	159
Of which:								
United States	25	23	39	35	50	7	31	38
Japan	5	31	18	36	54	41	24	21
Developing countries[3]	−1	·6	−3	9	−9	15	22	4
Offshore centers[4]	5	1	3	10	17	5	15	6
Countries in transition	—	−1	1	1	1	—	−1	−1
Of which:								
Former U.S.S.R.	—	—	1	1	1	—	−1	−1
Other transactors	3	2	−2	3	−1	3	−2	−2
Unidentified borrowers[5]	44	52	−6	44	53	−22	−20	25
Changes in liabilities to[6]	122	138	81	168	232	18	65	43
Industrial countries	60	53	50	107	120	−2	47	34
Of which:								
United States	26	23	21	6	28	−18	−9	−3
Japan	2	1	2	13	−3	−3	−2	−3
Developing countries[3]	3	15	18	33	27	−14	−10	−14
Offshore centers[4]	13	7	5	13	18	−4	1	4
Countries in transition	—	—	—	1	1	1	2	2
Of which:								
Former U.S.S.R.	—	—	—	—	—	—	1	—
Other transactors	−1	1	2	1	2	3	—	−2
Unidentified depositors[5]	47	61	6	14	64	35	25	19
Changes in net claims on[7]	−33	2	−6	18	33	77	75	147
Industrial countries	−22	25	31	13	84	97	80	125
Of which:								
United States	−1	1	19	28	22	25	40	42
Japan	3	30	16	22	57	44	25	24
Developing countries[3]	−4	−8	−21	−24	−36	29	32	18
Offshore centers[4]	−8	−6	−2	−4	−1	9	14	2
Countries in transition	—	−1	1	—	—	−1	−3	−3
Of which:								
Former U.S.S.R.	—	—	1	1	1	—	−2	−2
Other transactors	4	1	−3	2	−3	1	−2	−1
Unidentified (net)[5]	−2	−9	−12	31	−10	−58	−45	6

Sources: Bank for International Settlements, data reported to the IMF on currency distribution of banks' external accounts; International Monetary Fund, *International Financial Statistics*; and IMF staff estimates.

[1]Data on changes in claims and liabilities are derived from stock data on the reporting countries' assets and liabilities and are net of changes due to exchange rate movements.

[2]As measured by changes in the outstanding liabilities of borrowing countries, defined as cross-border bank credits to nonbanks by residence of borrower.

[3]Excluding offshore centers. Data include some accumulation of interest arrears and reduction in bank claims resulting from debt conversions, sales, and write-offs.

[4]The Bahamas, Bahrain, the Cayman Islands, Hong Kong, the Netherlands Antilles, Panama, and Singapore.

[5]The difference between the amount that countries report as their banks' positions with nonresident nonbanks in their monetary statistics and the amount that all banks in major financial centers report as their positions with nonbanks in each country.

[6]As measured by changes in the outstanding assets of depositing countries, defined as cross-border bank deposits of nonbanks by residence of depositor.

[7]Change in claims minus change in liabilities.

Table A9. Changes in Interbank Claims and Liabilities[1]

(In billions of U.S. dollars)

	1986	1987	1988	1989	1990	1991	1992	1993
Changes in claims on[2]	442	659	491	647	466	−165	122	67
Industrial countries	367	464	403	443	359	−162	44	31
Of which:								
United States	69	83	69	59	23	−13	42	45
Japan	148	192	185	136	47	−130	−131	−38
Developing countries[3]	3	16	−1	3	11	19	22	34
Offshore centers[4]	81	163	82	171	118	−10	11	−2
Countries in transition	4	1	4	6	−6	2	4	−2
Of which:								
Former U.S.S.R.	3	1	4	7	−7	3	7	—
Other transactors	−14	15	3	23	−16	−15	40	6
Changes in liabilities to[5]	465	626	437	655	436	−119	103	152
Industrial countries	363	440	320	467	370	−120	40	104
Of which:								
United States	56	35	63	61	−3	14	−33	−53
Japan	111	145	147	125	58	−44	−69	−39
Developing countries[3]	−8	33	15	37	53	34	36	45
Offshore centers[4]	117	137	95	135	33	−25	−15	−4
Countries in transition	−1	−2	4	3	−6	—	9	3
Of which:								
Former U.S.S.R.	1	−2	1	−1	−7	—	5	2
Other transactors	−6	18	2	13	−14	−9	32	4
Changes in net claims on[5]	−23	33	53	−8	30	−47	20	−85
Industrial countries	4	24	82	−24	−11	−42	4	−73
Of which:								
United States	13	48	6	−2	26	−27	75	98
Japan	37	47	39	12	−11	−86	−62	—
Developing countries[3]	11	−17	−16	−33	−42	−15	−14	−10
Offshore centers[4]	−36	26	−14	36	85	15	26	2
Countries in transition	5	3	—	3	−1	2	−4	−6
Of which:								
Former U.S.S.R.	2	2	2	8	−1	4	2	−2
Other transactors	−8	−3	1	11	−1	−6	8	2

Sources: Bank for International Settlements, data reported to the IMF on currency distribution of banks' external accounts; International Monetary Fund, *International Financial Statistics*; and IMF staff estimates.

[1]Data on changes in claims and liabilities are derived from stock data on the reporting countries' assets and liabilities and are net of changes due to exchange rate movements.

[2]As measured by changes in the outstanding liabilities of borrowing countries, defined as cross-border interbank accounts by residence of borrowing bank.

[3]Excluding offshore centers. Data include some accumulation of interest arrears and reduction in bank claims resulting from debt conversions, sales, and write-offs.

[4]The Bahamas, Bahrain, the Cayman Islands, Hong Kong, the Netherlands Antilles, Panama, and Singapore.

[5]As measured by changes in the outstanding assets of depositing countries, defined as cross-border interbank accounts by residence of lending banks.

[6]Change in claims minus change in liabilities.

Table A10. International Bond Issues by Developing Countries and Regions[1]
(In millions of U.S. dollars)

	1991	1992	1993	1993 1st qtr.	2nd qtr.	3rd qtr.	4th qtr.	1994 1st qtr.
Developing countries	12,438	23,780	59,437	10,109	12,117	13,492	23,717	17,628
Africa	236	725	—	—	—	—	—	877
Congo	—	—	—	—	—	—	—	600
South Africa	236	725	—	—	—	—	—	—
Tunisia	—	—	—	—	—	—	—	277
Asia	3,000	5,847	20,181	2,230	3,200	3,361	11,391	7,605
China	115	1,289	2,929	406	651	1,191	681	1,500
Hong Kong	100	185	5,785	657	—	590	4,538	1,305
India	227	—	546	—	—	65	481	439
Indonesia	369	494	485	30	—	—	455	659
Korea	2,012	3,208	5,864	671	1,343	725	3,125	1,273
Malaysia	—	—	954	—	500	—	454	230
Philippines	—	—	1,293	170	175	190	758	154
Taiwan Province of China	160	60	79	—	36	43	—	318
Thailand	17	610	2,247	296	495	557	899	1,728
Europe	1,960	4,561	9,638	2,863	1,257	1,988	3,530	875
Czech Republic	—	—	697	375	—	322	—	—
Former Czechoslovakia	277	129	—	—	—	—	—	—
Hungary	1,186	1,242	4,796	1,363	279	1,280	1,873	69
Slovak Republic	—	—	240	—	—	240	—	21
Turkey	497	3,190	3,905	1,125	978	145	1,657	785
Middle East	400	—	2,002	1,000	—	1,002	—	1,958
Israel	400	—	2,002	1,000	—	1,002	—	1,958
Western Hemisphere	7,242	12,577	27,396	4,017	7,559	7,022	8,798	6,313
Argentina	795	1,570	6,233	335	606	1,852	3,440	1,460
Bolivia	—	—	—	—	—	—	—	10
Brazil	1,837	3,655	6,619	1,327	1,635	1,583	2,074	1,095
Chile	200	120	433	—	333	—	100	—
Colombia	—	—	566	—	325	50	191	250
Costa Rica	—	—	—	—	—	—	—	50
Guatemala	—	—	60	—	—	60	—	—
Mexico	3,782	6,100	10,783	2,205	4,136	1,851	2,591	3,307
Panama	—	—	—	—	—	—	—	50
Peru	—	—	30	—	—	—	30	40
Trinidad and Tobago	—	100	125	—	—	—	5	—
Uruguay	—	100	140	—	140	—	—	100
Venezuela	578	932	2,348	150	385	1,626	187	—
Memorandum items:								
Issues under EMTN programs	375	1,215	3,713	607	393	1,439	1,274	374
Argentina	—	40	930	—	50	450	430	—
Brazil	—	110	422	62	110	100	150	35
Colombia	—	—	100	—	50	50	—	—
Korea	—	—	177	—	93	—	84	189
Mexico	375	665	1,741	545	90	646	460	150
Philippines	—	—	150	—	—	—	150	—
Thailand	—	—	194	—	—	194	—	—
Venezuela	—	400	—	—	—	—	—	—
Total bond issues in international bond markets	308,730	333,694	480,997	139,867	107,050	116,253	117,827	139,820
				(In percent)				
Shares of developing countries in global issuance	4.0	7.1	12.4	7.2	11.3	11.6	20.1	12.6

Sources: IMF staff estimates based on *Euroweek*; *Financial Times*; *International Financing Review*; and Organization for Economic Cooperation and Development, *Financial Market Trends* and *Financial Statistics Monthly*.

[1]Including note issues under European medium-term note (EMTN) programs.

Table A11. International Equity Issues by Developing Countries and Regions

(In millions of U.S. dollars)

	1991	1992	1993	1993 1st qtr.	1993 2nd qtr.	1993 3rd qtr.	1993 4th qtr.	1994 1st qtr.
Developing countries	5,436	9,259	11,865	1,000	3,179	2,351	5,312	4,018
Africa	143	270	8	—	—	—	8	—
Morocco	—	—	8	—	—	—	8	—
South Africa	143	270	—	—	—	—	—	—
Asia	1,022	4,732	5,673	653	826	1,244	2,927	2,508
Bangladesh	—	—	19	3	15	—	—	—
China	11	1,049	1,908	115	—	—	—	351
Hong Kong	140	1,250	1,264	374	—	250	640	72
India	—	240	331	—	—	137	194	1,310
Indonesia	167	262	604	74	67	263	200	342
Korea	200	150	328	28	150	. . .	150	150
Malaysia	. . .	382	. . .	. . .	. . .	. . .	. . .	—
Pakistan	11	48	5	. . .	5	. . .	. . .	—
Philippines	159	392	64	. . .	. . .	44	19	2
Singapore	125	272	613	41	171	. . .	401	70
Taiwan Province of China	. . .	543	72	. . .	72	. . .	424	—
Thailand	209	145	466	18	24	. . .	424	174
Europe	91	67	202	2	28	. . .	172	330
Hungary	91	33	17	2	7	. . .	9	—
Poland	—	—	1	—	1	—	—	—
Turkey	—	34	184	—	20	—	164	330
Middle East	60	127	257	38	22	189	8	4
Israel	60	127	257	38	22	189	8	4
Western Hemisphere	4,120	4,063	5,725	307	2,304	917	2,197	1,176
Argentina	356	372	2,793	—	2,095	380	318	197
Bolivia	—	—	10	—	—	—	10	—
Brazil	—	133	—	—	—	—	—	300
Chile	—	129	271	—	114	94	63	96
Colombia	—	—	91	27	—	—	64	—
Mexico	3,764	3,058	2,493	280	95	443	1,674	583
Panama	—	88	—	—	—	—	—	—
Peru	—	—	26	—	—	—	26	—
Venezuela	—	283	42	—	—	—	42	—
Total equity issues in international equity market	15,548	22,632	51,654	4,300	8,554	15,863	22,937	12,900
				(In percent)				
Share of developing countries in global issuance	35.0	40.9	22.9	23.3	37.2	14.8	23.2	31.1

Sources: *Euroweek*; *Financial Times*; *International Financing Review* (*IFR*); and *IFR* Equibase.

Table A12. Comparative Valuations Across Emerging Markets[1]

(In ratios; end-December 1993 data)

	Price-Earnings Ratio		Price-Book Value Ratio	
	Ratio	Relative to world	Ratio	Relative to world
Latin America				
Argentina	24.47	0.85	2.12	0.93
Brazil	11.69	0.41	0.69	0.30
Chile	20.04	0.70	2.22	0.97
Colombia	24.90	0.87	2.02	0.88
Mexico	19.70	0.69	2.75	1.20
Peru	39.19	1.37	3.77	1.65
Venezuela	26.07	0.91	1.32	0.58
East Asia				
China	. . .	. . .	. . .	. . .
Korea	25.13	0.88	1.38	0.60
Philippines	37.46	1.31	5.64	2.46
Taiwan Province of China	34.97	1.22	3.94	1.72
South Asia				
India	37.38	1.30	4.95	2.16
Indonesia	29.43	1.03	3.14	1.37
Malaysia	42.65	1.49	5.36	2.34
Pakistan	33.41	1.16	7.85	3.43
Sri Lanka	35.19	1.23	4.83	2.11
Thailand	28.27	0.99	4.89	2.14
Europe and Middle East				
Greece	9.67	0.34	1.85	0.81
Jordan	17.38	0.61	2.28	1.00
Portugal	16.96	0.59	2.03	0.89
Turkey	36.20	1.26	7.42	3.24

Source: International Finance Corporation.

[1]Relative to the Morgan Stanley Capital International (MSCI) World Index.

Table A13. Restrictions on Outward Portfolio Investment of Institutional Investors in Five Major Industrial Countries

	Restrictions on Foreign Investments of	
	Insurance companies	Pension funds
Canada	*Ceiling:* None. A June 1992 regulation removed ceilings on foreign investments, but limits may be imposed based on prudential considerations.	*Ceiling:* A December 1991 law progressively raises the ceiling on foreign investment from 10 percent to 20 percent in 1994.
Germany	*Ceiling:* Prohibitive at 5 percent of coverage fund. A European Community (EC) directive would raise the ceiling on foreign investment in 1994, but regulators are still expected to require assured returns on investments. *Other:* 100 percent matching of liabilities by assets in the same currency; restrictions on credit quality of investment.	*Ceiling:* Prohibitive at 5 percent of assets. *Other:* 100 percent matching of liabilities by assets in the same currency; restrictions on credit quality of investment.
Japan	*Ceiling:* Nonbinding at 30 percent of assets in the general account.[1] *Other:* Companies place tight restrictions on credit quality of investment; accounting incentives that bias investment in favor of high-income securities against those yielding potential capital gains.	*Ceiling:* Nonbinding at 30 percent of assets in the general account. *Other:* Pension funds place tight restrictions on credit quality of investment.
United Kingdom	*Ceiling:* None. *Other:* At least 80 percent matching of liabilities by assets in the same currency for liabilities in any currency that account for more than 5 percent of the total.	*Ceiling:* None. *Other:* Prudence.
United States	*Ceiling:* Varies by state and is typically prohibitive. New York State, which is the most influential state on insurance issues, raised the ceiling on foreign investments of insurance companies to 6 percent from 3 percent in 1990.[2] *Other:* Restrictions on credit quality of investment;[3] restrictions on composition of assets.	*Public pension funds:* *Ceiling:* Typical and often binding. *Other:* Charters of some pension funds impose restrictions on credit quality of investment. *Private pension funds:* *Ceiling:* None. *Other:* "Prudent man" rule and diversification;[4] charters of some pension funds impose restrictions on credit quality of investments.

Source: Chuhan (1994).
[1]Restrictions on Postal Life Insurance are more prohibitive.
[2]Does not include investments in Canada.
[3]Investments are rated by the National Association of Insurance Commissioners (NAIC).
[4]The Employee Retirement Income Security Act (ERISA) of 1974, which governs U.S. private pension funds, requires plan fiduciaries to exercise prudence in investment decisions. ERISA also requires plan trustees to diversify investments to minimize risk.

Table A14. Issues of Closed-End Funds Targeting Emerging Markets in Developing Countries and Regions
(In millions of U.S. dollars)

	1989	1990	1991	1992	1993
Developing countries	2,082	3,482	1,193	1,421	4,151
Global funds	76	36	253	137	2,669
Africa	—	—	—	—	66
Egypt	—	—	—	—	50
Mauritius	—	—	—	—	16
Asia	1,417	1,895	213	870	1,373
Multicountry	487	602	—	22	566
Specific country or region	930	1,294	213	848	806
China	—	—	—	646	456
India	168	105	—	—	—
Indonesia	199	312	—	—	—
Korea	—	478	140	170	110
Malaysia	150	292	—	—	—
Pakistan	—	—	23	6	178
Philippines	253	—	—	—	—
Singapore	—	—	—	—	—
Taiwan Province of China	56	—	40	26	—
Thailand	105	107	—	—	—
Vietnam	—	—	10	—	62
Europe	181	976	—	122	32
Multicountry	45	841	—	—	32
Country specific	136	135	—	122	—
Bulgaria	—	—	—	—	—
Former Czechoslovakia	—	—	—	31	—
Hungary	80	100	—	22	—
Israel	—	—	—	—	—
Poland	—	—	—	69	—
Turkey	56	35	—	—	—
Western Hemisphere	408	575	727	293	10
Multicountry	178	203	440	181	10
Country specific	230	372	288	112	—
Argentina	—	—	56	—	—
Brazil	—	—	—	112	—
Chile	230	180	—	—	—
Mexico	—	192	132	—	—
Venezuela	—	—	100	—	—

Source: Lipper Analytical Services.

Table A15. Details of Treasury Note Issues in China

	Amount _(In billions of Chinese yuan)_	Maturity _(Years)_	Interest Rate _(In percent)_[1]	Redemption _(In percent)_	Trading
1981	4.866	10.00	4.00	lottery	illegal
1982	4.383	10.00	4.80	lottery	illegal
1983	4.158	10.00	4.80	lottery	illegal
1984	4.253	10.00	4.80	lottery	illegal
1985	6.061	5.00	5.90	maturity	illegal
1986	6.251	5.00	6.10	maturity	illegal
1987	6.287	5.00	6.10	maturity	legal
1988	9.216	3.00	6.10	maturity	legal
1989	5.612[2]	3.00	14.00	maturity	legal
1990	9.328[2]	3.00	14.00	maturity	legal
1991	19.900[3]	3.00	10.00	maturity	legal
1992	30.000[4]	3.50	9.50;10.00[5]	maturity	legal
1993	30.000[4]	3.50	10.00;11.00[6]	maturity	legal

Source: Bi (1993).

[1]Where two interest rates are provided for pre-1989 issues, the higher rate was paid to individual investors, while the lower rate was paid to institutional investors.

[2]In 1989 and 1990 the authorities announced their intention to issue Y 5.5 billion, but ended up issuing more.

[3]In 1991 the authorities announced their intention to issue Y 10 billion.

[4]Refers to announced plans.

[5]The lower rate was paid to holders of the three-year bond.

[6]The lower rate was paid to holders of the three-year bond. These interest rates were increased to 12.52 and 14.06 percent, respectively, in May 1993 and to 13.96 and 15.86 percent, respectively, in July 1993.

Table A16. Bonds Issued by China

Issuer	Launch Date	Amount	Amount (*In millions of U.S. dollars*)	Coupon (*In percent*)	Spread (*In basis points*)	Maturity (*Years*)	Listing
1992							
TITIC	Jan. 1992	¥ 10 billion	80.9	6.5	109	5.0	. . .
CITIC	Mar. 1992	¥ 20 billion	150.7	6.4	93	5.0	Luxembourg
SITCO	May 1992	¥ 15 billion	115.0	6.4	95	5.0	. . .
Bank of China	July 1992	¥ 15 billion	120.0	6.2	124	5.0	. . .
GITIC	July 1992	¥ 15 billion	121.0	6.3	122	5.0	. . .
Bank of China	Aug. 1992	$150 million	150.0	. . .	. . .	5.0	. . .
PCBC	Nov. 1992	$150 million	150.0	. . .	55	7.0	Luxembourg
CITIC	Dec. 1992	¥ 30 billion	240.9	5.7	150	7.0	. . .
SITCO	Dec. 1992	¥ 20 billion	160.6	4.8	114	3.0	. . .
Total			1,289.2				
1993							
Bank of China	Mar. 1993	¥ 15 billion	127.9	4.7	60	5.0	Tokyo
Bank of China	Mar. 1993	¥ 15 billion	127.9	5.0	62	7.0	Tokyo
CITIC	Mar. 1993	$150 million	150.0	. . .	50	5.0	Singapore
Fujian	Apr. 1993	¥ 10 billion	88.5	4.1	40	2.5	Tokyo
GITIC	Apr. 1993	$150 million	150.0	. . .	55	5.0	Luxembourg
Bank of China	June 1993	$200 million	200.0	. . .	50	5.0	London
PCBC	June 1993	$50 million	50.0	. . .	50	5.0	London and Singapore
PCBC	June 1993	$70 million	70.0	. . .	60	7.0	London and Singapore
SITIC	June 1993	¥ 10 billion	92.9	. . .	112	5.0	Tokyo
CITIC	July 1993	$250 million	250.0	6.9	100	10.0	New York
CITIC	July 1993	¥ 30 billion	282.9	4.1	87	2.6	Luxembourg
China Investment Bank	July 1993	$100 million	100.0	. . .	53	5.0	Hong Kong
Hainan ITIC	Aug. 1993	$80 million	80.0	. . .	65	5.0	Hong Kong
DITIC	Sept. 1993	¥ 10 billion	94.9	4.2	101	5.0	Tokyo
People's Republic of China	Sept. 1993	¥ 30 billion	281.6	4.4	89	5.0	London
People's Republic of China	Oct. 1993	$300 million	300.0	6.1	88	10.0	Hong Kong and Singapore
SITICO	Oct. 1993	$70 million	70.0	. . .	98	5.0	Singapore
China Textile Machinery Stocks	Nov. 1993	Sw F 35 million	23.2	1.0	-300	5.1	. . .
GITIC	Nov. 1993	$150 million	150.0	6.8	115	10.0	. . .
ICBC	Dec. 1993	¥ 15 billion	137.6	3.4	105	5.0	Tokyo
Total			2,929.4				

Sources: *Euroweek*; *International Financing Review*; and IMF staff estimates.

References

"Administrative Arrangements Regarding the Auction of Government of Canada Securities," *Bank of Canada Review* (Summer 1993), pp. 71–76.

Altman, Edward I., "Research Update: Mortality Rates and Losses, Bond Rating Drift," Merrill Lynch Merchant Banking Group (1989).

Bailey, Warren, "Risk and Return on China's New Stock Markets: Some Preliminary Evidence," *Pacific Basin Finance Journal,* Vol. 2 (1994), pp. 243–60.

Bank for International Settlements, *International Convergence of Capital Measurement and Capital Standards,* Part II (Basle: Bank for International Settlements, July 1988).

——— *International Banking and Financial Market Developments* (Basle: Bank for International Settlements, February 1994).

———, and Group of Ten, *Report of the Committee on Interbank Netting Schemes of the Central Banks of the Group of Ten Countries* (Basle: Bank for International Settlements, 1990).

Bank of Japan, *Economic Statistics Monthly* (November 1993).

Bank of New York, *The Complete Depositary Receipt Directory* (New York: Bank of New York, 1993).

Basle Committee on Banking Supervision, "The Supervisory Treatment of Market Risks" (Basle: Basle Committee on Banking Supervision, April 1993).

Battley, Nick, ed., *The World's Futures Options Markets* (Chicago: Probus Publishing Company, 1993).

Bell, Michael W., and others, *China at the Threshold of a Market Economy*, IMF Occasional Paper No. 107 (Washington: International Monetary Fund, September 1993).

Bi, Keqian, "Credit Markets in China," *Columbia Journal of World Business*, Vol. 28 (Fall 1993), pp. 76–95.

Bikhchandani, Sushil, and Chi-fu Huang, "The Economics of Treasury Securities Markets," *Journal of Economic Perspectives*, Vol. 7, No. 3 (Summer 1993), pp. 117–34.

Blommestein, Hans J., and Michael G. Spencer, "The Role of Financial Institutions in the Transition to a Market Economy," IMF Working Paper No. 93/75 (Washington: International Monetary Fund, October 1993).

Board of Governors of the Federal Reserve System, *Flow of Funds Accounts, Third Quarter 1993* (Washington: Board of Governors of the Federal Reserve System, December 1993).

——— (1994a), *Federal Reserve Bulletin*, Vol. 80, No. 1 (January 1994).

——— (1994b), *Federal Reserve Bulletin*, Vol. 80, No. 3 (March 1994).

——— Federal Deposit Insurance Corporation, and Office of the Comptroller of Currency, "Derivative Product Activities of Commercial Banks: Joint Study Conducted in Response to Questions Posed by Senator Riegle on Derivative Products," January 27, 1993, Exhibit 1.

Bröker, Günther, *Government Securities and Debt Management in the 1990s* (Paris: Organization for Economic Cooperation and Development, 1993).

Campbell, John Y., and Kenneth A. Froot, "International Experiences with Securities Transactions Taxes," NBER Working Paper No. 4587 (Cambridge, Massachusetts: National Bureau of Economic Research, December 1993).

Chen, Yung-Sheng, "New Developments in Mainland China's Securities Markets," *Issues and Studies*, Vol. 27 (August 1991), pp. 82–103.

Chuhan, Punam, "Are Institutional Investors an Important Source of Portfolio Investment in Emerging Markets?" World Bank Policy Research Paper No. 1243 (Washington: World Bank, January 1994).

Collyns, Charles, and others, *Private Market Financing to Developing Countries*, World Economic and Financial Surveys (Washington: International Monetary Fund, December 1993).

European Community, Council Directive 93/6/EEC, "On the Capital Adequacy of Investments Firms and Credit Institutions," *Official Journal of the European Communities* (Luxembourg, June 11, 1993).

Evans, Nicolas, "The Global Bond Era Dawns," *Euroweek* (September 24, 1993), pp. 10–17.

Federal Register, Vol. 58, No. 176 (September 14, 1993), p. 48206.

Federal Reserve Bank of New York, "Administration of Relationships with Primary Dealers," Appendix E in U.S. Department of the Treasury, U.S. Securities and Exchange Commission, and Board of Governors of the Federal Reserve System, *Joint Report on the Government Securities Market* (Washington: U.S. Government Printing Office, January 1992).

Feldman, Robert, and Rajnish Mehra, "Auctions: Theory and Applications," *Staff Papers*, International Monetary Fund, Vol. 43 (September 1993), pp. 485–511.

"Financial Centre Germany: Underlying Conditions and Recent Development," *Monthly Report of the Deutsche Bundesbank*, Vol. 44, No. 3, March 1992, pp. 23–31.

Folkerts-Landau, David, and Peter M. Garber, "The European Central Bank: A Bank or a Monetary Policy Rule?" NBER Working Paper No. 4016 (Cambridge, Massachusetts: National Bureau of Economic Research, March 1992).

Giavazzi, Francesco, and Marco Pagano, "Confidence Crises and Public Debt Management," in *Public Debt Management: Theory and History*, ed. by Rudiger Dornbusch and Mario Draghi (Cambridge: Cambridge University Press, 1990).

Global Derivatives Study Group, *Derivatives: Practices and Principles* (Washington: Group of Thirty, 1993).

Goldstein, Morris, David Folkerts-Landau, and others, *International Capital Markets: Developments, Prospects, and Policy Issues*, World Economic and Financial Surveys (Washington: International Monetary Fund, September 1992).

—— (1993a), *International Capital Markets: Part I. Exchange Rate Management and International Capital Flows*, World Economic and Financial Surveys (Washington: International Monetary Fund, April 1993).

—— (1993b), *International Capital Markets: Part II. Systemic Issues in International Finance*, World Economic and Financial Surveys (Washington: International Monetary Fund, August 1993).

Goulder, Lawrence H., "Implications of Introducing U.S. Withholding Taxes on Foreigners' Interest Income," in *Tax Policy and the Economy*, ed. by Lawrence H. Summers (Cambridge, Massachusetts: MIT Press, 1990).

Greenspan, Alan, Testimony Before the Committee on Banking, Housing, and Urban Affairs, U.S. Senate (Washington, March 2, 1994).

Howell, Michael J., Angela Cozzini, and Luci Greenwood, *Cross-Border Capital Flows: A Study of Foreign Equity Investment—1991/92 Review* (London: Baring Securities, 1993).

—— *North America, Europe, Africa, Pacific Rim, and Latin America: Global and Emerging Markets Strategy* (London: Baring Securities, April 1994).

Hu, Yebi, *China's Capital Market* (Hong Kong: Chinese University Press, 1993).

Huizinga, Harry, "Withholding Taxes and the Cost of Public Debt," IMF Working Paper No. 94/18 (Washington: International Monetary Fund, February 1994).

International Finance Corporation, *Quarterly Review of Emerging Markets, Fourth Quarter 1993* (Washington: International Finance Corporation, 1994).

International Monetary Fund, *World Economic Outlook, October 1993: A Survey by the Staff of the International Monetary Fund*, World Economic and Financial Surveys (Washington: International Monetary Fund, October 1993).

—— *World Economic Outlook, April 1994: A Survey by the Staff of the International Monetary Fund*, World Economic and Financial Surveys (Washington: International Monetary Fund, April 1994).

Investment Company Institute, *Mutual Fund Factbook* (Washington: Investment Company Institute, 33rd ed., 1993).

Kleiman International Consultants, *Fifth Annual Emerging Stock Markets Survey* (November 1993).

Kroszner, Randall S., "An International Comparison of Primary Government Securities Markets," in *U.S. Securities Market: The Scholars' Assessment*, Vol. 1 (Chicago: MidAmerica Institute, April 1993).

Loser, Claudio, and Eliot Kalter, eds., *Mexico: The Strategy to Achieve Sustained Economic Growth*, IMF Occasional Paper No. 99 (Washington: International Monetary Fund, September 1992).

McDonough, William J., Remarks Before the Sixty-Sixth Annual Mid-Winter Meeting of the New York State Bankers Association (March 1994).

Miller, Merton, "Functional Regulation," Address at the Fifth Annual Pacific-Basin Capital Markets Finance Conference (Kuala Lumpur, June 1993).

Moody's Bond Survey, March 7, 1994.

Mullins, David W., Jr., Statement Before the Subcommittee on Securities of the Committee on Banking, Housing, and Urban Affairs, U.S. Senate (Washington, January 23, 1992); reproduced in Board of Governors of the Federal Reserve System, *Federal Reserve Bulletin*, Vol 78, No. 3 (March 1992), pp. 195–98.

Mussa, Michael, and Morris Goldstein, "The Integration of World Capital Markets," in *Changing Capital Markets: Implications for Monetary Policy* (Kansas City: Federal Reserve Bank of Kansas City, 1993).

Pensions and Investments, January 25, 1993.

——, January 24, 1994.

Pirrong, S. Craig, "The Market for Treasury Derivative Securities: Microstructure and Market Power," in *U.S. Treasury Securities Market: The Scholars' Assessment*, Vol. 1 (Chicago: MidAmerica Institute, April 1993).

Quale, Andrew, "Legal Primer for Non-U.S. Issuers Raising Financing in the United States," paper presented at the Second Annual Conference on Emerging Market High-Yield Sovereign and Corporate Bonds (New York, January 22, 1993).

Republic New York Securities, *Year End Hedge Fund Review 1993* (1994).

Rodriguez, Anthony P., "Government Securities Investments of Commercial Banks," *Quarterly Review*, Federal Reserve Bank of New York (Summer 1993), pp. 39–53.

Sargent, Thomas J., "Fact or Fiction: Shortening Debt Maturity Lowers Interest Costs" (Chicago: Catalyst Institute, December 1993).

World Economic and Financial Surveys

This series (ISSN 0258-7440) contains biannual, annual, and periodic studies covering monetary and financial issues of importance to the global economy. The core elements of the series are the *World Economic Outlook* report, usually published in May and October, and the annual report on *International Capital Markets*. Other studies assess international trade policy, private market and official financing for developing countries, exchange and payments systems, export credit policies, and issues raised in the *World Economic Outlook*.

World Economic Outlook: A Survey by the Staff of the International Monetary Fund

The *World Economic Outlook*, published twice a year in English, French, Spanish, and Arabic, presents IMF staff economists' analyses of global economic developments during the near and medium term. Chapters give an overview of the world economy; consider issues affecting industrial countries, developing countries, and economies in transition to the market; and address topics of pressing current interest. Annexes, boxes, charts, and an extensive statistical appendix augment the text.

ISSN 0256-6877.
$34.00 (academic rate: $23.00; paper).
1994 (May). ISBN 1-55775-381-4. **Stock #WEO-194.**
1994 (Oct.). ISBN 1-55775-385-7. **Stock #WEO-294.**
1993 (May). ISBN 1-55775-286-9. **Stock #WEO-193.**
1993 (Oct.). ISBN 1-55775-340-7. **Stock #WEO-293.**

International Capital Markets: Developments, Prospects, and Policy Issues
by an IMF Staff Team led by Morris Goldstein and David Folkerts-Landau

This annual report reviews developments in international capital markets, including recent bond market turbulence and the role of hedge funds, supervision of banks and nonbanks and the regulation of derivatives, structural changes in government securities markets, recent developments in private market financing for developing countries, and the role of capital markets in financing Chinese enterprises.

$20.00 (academic rate: $12.00; paper).
1994. ISBN 1-55775-426-8. **Stock #WEO-694.**

1993. *Part I: Exchange Rate Management and International Capital Flows*, by Morris Goldstein, David Folkerts-Landau, Peter Garber, Liliana Rojas-Suarez, and Michael Spencer.
ISBN 1-55775-290-7. **Stock #WEO-693.**

1993. *Part II: Systemic Issues in International Finance*, by an IMF Staff Team led by Morris Goldstein and David Folkerts-Landau.
ISBN 1-55775-335-0. **Stock #WEO-1293.**

Staff Studies for the *World Economic Outlook*
by the IMF's Research Department

These studies, supporting analyses and scenarios of the *World Economic Outlook*, provide a detailed examination of theory and evidence on major issues currently affecting the global economy.

$20.00 (academic rate: $12.00; paper).
1993. ISBN 1-55775-337-7. **Stock #WEO-393.**

Developments in International Exchange and Payments Systems
by a Staff Team from the IMF's Exchange and Trade Relations Department

The global trend toward liberalization in countries' international payments and transfer systems has been most dramatic in central and Eastern Europe. But developing countries in general have brought their exchange systems more in line with market principles and moved toward more flexible exchange rate arrangements, while industrial countries have moved toward more pegged arrangements.

$20.00 (academic rate: $12.00; paper).
1992. ISBN 1-55775-233-8. **Stock #WEO-892.**

Private Market Financing for Developing Countries
by a Staff Team from the IMF's Policy Development and Review Department led by Charles Collyns

This study surveys recent trends in private market financing for developing countries, including flows to developing countries through banking and securities markets; the restoration of access to voluntary market financing for some developing countries; and the status of commercial bank debt in low-income countries.

$20.00 (academic rate: $12.00; paper).
1993. ISBN 1-55775-361-X. **Stock #WEO-993.**
1992. ISBN 1-55775-318-0. **Stock #WEO-992.**

Issues and Developments in International Trade Policy
by an IMF Staff Team led by Margaret Kelly and Anne Kenny McGuirk

Since the mid-1980s, most developing countries have moved toward outward-looking, market-oriented policies and have liberalized their trade regimes. At the same time, industrial countries have acted to liberalize financial markets and foreign direct investment, deregulate services, and privatize public enterprises. This study discusses these and other developments in industrial, developing, and transition economies.

$20.00 (academic rate: $12.00; paper).
1992. ISBN 1-55775-311-3. **Stock #WEO-1092.**

Official Financing for Developing Countries
by a Staff Team from the IMF's Policy Development and Review Department led by Michael Kuhn

This study provides information on official financing for developing countries, with the focus on low- and lower-middle-income countries. It updates and replaces *Multilateral Official Debt Rescheduling: Recent Experience* and reviews developments in direct financing by official and multilateral sources.

$20.00 (academic rate: $12.00; paper)
1994. ISBN 1-55775-378-4. **Stock #WEO-1394.**

Officially Supported Export Credits: Developments and Prospects

This study examines export credit and cover policies in the ten major industrial countries.

$15.00 (academic rate: $12.00; paper).
1990. By G.G. Johnson, Matthew Fisher, and Elliot Harris.
ISBN 1-55775-139-0. **Stock #WEO-588.**

Available by series subscription or single title (including back issues); academic rate available only to full-time university faculty and students.

Please send orders and inquiries to:
International Monetary Fund, Publication Services, 700 19th Street, N.W.
Washington, D.C. 20431, U.S.A.
Tel.: (202) 623-7430   Telefax: (202) 623-7201